Managing Your Project
Achieving success with minimal stress

Andy Hunt

Copyright © 2016 Andy Hunt

All rights reserved.

ISBN: 1537212206

ISBN-13: 978-1537212203

CONTENTS

1. Introduction   1

Welcome !   1

1.1 The Purpose of this Book   1

1.2 The Sections of this Book   2

Section 1: Selecting and Starting a Project   3

Section 2: Organising Yourself - ideas, tools & techniques   3

Section 3: Time Management   4

Section 4: Planning, Writing, Thinking   5

Section 5: Communication - Writing and Speaking about your work   6

Section 6: Troubleshooting - Common Problems   7

Section 7: Towards the End of the Project   8

1.3 How and When to read this Book   9

Section 1 Selecting and Starting a Project   10

2. Choosing a Project   11

2.1 Read any Departmental Project Suggestions   11

2.2 Talk to previous project students   12

2.3 Initial Research   13

2.4 Engaging with potential Supervisors   15

2.5 Ranking your potential projects   17

What really interests you?   17

What work do you enjoy doing?   18

What response have you got from potential supervisors?   18

What information have you got?   18

What skills do you need for your career?   19

2.6 Making your Decision   19

2.7 Summary	19
2.8 Further Reading	20
3. Getting a Head Start	**21**
3.1 Read this book!	21
3.2 Follow up suggested links	22
3.3 Train yourself to be a professional researcher	22
3.3.1 Virtual Training Suite	23
3.4 Meet with your Supervisor	25
3.5 Studying Previous Reports	25
3.6 Summary	26
3.7 Further Information and Resources	26
4. Getting Started	**28**
4.1 If the project has begun and you've not read Chapter 3	28
4.2 Get to know your supervisor	29
4.3 Set up a Team	31
4.4 Set the Main Deadlines	33
4.5 Establish a method for taking notes, recording ideas	34
4.6 Write something as soon as you can	34
4.7 Establish when & where you will work	35
4.8 Summary	36
4.9 External References	37
5. The Supervision Process	**38**
5.1 Projects and supervisors	38
5.2 The real purpose of the supervision process	38
5.3 Does my supervisor have all the answers?	39
5.4 Pastoral support from the supervision process	40
5.5 Understanding the job of the supervisor	41
5.6 Working with your supervisor	42

5.7 Maximising the benefits of the supervision process	43
5.8 Summary	44

Section 2 Organising Yourself – ideas, tools & techniques   46

6. The 2-stage Work Process	**47**
6.1 Your new dual role	47
6.2 Some Doomsday scenarios	48
6.3 Manager and Worker roles you may know about	49
6.4 But there's only one of me	52
6.5 Your Supervisor is NOT your Manager	56
6.6 Summary	57
6.7 External Links	58
7. Taking Notes and keeping records	**59**
7.1 Capture the ideas while they are fresh	59
7.2 Summarise reading material	60
7.3 Paper versus Electronic systems	60
7.4 Computer-based note taking and storage	61
7.5 Example of an integrated electronic note system - Evernote	63
7.6 Summary	67
7.7 External Links	68
8. Mind Mapping	**70**
8.1 What is Mind Mapping?	70
8.2 How to make a Mind Map	70
8.3 Mind Maps for Note-taking	71
8.4 Mind Maps for Paper/Chapter Summaries	72
8.5 Mind Maps for Planning Talks and Reports	72
8.6 Mind Maps for taking Minutes of Meetings	74
8.7 Software for Mind Mapping	75

8.8 Personal Statement	77
8.9 Summary	78
8.10 External References	78
9. Setting up a Special Interest Group (SIG)	**80**
9.1 Your supervisor's time is limited	80
9.2 Motivating each other	81
9.3 Checking on each other	82
9.4 Proofreading and checking	82
9.5 Discussions	83
9.6 Testing things out	83
9.7 Giving presentations	84
9.8 Sharing Key Literature	84
9.9 Organising the SIG	85
9.10 Summary	87
9.11 External Links	88

Section 3 Time Management — 89

10. Time Management techniques and strategies	**91**
10.1 Introduction to Time Management	91
10.2 Reactive time management	92
10.3 Proactive time management	93
10.4 Methods of time management	93
10.5 Main principles of time management	95
10.6 Creating time with the 80:20 rule	97
10.7 Tools of time management	98
10.8 Time Management self-diagnosis	99
10.9 Summary	100
10.10 External Links	101
11. Establishing your best times for working	**102**

11.1 Daily Rhythms	102
11.2 Allocating tasks to appropriate times	103
11.3 Longer-time Rhythms	105
11.4 Summary	107
11.5 External Links	108
12. Introduction to GTD	**109**
Overview	109
12.1 Outline of GTD	109
12.2 Getting everything out of your head	111
12.3 Work out which things are Actionable and process these into an external system	114
12.4 The Weekly Review	126
12.5 Calendar and Context Lists	127
12.6 Keeping the system up to date	128
12.7 Summary	128
12.8 External Links	129
13. Email mastery -	**131**
how to get to INBOX zero	**131**
13.1 Inbox overload	131
13.2 The methodology for sorting emails	132
13.3 Identifying the email categories	133
13.4 An Empty Inbox	136
13.5 Processing the @Action folder	137
13.6 Summary	138
13.7 External Links	138
14. Calendars, time-tracking & reminders	**140**
14.1 Just Having a Calendar is not enough	140
14.2 Why do I need a Calendar? I remember everything!	141

14.3 Dangers of Multiple Calendars ... 142
14.4 Comparison of Paper and Electronic Calendars ... 143
14.5 Programs and Apps ... 145
14.6 How Calendars link with GTD ... 147
14.7 Using Calendars as Tickler notifications ... 148
14.8 How much to put in your Calendar? ... 149
14.9 Best practice in appointment planning ... 150
14.10 Thinking backwards from an event ... 151
14.11 Summary ... 153
14.12 External References ... 154

15. Project and Action Lists ... 155

15.1 The Limitations of a To-Do list ... 155
15.2 Project Lists ... 156
15.3 Action Lists ... 161
15.4 The Daily Planner ... 164
15.5 Summary ... 166
15.6 External Links ... 167

16. Technological Time Tricks ... 168

16.1 Paper or computer ... 168
16.2 Principles of using Electronic Time Management tools ... 169
16.3 Summary of a Working System ... 170
16.4 Alternative Technological Solutions ... 177
16.5 Be willing to experiment ... 179
16.6 Summary ... 180
16.7 External Links ... 181

Section 4 Planning, Writing, Thinking ... 183

17. Title, Aims and Objectives ... 185

17.1 Setting the overall focus ... 185

17.2 Techniques for generating ideas	*187*
17.3 Developing your Title, Aims & Objectives	*190*
17.6 Bringing together Title, Aims & Objectives	*194*
17.7 Summary	*195*
18. The Project Proposal	**196**
18.1 Your first report	*196*
18.2 Structuring your report	*197*
18.3 Summary	*200*
19. The Literature Survey	**201**
19.1 The importance of setting your work in context	*201*
19.2 What has been done?	*202*
19.3 Different types of information source	*203*
19.4 Learning from other people	*209*
19.5 Writing the Literature Survey	*211*
19.5.3 Arguing your case	*212*
19.6 Plagiarism	*215*
19.7 Summary	*215*
20. Successful Project Planning	**217**
20.1 Turning Objectives into Tasks	*217*
20.2 Project storyboarding	*220*
20.3 Criteria for success	*223*
20.4 Establishing Key Deliverables	*225*
20.5 From Objectives to Work Packages	*226*
Work Package 1: Research	*228*
20.6 Relationship between Work Packages and Timing	*229*
20.7 Summary	*229*
20.8 External References	*230*
21. Detailed Time & Project Planning	**231**

21.1 Establishing all external deadlines — 231
21.2 Working backwards from fixed deadlines — 232
21.3 Working forward to allocate time — 232
21.4 Storyboard or time-chart — 233
21.5 Creating a time-chart — 235
21.6 Being realistic about what time you have — 236
21.7 Summary — 237

Section 5 Communication
– Writing and Speaking about your work — 238

22. Structuring your Communication — 239
22.1 Other people's mind-sets — 239
22.2 Revealing information logically — 240
22.3 Your starting-point is not theirs — 242
22.4 Different forms of direct communication — 243
22.5 Social Media — 246
22.6 Asking people for help — 251
22.7 Summary — 254
22.8 External Links — 255

23. Giving Presentations — 256
23.1 Presenting your ideas to others — 256
23.2 Establishing the audience — 257
23.3 Methods of presentation — 257
23.4 Planning the presentation — 260
23.5 Giving the talk — 261
23.6 Summary — 262
23.7 References — 263

24. Organising the Final Report — 264
24.1 Introduction — 264

24.2 Report-writing as an ongoing process	264
24.3 Writing as a daily activity	266
24.4 Scoping your writing time	267
24.5 Contents as a springboard for writing	269
24.6 Backing up your work	270
24.7 Summary	271
24.8 Further Reading	272
25. Writing Style and Format	**273**
25.1 Establishing the readership	273
25.2 House-styles	274
25.3 Tenses and 3rd vs 1st Person	275
25.4 Revealing information to the reader	277
25.5 Writing flow	278
25.6 Use of Diagrams	279
25.7 Appendices	280
25.8 Submitting Electronic information	281
25.9 Summary	283
25.10 Further reading	283
Section 6 Troubleshooting - Common Problems	**285**
26. Procrastination	**287**
26.1 Stalling Activities	287
26.2 The Psychology of Procrastination	288
26.3 When is it NOT Procrastination?	289
26.3 The Solution	290
26.4 Positive and Negative Procrastination	293
26.5 Summary	294
26.6 Further Reading	295
27. Perfectionism	**296**

27.1 Striving for Quality is good	296
27.2 What is Perfectionism?	296
27.3 Managing Perfectionism	300
27.4 Summary	302
27.5 External References	303
28. Getting Stuck	**304**
28.1 Introduction	304
28.2 Why are you really stuck?	305
28.3 Exactly what is stuck?	306
28.4 What will 'being un-stuck' look and feel like?	307
28.5 How can I put this into action and get un-stuck?	308
28.6 Summary	309
28.7 External links	310
29. Losing Focus	**311**
29.1 Identifying your loss of focus	311
29.2 How your focus is lost	312
29.3 The importance of regular Manager meetings	313
29.4 Managerial Self-Assessment	314
29.5 Summary	316
30. Losing Motivation	**317**
30.1 What does losing motivation feel like?	317
30.2 Project – Work - Play balance	318
30.3 The effect of tiredness	318
30.4 The importance of perspective on motivation	319
30.5 Summary	321
30.6 Further Reading and External Links	322
31. Discovering Similar Work	**323**
31.1 Someone else has done it already	323

31.2 Updating your Literature Survey   324
31.3 Idea Particles   324
31.4 Using the new ideas   325
31.5 Summary   327

Section 7 Towards the End of the Project   328

32. The Closing Stages   329

32.1 Running out of time   329
32.2 Don't forget to Manage   330
32.3 Don't overwork   332
32.4 Identify the Critical Path   333
32.5 Form a Countdown plan   333
32.6 Use Storyboards to gracefully manage Further Work   335
32.7 Build in Review and Proofreading time   337
32.8 Summary   337

33. Finding out how your project will be marked   339

33.1 Marking Guidelines & Markers   339
33.2 Using the Marking Guidelines   342
33.3 Looking at previous work   343
33.4 Summary   343

34. The Viva   345

34.1 Purpose of the viva   345
34.2 Challenging Questions   346
34.3 Preparation for the viva   347
Project: Self-Assessment Form 2   349
34.4 Presentation time within the viva   349
34.5 Summary   350

Managing Your Project

35. Publishing your Work	**352**
35.1 Why publish?	*352*
35.2 Should you publish?	*353*
35.3 Which publication?	*354*
35.4 Summary	*356*
35.5 External References	*357*
Final words	*358*

1. INTRODUCTION

Welcome !

You're probably reading this because you have a major piece of solo work ahead of you, and it all seems a bit daunting. This book is written based on the experience of supervising students for over 25 years, noting carefully all the things that work and do not work. It is really quite fascinating how something as *individual* as a solo project can often cause the *same* problems and reactions in every student.

This book aims to help you to succeed in the project process, whether it is ahead of you, or whether you are in the middle of it wondering why things aren't working out as well as you'd hoped.

Do take some time to look at this Introduction, see what's ahead, and work out for yourself the best way of using the advice.

1.1 The Purpose of this Book

Most courses in higher education include a major element of individual work. Universities and Colleges use different names, such as:

- solo project
- individual (or independent) study module (ISM)
- dissertation
- thesis.

Whatever the name, the solo project is a significant challenge to most students because it is so different from the other modules in the course. For a start, there are usually no lectures. The timetable for it is typically just a large block of time, rather than the carefully crafted set of lectures, tutorials and assignments that you may be used to. All of a sudden it seems that a huge managerial, motivational and organisational burden has been placed upon you. This is exactly the intention, because - when graduate students look back on their degree - it is during this period that most will say that they 'grew up' or 'learned to stand on their own two feet'.

However, just *knowing* that there are a whole new set of pressures and challenges on you does not actually help you to *cope* with them. In fact it can be a heavy burden for many students and can, initially at least, be a fearful process.

The purpose of this book is to help you manage yourself, your work, your time, and your interaction with other people during this extended period of solo work. It is written from the experience of both students and supervisors over many years of project work at different levels of study, including undergraduate final projects, solo dissertations at Masters level, and PhD study towards a thesis. What is interesting is that - though the topics of study vary, and the academic levels and requirements are different - there are many common traits which continually come up.

Over the years I have noticed, in my own supervision meetings (and those of other supervisors) with different students, that a large proportion of the discussion and training given is in common to all. In other words it seems that there is a 'curriculum' required for doing individual study – independent of subject or level. This book gives you a head start, by identifying that previously invisible curriculum, and by distilling into one place the various things that students need to know in order to carry out a successful final project.

This will never replace the supervision process itself, but it should certainly help it, by letting you deal with each of the issues in your own time, rather than relying on the supervisor to train you in everything outlined here. This should have two specific effects:

1) It should free up the supervisions for more focussed discussion on your particular topic and research (rather than taking up most of the time covering common issues);

2) It should help you 'find your own feet' much faster and with more understanding and confidence than otherwise.

1.2 The Sections of this Book

Managing Your Project is divided into 7 major sections, representing different skills or requirements of an individual project. Each section is made up of a number of chapters.

Section 1: Selecting and Starting a Project

Ideally this should be read as you are preparing to choose your project and select a supervisor, and then during the very early stages of carrying out the project. It includes the following chapters:

Ch. 2 Choosing a Project – *advice on selecting the best topic and a suitable supervisor.* This chapter helps you with how to find out about the projects on offer, how to develop your own thinking, and how to make connections with others.

Ch. 3 Getting a Head Start - *maximising the benefits of the project period by starting ahead of time.* There are many things that can be done in advance of the actual project start-time. Many of these are to do with training yourself in the skills that you will need throughout the project. This chapter, and indeed the whole book, will help you in this process.

Ch. 4 Getting Started - *making the most of the very early stages of the project.* This chapter helps you in setting up support networks, getting yourself organised, and formulating an effective project plan.

Ch. 5 The Supervision Process - *understanding the role of your supervisor.* This chapter gives you some insight into what it's like to be a supervisor, and what are some of the best ways of making the supervision process as effective as possible. The overall point of the supervision process is to encourage you to be an independent researcher.

Section 2: Organising Yourself - ideas, tools & techniques

This section contains a series of chapters covering some of the most important skills needed to navigate the solo project process. This section applies not just to the start of the project, but to the whole process and the way you organise your work in general.

Ch. 6 The 2-stage work process - *understanding that your role now includes much more management and organisation than before.* You need to be both Manager and Worker, both Planner and Implementer. This chapter talks you through why this dual process is important, and why it is a distinct and necessary part of solo project work.

Ch. 7 Taking notes and keeping records - because (especially in the early stages of the project) you will be encountering masses of new material, and having lots of new ideas. It is essential to the success of your project that you find an effective way to capture and process these ideas.

Ch. 8 Mind-Mapping - *a graphical note-taking and planning technique which should be more widely taught.* Using graphical pen-and-paper or computer software, mind-mapping helps you with effective planning, note-taking, meeting planning, document development and project planning.

Ch. 9 Setting up a Special Interest Group (SIG) - *because doing a solo project can be lonely work, and it is vital to set up and maximise the use of a support network.* A superb way of doing this is to gather a small group of students doing similar and related work in order to support each other.

Section 3: Time Management

Time Management is all about self-organisation, and so could just as well have been covered in the section above. However, it so important that it really does deserve its own section. Poor time management is often considered to be the biggest single reason for project failure and poor marks in higher education, and yet - as a topic - it is rarely taught. As a student you are expected to instinctively adopt a professional attitude to managing yourself, your time and your work. But many students find that this does not come naturally, and are perpetually disorganised, feeling that this is just 'their lot' and not something which can be changed. Quite the opposite is true, however.

Therefore this section focuses on many different aspects, skills and techniques, which could be sensibly covered by the phrase "Time Management".

Each of its chapters covers a particular topic which can be read at any time of the project, but which will be useful to read as you begin the project process:

Ch. 10 Time Management Techniques and Strategies - *finding the best method for you.* This chapter gives a summary of some of the most popular systems of time management and distils them into a series of actions that you should carry out on a regular basis in order to master your time. Each person is different, so it's important to experiment until you find a methodology that suits you.

Ch. 11 Establishing your best times for working - *finding out which parts of a typical day you are at your most productive, and then planning your work around this.* Even though every day is different and has its own challenges, students usually discover that their brains and bodies run to a cyclic pattern, and you can use that knowledge to your advantage when planning your work. A lot of time can be saved by avoiding fruitless working hours.

Ch. 12 Introduction to GTD – a summary of the popular and very useful Getting Things Done (GTD) methodology which has swept the business world, basically because it seems to work for lots of people. David

Allen has studied people's working habits over decades and has distilled the essence of how to best use your brain to organise and effectively carry out all the things you need to do.

Ch. 13 Email mastery - *how to get to 'INBOX zero'*. Nowadays we are bombarded by incoming information, and one source which regularly gets out of control is the email inbox. Many people in the professional world use a few relatively simple techniques, carried out regularly, in order to keep their email inbox empty. Those with thousands of emails in their inbox often don't even realise there is a problem, or that 'zero' is even possible. However, once you have seen this in action, and realised how it kick-starts your organisation system, you'll probably never want to go back to your old ways.

Ch. 14 Calendars, Time-tracking and reminders – *looking at best practice in managing your schedule and commitments*. Early on in higher education your time management consists mainly of getting to the right place at the right time. But now, you need to be generating your own deadlines and internal commitments. This chapter explains the most effective methodologies for using a calendar or planner, and explains why you really should use one.

Ch. 15 Project and Action Lists – *because most 'To-Do' lists have their limitations*. In this chapter we examine how to best keep track of all the higher-level commitments in your life – using the generic term *Projects*. There are methodologies for converting these into working weekly and daily action lists, which are much more effective than a simple To-Do list.

Ch. 16 Technological Time Tricks - *using modern technology to help you manage your time and your work*. The previous chapters focus on the methodology behind time management, which works just as well on paper as with electronic gadgets. This chapter, distilled from my own experience and that of my students, explains some of the best ways to use technologies (computer, gadgets and various Apps and software) to build an effective management system. It's not for everyone, and you may well be a 'paper person', but read this to find out if this would suit you. For those people it suits, it can be a life changer and they never look back.

Section 4: Planning, Writing, Thinking

This section brings together some of the key project-oriented information that you'll need as you progress through the project. Some of these chapters are best read right at the start of the project, but can also be useful if you are approaching this later on.

Ch. 17 Title, Aims & Objectives - *how to set and develop the main goals of the project.* This chapter looks in some detail about how to encapsulate what you really want to do in a series of vital project elements that drill down into more detail. This helps you not only to focus effectively but to communicate clearly about your work.

Ch. 18 The Project Proposal - *many departments require that you write an initial report after several weeks of work, and for good reason.* It establishes the basis for the project, acts as a 'contract' between you and your supervisor, gives you valuable feedback, and works as a starting-point for the all-important final report.

Ch. 19 Literature Survey - *often an integral part of any research report, the Literature Survey is your statement of what is already 'out there'.* This chapter gives you hints and advice about writing about other people's work, and how to make it lay the foundations for what you are going to do in your own project.

Ch. 20 Successful Project Planning - although this whole book is about helping you carry out a successful project, there are various tools and techniques which help you manage the project in a professional way. This chapter takes you through these techniques and explains a method of devising Work Packages for all the major sections of your project. This also has the advantage of introducing you to a popular planning method, often used in research grants and industrial organisations.

Ch. 21 Detailed Time and Project Planning – *specific tools and techniques for managing time and uncertainty in projects.* For many people GANTT charts and other timing diagrams are what they think of when considering the words 'Project Management'. Graphical time-plans are indeed an important part of project planning and they are covered in this chapter. However, the rest of the book shows that they are just *part* of a much bigger self-organisational task that needs to be done, which is why time-charts *on their own* are rarely effective.

Section 5: Communication - Writing and Speaking about your work

Your project, however brilliant, is no good to anyone else if it just remains in your head. You have to find ways of communicating your ideas, plans and results to other people. This section helps you to communicate with others more clearly, and with the reader/listener in mind. It breaks down the process into the following sections:

Ch. 22 Structuring Your Communication – *because most project students find it quite difficult to write an effective report and speak about their project.* This is usually because not enough thought has been given to the point of view of the reader or listener. This chapter explains the importance of logical flow, setting the context, and focussing on a specific audience. It also considers your everyday communications and how to get the most out of them.

Ch. 23 Giving Presentations - *describing your project effectively by talking about it to other people.* Though many say that Public Speaking is their worst fear, it's an important part of communicating your project plans and results, and is often a key part of the project process. This chapter guides you through the process of planning and presenting a talk to an audience, and explains why it's a superb way of organising your thoughts.

Ch. 24 Organising the Final Report - *the most important part of your project.* This chapter gives some good and bad examples of planning and writing your final report. It's a major undertaking, and needs to be given high priority in your planning. Guidance is offered here about how to start, how to write regularly, and how to cope if you are running short of time.

Ch. 25 Writing Style and Format - *how the report should be actually written.* Although each subject and department will have its own guidelines, this chapter takes you through some common considerations that all project authors should think about when writing their final report.

Section 6: Troubleshooting - Common Problems

This section contains a series of chapters focussed on particular problems which seem to strike project students at various times. Over the years I've noticed which negative situations are most common, and have spent lots of time helping students through these times, working out solutions, overcoming the problem, and often turning it into a positive strength. For easy reference each chapter deals with a particular problem.

Ch. 26 Procrastination – *when you can't get going.* We can be incredibly creative at finding ways *not* to work. Sometimes this provides a useful break or release, but it can easily become a painful time of stagnation. This chapter looks at *why* we put things off, and gives some advice about how to kick-start yourself into action again.

Ch. 27 Perfectionism – *when you don't know how to stop!* Perfectionism in mild doses can help you to improve your work, which is a good thing. However, it can rapidly get out of control and become a real problem, leading people to get caught up on certain activities at the expense of others, and to never be happy with their work. Here we look at the causes and solutions to strike a good working balance between self-critique and finishing promptly.

Ch. 28 Getting Stuck - *when you can't see a solution.* If you come to a halt, this chapter will help you get moving again. It includes a series of methods that help you to address the problem, think around it, and involve others where necessary; all with the aim of getting you *un*stuck.

Ch. 29 Losing Focus - *when you're not entirely sure that you're working on the right thing.* This can be a tricky situation because you can find yourself slogging away at something, but at the back of your mind you are really not sure that you're making progress on your project. This chapter helps you regain focus by re-launching some of the management techniques covered in other parts of the book.

Ch. 30 Losing Motivation - *when you just don't feel like working.* This is an important issue to address because it can have many causes, each of which is addressed with its own recommended solutions. This chapter helps you to identify the cause and suggests appropriate remedies.

Ch. 31 Discovering Similar Work - *when you find out that somebody else "is doing your project".* This is a situation which happens more often than you might expect. You spend a lot of effort coming up with what you think is a unique project, then - half-way through - you find that someone else around the world is doing the same thing. This chapter helps you convert the initial disappointment into a series of positive drivers for your project.

Section 7: Towards the End of the Project

This final section contains a set of chapters which come into play in the latter stages of the project, and after its completion.

Ch. 32 The Closing Stages - *keeping cool towards the end.* Much of the earlier parts of the book rightfully concentrate on setting up a management system and 'getting going'. However, this chapter helps you to accept that running out of time is inevitable, and suggests ways of handling this positively and gracefully, thus bring the project to a successful and well-managed conclusion.

Ch. 33 Finding out how your Project will be Marked - *allowing you to focus effectively in the latter stages.* Knowledge of your marking scheme and markers - if handled well - can give you an advantage by helping you to concentrate on the most important elements of your project in the last months and weeks. This chapter describes several strategies to discover your marking scheme and to use it to manage the closing stages.

Ch. 34 The Viva - *talking about your project effectively.* Many projects conclude with a face-to-face spoken examination called a 'viva-voce' or commonly 'viva'. This chapter helps you prepare for it by giving you an idea of what to expect in that exam, what sort of questioning you may face, and how to handle this effectively.

Ch. 35 Publishing Your Work - *sharing your project results with a wider audience.* This final chapter considers how to summarise your work in the form of papers, and how to present it at conferences. If your project is successful, then other people are going to want to hear about it, and this chapter gives some advice about how to make that happen.

1.3 How and When to read this Book

The chapters are ordered so that you can read the whole book from start to finish if you like. It roughly follows the time-flow of the project itself, so ideally you should read Section 1 *before* you begin the project. But don't worry if you're coming to this later on in the process. You will still gain important ideas if you've already started. In fact you can compare what you're already doing with what's written here, and only implement those things that you think will give you an improvement.

If the project has just started, you might want to complete Section 1, and then go straight to Section 4, which contains many of the initial activities on a typical project. Please remember to go back and work through Sections 2 and 3, because this is where the complex issues of personal and time management are covered. The earlier you read these and develop your own management techniques, the better your project will flow.

As a totally different approach, you can just 'dip into' the book as and when you need it. The chapters have been written to address a particular topic, and to be fairly self-contained. So, if you prefer, you can treat this book as a collection of smaller topics which you can read when the situation arises. The only problem with this approach is that you may miss something you haven't thought about, i.e., you may be working away without realising that you are storing up problems for yourself later.

So, in summary, I'd recommend that you use a combination of the above two approaches. Take time now to read through from start to finish, and then later you can dip into chapters in more detail as and when you need them.

Wishing you all the very best with your project, and I look forward to accompanying you along the way!

SECTION 1
SELECTING AND STARTING A PROJECT

Ideally this should be read as you are preparing to choose your project and select a supervisor, and then during the very early stages of carrying out the project.

- **Ch. 2 Choosing a Project** – *advice on selecting the best topic and a suitable supervisor.* This chapter helps you with how to find out about the projects on offer, how to develop your own thinking, and how to make connections with others.

- **Ch. 3 Getting a Head Start** - *maximising the benefits of the project period by starting ahead of time.* There are many things that can be done in advance of the actual project start-time. Many of these are to do with training yourself in the skills that you will need throughout the project. This chapter, and indeed the whole book, will help you in this process.

- **Ch. 4 Getting Started** - *making the most of the very early stages of the project.* This chapter helps you in setting up support networks, getting yourself organised, and formulating an effective project plan.

- **Ch. 5 The Supervision Process** - *understanding the role of your supervisor.* This chapter gives you some insight into what it's like to be a supervisor, and what are some of the best ways of making the supervision process as effective as possible. The overall point of the supervision process is to encourage you to be an independent researcher.

2. CHOOSING A PROJECT

If you have already chosen your project, or have made a start on it, or indeed have been *allocated* a project to do, then you may safely skip this chapter.

Choosing a project can be a daunting process. You are keenly aware that your project will be responsible for a relatively large part of your degree, so you want to make the right choice. However, this puts you under extra pressure to make the 'right' decision.

Ultimately, the choice is yours, but the purpose of this chapter is to give you some suggestions of things to do that should inform your decision-making process and make you feel more confident about your eventual choice.

2.1 Read any Departmental Project Suggestions

Different education institutions, and departments within them, have very different ways of matching students to projects. Here are 3 common methods:

a) Students are allocated to projects (in which case there is no need for you to read any further in this chapter);

b) Students are expected to entirely form their own project suggestions and to find a suitable supervisor (in which case, skip now to section 2.2);

c) There is a managed process of advertising projects, students selecting choices, and the department determining the 'best-fit' allocation of projects and supervisors to students.

If your situation is most like c) then your department will communicate with you where to look at a list of potential projects. For example, you may be emailed a link to a web-page giving a list of project choices that have been suggested by supervisors.

Your first task, therefore, is to allocate some time to read through this list. At first, just skim through the list looking at titles and supervisors and see if anything catches your eye. Students have reported that often their 'gut reaction' turned out to be their final choice. Some students describe looking through the list and seeing just one project that jumps out at them. Sometime it's not the project that catches your attention, but the supervisor. Maybe there was a course or module that you particularly enjoyed, and you can imagine working in that area. Perhaps you have heard something about the supervisor's research work and you realise that it's something of interest.

Secondly you should 'drill down' into any projects that you are interested in. The departmental project database may provide you with clickable links to reveal more detailed information about the project. This will give you a better impression as to what is expected by the supervisor, and what sort of work the project will involve. During this process it's a good idea to make your own notes. A super way of doing this, if you've not come across this before, is by making a Mind Map (covered in detail in Chapter 8).

Don't worry if you cannot see the perfect project, as there is always the opportunity to customise one of these projects to be more in line with your own goals and interests. The idea is to use the department's suggestions as a *starting-point*. So, at the end of this process you should have a list, or mind-map, of projects on offer that you are potentially interested in.

2.2 Talk to previous project students

It can be really helpful to search out people who have experience of the project process. Look through your contacts list and see if it contains anyone who has done (or is in the process of doing) a project similar to yours.

Perhaps you know (or know people who know) some of the following:

- current undergraduate finalists - those currently doing projects;
- postgraduates - those who have survived the process and liked it so much they have stayed on to do more!
- people who've already been through higher education.

It can be a very useful experience to talk to people *currently* doing projects. You will get a good idea of what it is really like to be in the middle of a large process. If you can find people working in the area in which you are interested, then this is doubly useful, because you can find out more about the topic and what makes good research in this area. If you can find someone who is currently being supervised by a supervisor you are interested in, then this is triply useful as you can gain some invaluable insight into what it is actually like to work with this supervisor for a prolonged period. Don't be shy about asking. You might be surprised how willing people are to talk about their work. Sometimes it can be a lonely experience doing a solo project, and it's a great boost to find someone who's interested to hear about what you're doing.

Talking to postgraduates can be a very enlightening experience, because they have completed their undergraduate studies and have organised their life to stay on and do more of the same, and in more detail. So you can learn a great deal from them about what they did at undergraduate level, what they discovered, and what made them stay on to do more.

Take the opportunity, if possible, to talk to people who did their research / solo projects some years ago. They can give you a interesting perspective looking back at the project experience. Maybe you will find out how it has influenced their career, or what skills they developed during the project period that have turned out to be the most useful in later life.

2.3 Initial Research

A very good starting-point for any research project is to find out what *other* people have done on the topic, and what is currently being done in related fields. You cannot be sure that your idea is new until you have a solid idea of what already exists.

Also, by finding out as much as possible about the topic, you get a much better idea of where your intended work will 'fit in'. Many researchers talk about finding a 'niche' in their larger research topic that needs more work.

The main reason - at this stage - for finding out all this information is so that you can be informed when first talking to your supervisor. As a supervisor it makes the world of difference whether someone is prepared or not.

Compare the following two conversations, and imagine you were the supervisor meeting a potential student for the first time:

Student / Potential Supervisor: Meeting 1

STUDENT: Thanks for meeting me. I'd like to do your project on Film Music and Sound Design.

SUPERVISOR: That's great. Tell me why.

STUDENT: Don't know really. It's just that I liked your first year welcome lectures and thought you'd be a good supervisor.

SUPERVISOR: Ok, thank you! But what about the *topic*? What are you interested in *doing* for the project?

STUDENT: Well, I like music. And I watch a lot of films.

SUPERVISOR: Ok, but what *specific* area are you interested in? How do you hope to contribute to the research in this area?

STUDENT: Well, I suppose I was rather hoping you would tell me what to do. After all, *you're* the expert.

Student / Potential Supervisor: Meeting 2

STUDENT: Thanks for meeting me. I'm really interested in your project on Film Music and Sound Design. I'm thinking of putting it down as my first choice.

SUPERVISOR: That's great. Tell me why.

STUDENT: *(Brings out a notepad)*. Well, I saw that in your project advert that this topic was about new methods of computer-based sound design in films. I'm really interested in films and their soundtracks, but I'd not thought about the computers used in their making before. So, what I've done is to make this Mind-Map *(shows a colourful diagram, split into topics)* to summarise what I think are the main issues involved. And, I've been looking around online and I've come across these books on the subject *(shows a draft Literature List)*. Also, there are several discussion groups on the use of sound in films. I've listed them here. I had no idea how much went on behind the scenes!

SUPERVISOR: Ok, thank you! But what about the topic? What are you interested in doing for the project?

STUDENT: Well, I'm keen to find out how you would like the project to go. But for me, I guess - looking at all these possible avenues *(pointing to the Mind-Map again)* - that it's the area of new audio processing software that interests me; finding out what works for the film makers and what's still required but not implemented yet.

Notice that the supervisor's response is similar in both cases. But if you were the supervisor, and you had these two meetings in the same morning, with both the above students. Which one would you prefer to take on as a research student? Remember that you're going to be seeing this student at least weekly for the next several months, and giving feedback and marking them etc. You may also be looking for some new postgraduate students, people with potential who might like to stay on and research in this area after this project.

Student 1 is flattering and enthusiastic, and has at least bothered to arrange a meeting with the supervisor and has turned up on time! However, Student 2 really looks like they've put a good deal of effort into preparing for the meeting, and already has started to engage with the topic and to have some views on the subject.

So take some time to find out about the key topics in this area. Here are a few questions for you to ask and look into. As you do this you will find that you are gathering information to build up your Literature List or Mind Map to show your potential supervisor:

- What are the best-known books and research papers?
- Can you get hold of some of these and start having a look through them?
- Has anyone written any summaries or discussions about these key works?
- From an internet search - can you find out people and organisations who are working in this area?
- Are there educational courses on the subject around the world? (and if so, what project topics do the students look at?)
- Are there discussion groups or social networks dedicated to the topic?

2.4 Engaging with potential Supervisors

This stage is the most important part of the process, yet one which many students ignore. You should take the time to ask to meet with any of the supervisors whose projects you have identified in the above process.

Doing this has several advantages:

- you get to decide whether you could work with this person for a sustained period
- you can ask specific questions about the project

- you get to hear about any updates on the project suggestion (as sometimes the descriptions on-line are generic, or maybe a little out of date)
- you can discuss your own interests and goals with the supervisor
- the supervisor gets to see that you are genuinely interested in their work (and so if asked later on to choose between several students, you will be memorable).

Before you arrange to meet the supervisor, make sure that you are fully prepared for the meeting so that you can maximise the time. Things you may want to think about in advance are:

- what *you* think the project is about, as a starting-point for the conversation
- questions you want to ask about the project, to clarify what it's really all about
- ideas of your own that you would like to discuss
- some idea of what are the current and previous research questions in this area (see the section 2.3 above)
- where on your list of priorities is this project (is this a marginal interest, or the main thing that you would like to do)?

To make sure that the meeting with the supervisor is a *two-way* process (and to demonstrate that you've been doing some active thinking) it's important to prepare some questions to ask. Here are some ideas for things that you could ask (but you will feel much more comfortable if you prepare your own).

- Could you give me a summary of your research work, so I can set this project in context of the other things you're interested in?
- How many other people have asked you about this project?
- How many people are you willing to take on this subject?
- What do you think would be the best focus in this area?
- Do you think my idea of . . . would fit into this project?
- Is there any specific reading that you would recommend I do before making a final choice?
- Is there anyone else I should be talking to about this?

To set up the meeting itself you'll need to be proactive and email the supervisor. In this email it is good to name the project that you're interested in, and give a short summary of what you would like to meet to discuss.

Then give plenty of suggested times when you could be free to make it easier for the supervisor to just pick a suitable one and email you back. As a supervisor it's frustrating to be told "just look at my timetable" as we do not always have ready access to individual student's commitments. Also there are many times when I *have* searched out the specific timetable, compared it with my calendar, found a slot, sent a message, and then a week later received the reply "oh sorry, I've got football practice then; have you got any other times?" And thus the whole process gets off to a clunky and rather unsatisfying start.

The other advantage of setting up the meeting by email is that you and the supervisor have a record of the contact. Later, when the supervisor might have to choose between several potential students, your email is there as a reminder.

Remember that the best projects are those which are a *collaboration* between student and supervisor. At the end of the process a good project will be your *own work*, but that *fits in* with the research and interests of the supervisor and the wider community. So an early meeting to discuss the project is one of the best ways of getting the project started on the correct footing - that of a research collaboration.

2.5 Ranking your potential projects

This section summarises a few ideas of things that you might want to think about in order to help you choose a project.

It may be that there is only one obvious option for you, and you are already very happy with it, in which case you can skip this section.

More often than not though, students at this stage will have several project ideas, maybe involving a choice of supervisor as well as project focus. So, start off by summarising your project choices into one place (one piece of paper, or a single screen of text, or a Mind-Map), and then ask yourself the following questions.

What *really* interests you?

Look over your list and rate each project in terms of how fascinated you are in the topic being proposed. If you're deeply intrigued by a project, or interested in its implications, then this can provide you with a lot of motivation along the way.

What work do you *enjoy* doing?

Think about the essential work involved in each project. Is it mainly reading, talking to people, processing data, writing computer code, creating artwork, etc.? What will it be like working on this day after day? And how do you feel about that?

To help you answer this question, you might want to re-contact the people who have done similar projects before, to discover what day-to-day activities are required. For example, if you choose that project on Film Music Sound, and you are mentally picturing yourself walking around a Hollywood Studio, you might feel let down if you discover too late that in practice you will be spending your time writing low-level computer code. Or that might be your idea of Heaven. The point is that you need to be comfortable with the main tasks required for the project.

What *response* have you got from potential supervisors?

You may have sent messages to several supervisors but only received replies from a few. Now, it could be that they are away or very busy, but still might be the ideal supervisor for you.

You may have met with more than one person. Assess the responses that you got from the supervisors that you have met. This will help you to decide whether or not you would be comfortable working with this person for the duration of the project. The sort of issues that turn out to be quite important are:

- whether you share the same view of the project's goals
- whether there is room for your opinions and contribution
- how you get on personally
- whether you can agree on how the project will be managed.

What information have you got?

Look at what you have managed to find out about the project from others, and from your own research. It may be that one project has plenty of information from previous students, and you have a detailed idea of what is involved.

Don't rule out a project because you cannot find out much about it (as it may be a cutting-edge idea, with little previous work, and not much available 'out there'). However, you need to be comfortable with the amount of information that is there, and this may help you to rank your choice.

What skills do you need for your career?

It may be that one project looks great fun and is with your favourite supervisor, but another one provides you with valuable experience for a favoured career or course of further study. Add this to your list. This is a hard decision to make, and only you can make it. In some situations it is best to invest in the longer-term plan, and in others it's more sensible to make your life easier by going for the more 'fun' choice.

2.6 Making your Decision

After asking yourself all the above questions, and making notes against each possible project, you will need to make a choice. Some Departments will ask you to rank your choices in order of preference, and then they will try to allocate you a project as high up your list as possible. Others require that you choose one project and agree that with the supervisor.

Sometimes students ask whether they can alter their choice later, if needed. There may be a time-frame within which this is possible. However, I would strongly advise against this (unless it's clear that a disastrous decision has been made) because you will have to re-think everything again, form new relationships, read new material, and you could rapidly get behind schedule. MUCH better is to take a longer time to make your initial project choice. If you're not sure, then go around the process again, maybe narrowing down the number of options you are giving yourself. Ask for another meeting with the supervisors. Go back to the previous students. Read up more on each subject. Effort invested at this point is not wasted, and you will end up feeling much more confident about your decision.

When you submit your choice, or choices, make sure you understand the procedure for the allocation of projects, especially finding out when you will know for sure.

The next chapter looks at what you can do to prepare for your project work before the official start-date, but it really helps if you know when the projects will be allocated.

2.7 Summary

Find out as soon as possible how your department allocates projects, and how much say you have in the discussion. If there is a list of suggested projects and supervisors then read this through carefully, taking note of the ones that are most of interest.

If possible, try to find people who have successfully completed projects in this area, or who have worked with that supervisor, and meet them to discuss their work and how they have found the experience.

Do some initial research on the topic, and on what information is currently out there. Think about what you would like your own contribution to be. When you feel adequately prepared, arrange a meeting with each potential supervisor and discuss the project, the area, their hopes for the project, and your own ideas. Ask lots of questions and aim to get as much information and discussion as possible within your meeting by preparing lists of questions in advance. This also shows the supervisor that you are keen, and willing to put in some effort.

When making your final choice of project make sure you take into account what *really* interests you; what type of work the day-to-day project execution will actually entail; your responses from the supervisors; the extent of starting information available; and the skills you need to develop for your career.

2.8 Further Reading

Find your own Department's guidelines for choosing and allocating projects and make sure you read these thoroughly.

3. GETTING A HEAD START

This chapter takes a look at what you can do to make a solid start to the project by preparing yourself during the time leading up to the start of the project. I've often noticed that it's the students who ask for 'summer reading' or enquire whether 'you would meet me before we officially start the project' who invariably are the most dedicated and thus end up with the better results.

So, think of this chapter as suggesting a *warm-up* routine; a series of activities that will get you set up - and indeed even making progress towards your project goals - *before* the official starting-date.

3.1 Read this book!

That may sound like a daft thing to say, especially as you are in the process of reading it right now. However, it may help you to plan some time now to read through the whole book.

Some of the later chapters deal with issues that are clearly intended for the end of the project process (such as planning for a spoken - viva - exam, and publishing your research work). It may seem a long way off at this point to be thinking about the end of the project, but you have probably heard the advice "Begin with the End in Mind" (Covey, 1989), which suggests that a project which is outcome-focussed is much more likely to become successful.

The earlier chapters of this book deal with more immediate issues of starting the project, maximising the effectiveness of the supervision process, how to manage yourself and your time, how to take notes and manage ideas, how to make the most of the other people working in this area, dealing with the main phases of the project and its planning, etc.

These chapters are much more useful if you can take the time to work through them and practice their ideas BEFORE the start of the project, because this way they will not detract from the project time. (However, if you are reading this later in the process, you will still gain benefit by taking some time out to learn how to work more effectively.)

So, why not take whatever diary system you currently use (this will be challenged and possibly expanded later in the book) and enter in something like reading a chapter a day, or some other schedule that will help you work through this book in small chunks.

3.2 Follow up suggested links

Some chapters suggest further information on a subject. If you are particularly interested in a certain topic, or you highlight a particular training need in yourself, then take some time to follow-up these links.

At this stage of the project, there are three types of follow-up links that are particularly useful:

1) **Topic-specific information**; obtained from your supervisor or department (e.g. previous student reports, or recommended papers and books to read) or your own explorations of the topic from Library and web-searches.

2) **Project management techniques**; even though I have tried to encapsulate most of what you need in this book, there are many places where you might want to follow-up a particular skill or technique (such as Mind Mapping). Links are listed at the end of chapters.

3) **Inspirational reading**; Many people who are at a transition stage in their life or career find it useful to put aside time for reading inspirational writing. This can be practical, spiritual, or motivational.

The main purpose of *this* book is to give you ideas and hints and links about 2) above. Topic-specific information (1) is best obtained from those directly involved in your project. For inspirational reading (3) I hesitate to give you my recommendations because this is such a personal issue that we are bound to find different things useful, acceptable, or relevant.

3.3 Train yourself to be a professional researcher

As you work through this book you will probably become aware of things that you want to improve (such as your note-taking, time management, etc.). It is important to schedule time to actually DO something about this.

Managing Your Project

The phrase "the road to Hell is paved with good intentions" often, sadly, applies to projects. If you simply are 'aware' of things that must be done or improved, but you do nothing about them, you live in a state of guilt and failure, and I guess that's a pretty good description of Hell. On the other hand, by addressing each issue, finding out about it, scheduling time to practice it, keeping a record of your progress, etc. you will find that you gain a great sense of satisfaction AND you are getting things done and moving the project on.

So, there are a number of things that you specifically can do to become a better project manager and researcher:

- get to know the field or topic in which your project lies
- take notes about the key papers and books
- develop your note-taking skills
- study what previous students have done and written
- get some general research training (see next section)

We will be covering all of the above topics very soon, but for the last point - on general research training - there is a specific online resource which is extremely useful.

3.3.1 Virtual Training Suite

Many of the general and specific skills you need to be a researcher in a particular field are summed up - highly visually - in a super set of web-pages under the banner Virtual Training Suite, commonly known as VTS Tutorials (www.vtstutorials.co.uk).

Each tutorial is based around a particular subject (listed on the front page alphabetically: starting with Aeronautical Engineering, Agriculture, Allied Health, American Studies, Anthropology, Archaeology, Architecture etc. – see Figure 3.1). Even if you can't quite find your exact subject, these are so useful that you should try picking something as close as possible to the topic of your project. They are designed to take about an hour to complete, but you can revisit as many times as you like.

For each topic, there is a summary of some of the best specific resources on the web for finding information about your particular subject area. These have been designed by university subject specialists and librarians and so give a good insight into the main places to visit on the web.

Figure 3.1 Front page for http://www.vtstutorials.co.uk/

On the way you will learn about (or get a refresher on) Academic Research - its principles and practices, and hints about how to do well, and warnings against common bad practices in research. There is also an overview of the different types of publication (books, journals etc.) and their relative advantages and disadvantages.

You will also get many subject-specific hints about how to find more detailed information about particular topics or papers.

There's also a lot here about the critical thinking and analysis that is necessary to understand and produce research papers and reports.

We will be covering a lot of the above areas later in the book (specifically in Chapter 19 on the Literature Survey), but this site gives an appealing and very well-constructed introduction to research in your specific topic area that would be very useful for giving you a head start.

3.4 Meet with your Supervisor

If your supervisor is willing and available, set up some occasional meetings to discuss your project - even though the official project period hasn't started yet. This not only demonstrates that you are keen, but it gives the supervisor hope that this is going to be a good project. If the supervisor is away, or you are in different places (e.g. during the summer vacation) then some email exchanges can be beneficial.

In the few projects I have supervised where things have gone really badly for the student, it has been because they have not been turning up or engaging with the material. Making a head-start on the project is an excellent way of developing good habits, and indeed setting up the student-supervisor relationship, which we shall look at in more detail in the next chapter.

3.5 Studying Previous Reports

One of the most useful ways of preparing for a project is to see some finished project reports. There are several reasons for this:

a) you get a crash-course in your particular topic area

b) you see some examples of your ultimate 'deliverable'

c) you can analyse which reports did well, and why

d) you get lots of ideas about layout, referencing, use of diagrams, and writing style.

If you are having a meeting with your supervisor during the preparation phase of the project, ask your supervisor for copies of previous reports in the same area as your project. Sometimes your project might be a direct 'follow-on' from a previous student's project, in which case it is *essential* to read and get to know the prior work. In other situations, you will get a report that is *related* to your project area.

If possible, ask for some indication of the mark that the report achieved. Studying a project that has achieved a good mark can give you lots of ideas of what you need to do to achieve the same. There is no way that you should copy or try to emulate the project on a surface level, but instead try to understand what it is that the student has achieved and presented, and then try to work out how you could produce something of a similar quality. Looking at a previous good project is not a short-cut to success, but it may well be an inspiration.

If it is a fairly recently completed project, your supervisor might be able to remember more details of the marking process, and might be willing to explain what it was that was particularly good about the project and report. I'd recommend not bothering to ask about those reports and project which didn't do well. There are *many* ways to do a 'bad' project, and - to be honest - you shouldn't be filling your mind with them. Instead, look for the inspirational projects, and target your work from the start to be as good as them.

3.6 Summary

There's a lot to be gained by getting a head-start on your project, and preparing yourself before the official starting date. Begin by reading this book so that you know what lies ahead.

Start reading and preparing as soon as you can. Typically it is useful to find:

- Topic-based information from supervisor, previous reports and your own research
- Project management techniques from this book
- Inspirational reading

Begin the process of becoming a professional researcher by reading up about research skills, and I recommend the Virtual Training Suite (http://www.vtstutorials.co.uk/).

Meet with your supervisor ahead of the official start if possible, and get recommendations for any previous student reports in this area. Then schedule time to read them, as they are a great source of information and inspiration.

3.7 Further Information and Resources

3.7.1 VTS Tutorials (www.vtstutorials.co.uk)

As described in section 3.3.1 above, these are an integrated online tutorial suite for students new to university-level research. Ordered by academic topic, they take the student through the principles of research and academic critique, as well as giving a thorough guide to the internet resources in each subject area.

3.7.2 Seven Habits of Highly Effective People

This classic self-help book by Stephen Covey has been top of the bestsellers list for nearly 3 decades now. If you're looking for a guide to planning, getting motivated, aiming high, working out how you can be more effective etc., then this book might be worth a read (see reference below).

(Covey, 1989) Stephen R. Covey, Seven Habits of Highly Effective People: Powerful Lessons in Personal Change, Simon & Schuster Ltd; Reprinted Edition (4 Jan 2004), ISBN-10: 0684858398, ISBN-13: 978-0684858395

4. GETTING STARTED

So, it begins.

The start of a major project can be a really exciting experience, but at the same time a rather daunting one. There is so much to be done, but it is often not clear precisely what should be done. Many times this leads students to not doing anything, and bad habits are set up. This chapter deals with the beginning of the official project time, and walks you through a number of things that you can do to really kick the project into action.

It can be read as an independent chapter if needed, but it works best of all if it's read as a follow-on to Chapter 3 (Getting a Head Start). The *ideal* situation is that you have read Chapter 3 and implemented its advice *before* the official project period began. If you've done already this, then please feel free to skip section 4.1 and go straight to 4.2.

4.1 If the project has begun and you've not read Chapter 3

It's not always possible to start work on a project before the official project period begins. You may be arriving at your new educational institution and the project begins immediately, giving you little time for advance preparation. You might have only just discovered this book, and are reading it to find out what you should have done earlier.

It's worth reading Chapter 3, because it's all about getting yourself prepared mentally for the project. Read it, but look out for those things you can do which will prepare the groundwork for your project, and your own working practices and research techniques.

If you look again at its summary, these are basically the things it advises:

Managing Your Project

- Set time aside to read through this book
- Follow up its links & references
- Set out to be a professional-quality researcher; and schedule time to get there
- Meet with your supervisor, to discuss the project topic and plans
- Get hold of previous (good) project reports and study them carefully for insight.

In other words, it is advisable to set aside time to prepare yourself for this huge task by reading all about the topic, taking advice about project management, getting ideas on research techniques, talking to your supervisor, and reading any previous student reports in your topic area.

4.2 Get to know your supervisor

One of the most important first steps in a new project is to meet with your supervisor to discuss the project. Therefore it's important to organise a meeting as soon as possible.

4.2.1 Setting up supervision meetings

Some universities and colleges will do this for you and will timetable your supervisions. Occasionally a supervisor will send out a meeting request to you, possibly containing a timetable for supervisions. More often, though, it will be up to *you* to initiate the contact, and negotiate a meeting date, time and place.

This can be your first taste that this large Project is going to be different from what you are familiar with. You have probably been used to being told when and where to go for your lectures, seminars, labs, workshops etc. Now, you are being asked to organise something. And so it should be like that, because this is *your* project and you are the manager (but more about this later, particularly see Chapter 6 - the 2-stage work process).

Therefore you need to take the initiative on this. Look at your own schedule and come up with a series of suggestions for meeting times. Usually email is a good way of setting this up, but don't be worried about following this up with a phone call or a visit if you haven't had a reply within a few days. The meeting place will usually be the supervisor's office, but occasionally it can be somewhere else such as a coffee bar.

The following chapter gives you more of a detailed insight into the supervision process itself, and how to get the best out of it.

4.2.2 What to discuss in your first supervision

a) Project Aims. The most important thing to do in your early supervision meetings is to talk through the project aims and try to align your thinking with that of your supervisor. The supervisor may have a very clear idea about where the project should be heading, and you may have your own equally clear idea of what you think you will be doing. It's vital that you discuss these aims to make sure that you are heading in the same direction. You and your supervisor will be working as a team and you need to make sure you are working on the same project! Be prepared for this to take a bit of time to sort out - that is perfectly normal. There's a whole chapter coming up on setting your Aims and Objectives (Chapter 17), so you might like to study that in more detail nearer the time of your first supervision.

b) Recommended Reading. You can also use the first supervision meetings to ask for some recommended reading, such as previous projects, useful web links, academic papers on the subject. What to do with these reports is discussed in Chapter 3: *Getting a Head Start*.

c) Set up Supervision Meetings. Determine with your supervisor how you are going to organise supervision meetings. Some universities will prescribe these meetings (e.g. once per week in the first term of the project) and even timetable the meetings for you. However, it is common practice for this to be left up to the student and supervisor to sort out for themselves. Therefore it's important to discuss this at your first meeting.

There appear to be three common ways of handling this:

1) **Agree together a fixed schedule of supervision meetings** (e.g. once per week or every two weeks at a fixed time in the supervisor's office). This gives you solid points of reference to put in your calendar or diary, and is a good way of getting used to the regular commitment required. Advantage: Fixed, regular meetings you can rely on and plan around. Disadvantage: Sometimes there may not be much to talk about.

2) **At each meeting, get your diaries out and agree the time and place of the NEXT meeting.** Advantage: The meetings can be more flexibly allocated to account for varying timetables, and varying workload. Disadvantage: There's a time/effort overhead involved in setting up every meeting, and there can be more of a temptation to skip a meeting.

3) **As a student, you request a meeting when you need it.** *Advantage:* For students with experience in project management this can suit a highly flexible arrangement. Meetings are not held for the sake of it, and are more likely to be targeted at a particular student need.

Managing Your Project

Disadvantage: If you are new to project management, you are not as likely to know when you should be meeting, as you are not familiar with the processes or what is required. In that case this method is likely to result in a lack of supervision, and the student 'drifting'.

If you and your supervisor don't really mind I would recommend style 1) for an undergraduate project, 2) for a Masters project, and 3) for a PhD.

d) Agree a communication method. Individual supervisors have different ways of managing their time and their diary. Some may have their own admin staff or Personal Assistant (PA), but many will be juggling multiple conflicting demands as well as managing their own systems. It's important to have an open discussion about the best method of communicating with your supervisor.

Some people run an 'open-door' policy, which effectively means 'if you can see that I'm free, please drop in for a chat'. Others may have 'open office hours', where there are some timetabled slots where the open-door policy applies. Others may be so busy they can only operate by a strict appointment system. Still others may prefer contact by a particular method, such as email, phone, internal appointments system, etc.

My personally preferred method is **email** (even if it's used to set up a face-to-face meeting) because it's an asynchronous medium. This means that you send the message when it's convenient for you, and I receive the message when it's convenient for me. (Note that with email, you only disturb people if they have chosen to indicate an incoming message with an alert, and this is their *choice*.)

You will also need to do a bit of experimentation with what actually works best in practice. (As an aside, this is a really useful tip for life in general. There is no single communication method that works for everyone. When you need to have regular communication with someone, actually discuss what they prefer, and then monitor the situation to see if it actually works).

You might find that some supervisors are slow to answer their email, and that phoning, or asking an admin assistant is a lot more effective. For some people the open-door policy works, but in practice you might find it frustrating to turn up, only to find your supervisor busy with a queue of other people.

4.3 Set up a Team

For a solo project, it is clear from the name that it is mainly going to be one person - i.e. you - doing the work. You will be meeting with your supervisor, hopefully on a regular basis, but it's important to involve other people wherever possible.

Try to establish a *team* of people who are working in a similar area, and others who can give you some support. There are different ways of finding those working in your topic area. Your supervisor is a good place to start. Sometimes they will actively set up discussion groups with various students doing their projects. It's very likely that these will all be in very similar subject areas. If there is nothing formally arranged for you, please consider taking the initiative and setting this up for yourself. If there are no other students studying with your supervisor, look wider. Try for other students doing a similar project with other supervisors. What's important is that they are following the same timing structure as you, and are doing projects with similar expectations and demands.

You may wonder what is so important about getting other people involved in what is meant to be an individual project. Whilst it is true that your topic should have an individual focus, it is the management of the whole complex process which benefits from having a group of peers. These are the main reasons to include others:

- Your **supervisor's time is limited** and shared between many people and conflicting responsibilities, so should not be your *only* source of support.

- You give each other **Motivation** - someone else to talk to who is going through similar demands and pressures.

- **Checking on each other** - making sure you're all working towards upcoming deadlines, and are making progress on your work.

- **Proofreading** and checking - we will see later in the book that it's often very hard to spot errors in your own work, so you can provide a free service to each other (with a group of people who are likely to understand your topic).

- You can set up **meetings to discuss concepts and problems**. Often there are common issues to address, and this gives you a ready-made group who don't mind spending their time because you all benefit.

- You get a ready **group to try things out on**, such as a survey or a computer program. Many projects produce ideas or prototypes which need testing. Try things out on your friendly and understanding group first.

- Giving **presentations** to your team. If giving talks is part of your course, or training, then what better than an audience who have a vested interest in your general topic area?

Chapter 9: *Setting up a Special Interest Group (SIG)* covers each of the above points in detail. Don't wait until later in the project when you might suddenly be aware of the need for help, but try to get the group established at the start of the project.

Schedule some meetings, or at least an initial time to meet, so that discussions can begin. Maybe invite the others via email, and if you'd like to recommend the book while you're doing it ... ;-)

4.4 Set the Main Deadlines

It's important from the start to establish the main deadlines and expectations for the project. The irony is that on such a big project there are often *few* deadlines (maybe an initial report, final report and possibly a presentation or demonstration). This raises the importance of planning for these big deadlines carefully, right from the start.

Look up your university's assessment information, and make sure you understand exactly what is required, by when, and in what format. Check with your supervisor if you are not sure.

In the later sections on Time Management and Project Planning, we will see how important it is to create a whole set of carefully structured sub-deadlines, which will guarantee to get you delivering the big ones on time and up to standard.

Some people recommend putting some sort of chart or timing diagram on your wall (or somewhere that you will see it daily) showing where you are now, and what is coming up in the future - including your various required submissions. This can help you see the 'big picture' on a daily basis, which can be a useful motivator for managing your project effectively.

Take note - one of the VERY WORST things you can say to yourself (and I have seen this happen *so* often) is this:

"Oh, the main deadline is ages off. It doesn't concern me now. No need to sweat on my project. I'll use all this 'free time' for ... <insert favourite distraction here>"

The main deadline will sneak up on you like a train coming at you down a tunnel, and you will wonder where all the time went. Free time is important, and you must plan for it. But Project time is not free time.

4.5 Establish a method for taking notes, recording ideas

Particularly in the early stages of the project you will be gathering information. In fact that really ought to be your *main* occupation. This information may come in many forms, such as:

- instructions from your supervisor
- ideas from your own head about the project
- web-searches for related topics and papers etc.
- lists of books to read
- previous reports to read (and the rich sources of information inside them)
- ideas from discussions with fellow students.

It is really important that you find a way of keeping all this information, firstly so that you can effectively capture it, and secondly so that you can retrieve it when needed.

Nowadays there are various electronic (computer-based) methods of storing and filing information. It is really worthwhile considering setting up a comprehensive electronic system. Because quite a few of your ideas will already be in computer-based form (e.g. a web-search) it can save a lot of time and printer ink if you can save this electronically. However, many people feel instinctively that paper-based records are more tangible and somehow more 'real'. You will need to examine, from the outset of the project, your preferred method for keeping notes and tracking all your incoming information. If you don't have some sort of system, you are bound to lose valuable ideas.

Chapter 7 - *Taking Notes and keeping records* covers this topic in more detail and considers the advantages and disadvantages of each of the options.

4.6 Write something as soon as you can

One of the biggest mistakes in a large project is to think that the only writing you need to do is for your final report, so you can leave thinking about that towards the end of the project. On the contrary, because the final report is such a big part of the project and its mark, you need to practice writing from the outset. But there are other benefits beyond 'rehearsing' for the end report.

Often writing things down is a really helpful way of getting your thoughts out in the open so that you can assess them and refine them. It allows you to capture fleeting ideas. It has been said that the best way to get a *good* idea is to have *lots* of ideas (of variable quality) and then evaluate each one. You can also show your writing to other people, including your supervisor, and ask for feedback.

If you feel daring, why not establish a *daily* writing routine. Many authors will tell you that the concept of 'morning pages' helps them produce book after book, or paper after paper. The idea is to write about 3 pages of text every day. This can be free-flow thoughts, or it might be the next bit of a larger project you are working on.

You might be interested to know that this book was mostly written using this method. The ideas were stuck in my head, waiting several years for an opportunity to emerge, but there was never a suitable time to just sit down and write it. By chance I came across the website *750words.com*, which was set up by Buster Benson to encourage people to develop this regular writing habit. If you subscribe, you get daily reminders, a place to write your words without distraction, archiving of material, encouragement from a worldwide peer group of people writing, and statistics and 'accomplishments'. This is the first thing that has worked to get me writing every day, and it has suited my style of working. You may want to try this or something similar. The advantage of daily writing is that you develop the habit, and you surprise yourself not only with how many ideas you already have, but with what you actually write. Some of it will be useful for your final purpose (e.g. this book, or your report), but it's also about the process.

The important thing is to get your ideas down and stored, whether electronically, or on paper.

4.7 Establish when & where you will work

We're going to be looking in detail at issues of time management and planning, but from the very start it's worth setting up a Workspace. This is somewhere that you can do the majority of your project work; somewhere that you will *associate* with focussing on your project and being productive.

Everyone's workspace is different. Here are a few ideas that people have found to work for them. Not every one will appeal to you, but you might get some inspiration about setting up your own:

- a special room which you dedicate to becoming your office. As you walk in, this is your working environment.

- a particular project lab or computer space at your university.

- one corner of your study-bedroom, where the desk is, that you customise to have all your project material at hand.

- taking a laptop to a quiet room (e.g. a library) where you will not get disturbed, or where the atmosphere is of people quietly and diligently working.

- sitting in bed with a cup of tea and a laptop computer to do your main planning.

- outside on a bench with a cup of coffee and a notepad, absorbing the sun and having time to think and jot down ideas and plans.

- working on any computer, but arranging your web-browser so that it has access to your on-line files and notes, and with a set of headphones to allow you to listen to your favourite music or maybe a noise-generator to help with concentration and to drown out surrounding noise.

(I can hear a few of you laughing at the impossibility of some of the ideas above, but they all work for someone. The important thing is to establish your own special space.)

As important as deciding *where* you're going to work, is that you plan for WHEN you will work. This is clearly a time management issue, but in the early days of the project, you need not make this too complicated. Find a few hours each day when you are at your best, and dedicate this to the project. Your job is then to find the appropriate work that needs to be done to fill this time. Too many students don't think in detail about what they specifically need to do, and end up squandering huge amounts of precious project time. Many an exasperated and stressed-out student will be found saying towards the end of the project *"IF ONLY I had got my act together and started working early!!"*

4.8 Summary

Arrange a meeting with your supervisor as soon as possible. If nothing is scheduled for you then take the initiative and arrange this via email. At that meeting make sure you discuss and agree on the Aims of the project, as you will probably both have different ideas. Also use this first meeting to agree on the scheduling of future meetings, and the communication methods for the project (phone, email, drop-in, etc.).

Set up a team of people to help with mutual support in the project process. These can be students with the same supervisor as you, or working in a similar area. Your supervisor's time is limited, and with a support team you can help each other with motivation, proofreading, testing, discussing, and just having others to talk things through with.

Acknowledge your project's main deliverables (initial report, presentation, final report, viva, etc.) right from the start, and begin the planning process immediately. Some of these are huge requirements, which need a slow, sustained commitment, rather than a last-minute rush.

Discover your preferred way of making notes and storing ideas (e.g. paper-based filing system, or computer-based note system etc.) and use it regularly to capture ideas from your own head (they may not visit you again!) and from your supervisor and support team. Use it also as the core of your research and reading information storage.

Begin the process of writing as early as you possibly can. It's a mistake to leave this until some mythical time in the future when you will finally be ready to write your report. Writing is a habit, and you might like to look at something like 750words.com to get yourself writing regularly.

Find a place or environment that can be used as a Workspace (this can be a specific room, or area, or a certain set of cues that get you into the working mood). Decide when you are going to work, on a regular basis, and find the most appropriate tasks for you to do on the project during those times. This is an antidote for the all-too-common "I'll leave it for now and work harder later".

4.9 External References

http://750words.com/ - a website that encourages you to write about 3 pages of text every day. This book was written using this technique, and it just might help you to tackle the major reports in your project.

On-line noise generators, such as http://mynoise.net/ allow you to customise some masking noise, which many people find helps them to concentrate on work, as well as cancelling out disturbing sounds around you.

5. THE SUPERVISION PROCESS

The working relationship between student and supervisor is a vital one for any project. In this chapter we take a step back from the details or the specifics of your particular project to consider how to make sure that this relationship works well.

5.1 Projects and supervisors

For many small-scale projects and assignments (such as those encountered in your studies so far) there may not be a supervisor, and you are entirely responsible for managing, making decisions and completing the assignment. Or indeed it may be a group-based project with a supervisor whose main job is to oversee whether the group itself is operating effectively. This chapter assumes that you are dealing with a major project with an assigned or chosen supervisor who indeed might have set the project in the first place. The interaction between you and your supervisor is the primary communication path in your project, so it is important to look at ways of maximising the benefits of this relationship.

5.2 The *real* purpose of the supervision process

You can think of the supervision process as the meeting of two minds. Your supervisor usually has more experience in the general topic area, and you will have more time available to work on a subset of the topic area. Therefore at the end of the project, it is *you* who will be the expert in the sub-topic you have studied. Indeed, if you are studying at a higher level, such as a PhD, you could well end up being the *world* expert in a specifically focussed area. Understanding this dynamic is the key to a successful relationship.

Managing Your Project

The supervision process is actually necessary for most research to proceed, primarily because of this partnership between a dedicated researcher (with plenty of time to focus, think, search for information, test and try things out) and someone who usually has more experience of carrying out and overseeing projects, and can offer ideas and perspectives not yet available to the new researcher. On your part you will, quite rightly, value the supervisor as a guide to the whole process, and someone to turn to for advice and support. On the other hand the supervisor gains a lot from the relationship too; they have someone available to focus on some research that they do not have the time for, and who will probably come up with a whole new set of ideas they never thought of before.

The idea of the supervision relationship being a *dynamic* one is important. The project period allows you the time to make the transition from 'being rather new and unsure of how to proceed' to 'being a confident and independently-driven researcher'.

5.3 Does my supervisor have all the answers?

Hopefully, you will have enough of a feel for research to know that *nobody* has all the answers. However, it is shocking how many students consider their supervisor as some sort of 'guru' - an informed guide who already knows the solutions to their problems.

The supervisor can indeed guide you at all stages of the process, but remember that, in a good research project, you are both working on something new, so there are no ready-packaged 'right answers'. Supervisors are often likely to answer your questions with another question, and for good reason. Consider the following two conversations.

Supervision 1

Student: I'm really stuck on this tricky problem. I need to make a decision, but should it be 'path A' or 'path B'?

Supervisor: Path A

Student: Ok thanks.

Supervision 2

Student: I'm really stuck on this tricky problem. I need to make a decision, but should it be 'path A' or 'path B'?

Supervisor: Mmmm – that *is* a tricky problem! What do *you* think is the solution?

Student: Er, *(pause)* well, path A might be the easiest to get going with, but B is the most elegant solution. However it will be expensive and will take me ages.

Supervisor: Ok, so what do you think you should do then?

Student: Well, I suppose we could *try* path A, because at least I can get on with it. Then we could meet again to discuss how it went, and if it was no good, then we would have to think again about path B.

Supervisor: Seems like a good idea. Are you happy to get on with that?

Student: Ok thanks.

Notice that in both conversations the opening and closing sentences are the same. But do you notice how the learning process is very different? The irony is that many students actually *want* the first conversation. They want to 'learn from the guru', and 'be told the right way to go'. Look again at the first conversation. The student is left with the feeling that the supervisor already knows the answer, and that their supervisor really is a guru with all the answers. The student probably has no idea of why path A has been chosen, so really not much has been learnt. Worse still, in the final examination someone might ask "Why did you take path A?", and the honest (but not very impressive) reply is "because my supervisor told me to". In other words, it reinforces the student's view that they do not know the answer, and that other people are somehow better than them at being able to find an answer.

In contrast, in the second conversation, because the supervisor holds back from giving a straight answer, several things have occurred:

- The supervisor demonstrates that there is no easy/obvious choice
- The student feels that they have an important say in the process
- The student has been allowed to come up with their own reasons for the choice
- The student will be able to justify this decision to anyone else in the future.

5.4 Pastoral support from the supervision process

In addition to your project supervisor, it is probable that you will already have an academic supervisor, whom you have known from when you first joined university. The academic supervisor is your main link with your educational establishment. So, he or she needs to know as soon as possible if anything goes wrong (illness, lack of focus, or any other circumstance that affects your work). It may be that by the final year, you are seeing less of this supervisor, but do remember to keep them in touch with anything that affects your progress.

The project supervisor will probably be seeing you a lot more often than your academic supervisor, and so may be an important person to talk to about problems that are wider than your immediate project challenges. Some students prefer to keep these two roles quite distinct, choosing to only inform their academic supervisor about 'life' problems, and only talking about the project with the project supervisor. This is certainly one way of working, and it does keep the roles distinct. However, there are some benefits to sharing more freely with both supervisors. Your academic supervisor has known you for a lot longer and thus may be able to offer some useful perspectives on your project, even though it might not be their specialist subject. The project supervisor will probably notice if you are not making progress, and it is often useful to let them know if you are facing some external problems.

From this point onwards in the book, we will no longer refer to your academic supervisor, but will assume that the word 'supervisor' refers solely to the person allocated to helping you through the project process.

The supervisor can also help you to be aware of the arrangements and deadlines that concern your project, but remember that it is *you* who needs to manage the details of your workload so that those deadlines are met.

5.5 Understanding the job of the supervisor

As a general rule, whenever you are communicating with other people, you should try to be aware of some of their concerns, demands and priorities. This usually makes for better communication and understanding between people.

Quite naturally you will initially regard your supervisor as "the person who helps me with my project". The purpose of this section is to explain that, although that is true, it is not how life looks from the supervisor's perspective.

Whilst it is true that your supervisor has the very important role of helping you in your project, they also have hundreds of other tasks to do. A university supervisor, for example, has all their other students to supervise (at both undergraduate, masters and doctoral level), each with different topics and schedules to manage. Even so, you might be surprised to find out that all of these supervision commitments constitute just a small part of the job. You might refer to him or her as 'my supervisor' but the job role of 'lecturer', for example, extends way beyond looking after project students. There are the regular lecturing commitments (and preparing a lecture takes a *lot* longer than the hour or so it takes to deliver it, often days of work for each lecture). Then there is the Research role, by which many academics and universities are assessed. Research applications take months to prepare and a high proportion face rejection; but credit is only given for those very few that are accepted. When grants are awarded, then the work is committed to be carried out; large-scale, risky, experimental projects and teams of people need to be managed. Then there are the administrative tasks; Boards of Studies to manage the curriculum, exam marking and feedback (Reading maybe 80 papers and filling in a page of feedback for each, multiplied by the number of modules they teach), Exam Meetings, Disciplinary Procedures, letters of reference to write for past students (all of which begin with something like "I know you haven't heard from me for years but please read my CV, this application pack, and write me a 2-page reference by tomorrow"), staff-student liaison meetings, and minutes to prepare, new courses to develop, interviews for prospective students and researchers, journal papers to be written (again on which you are assessed and judged), books to write, conferences to referee, conferences to attend, plan and present ongoing work at . . . and the list goes on and on.

This is not intended to make you feel sorry for your 'poor old supervisor', but it is intended to help you to understand the commitments and perspective of the 'other half' of your supervision process.

5.6 Working with your supervisor

Understanding these other pressures and commitments will help you in the way that you communicate with, and plan work with, your supervisor.

As a specific example, imagine that you would benefit from some feedback on something you have written (perhaps 20 pages of a project report). Because you have decided that this is important to you, it would be easy to think of your supervisor as some sort of 'feedback service', and ask them to "look at this before our meeting tomorrow". However, now that you are aware of some of the commitments that your supervisor is already dealing with as a matter of course, you might find other ways of approaching the issue, such as:

"I would really like some feedback on chapter 1 of my report. Ideally I need this by the end of the month to allow me to respond to any feedback while writing my next chapters, which I hope to do next month. Do you have any time in the next two weeks to look at this?"

Note that in order to allow this much time (i.e. waiting two weeks for feedback) you will have had to identify the need early. In other words - as a general rule - if you wish to effectively (and courteously) use someone else's resources it is important to plan ahead.

Knowledge of your supervisor's other commitments will also help when you are structuring your regular contact with them, as we will see in the next section.

5.7 Maximising the benefits of the supervision process

There are no fixed rules about supervisions. As explained in Chapter 4 - *Getting Started* you should arrange with your supervisor how often you plan to meet, and whether to pre-book those meetings in advance, or to 'wait until one is needed'.

In the next three paragraphs we will look at three issues that will transform those meetings, and in fact the whole supervision process:

- Preparing for meetings
- Cooperating in research
- Moving from dependence to independence

a) Prepare for Meetings by ensuring that you know what you want to get out of each particular meeting and letting your supervisor know this in advance. You may want to try producing an *Agenda* (a structured plan of issues to be discussed), which can be sent to the supervisor ahead of the meeting. This helps you both to be clear about what you want to achieve. Your supervisor can add extra items to that agenda, and this results in a joint list of what needs discussing. This is not to imply that your meetings need to be terribly formal, but rather that you both take part in the meeting knowing what you want as outcomes. This also helps your supervisor to 'tune-in' to your specific research topic and problems, given that for hours beforehand they will be working on many of the other commitments outlined above.

b) Cooperate in research by showing an interest in the other things that the supervisor is involved with. People generally enjoy discussing their work with other people, so why not ask your supervisor about his or her other research projects? By this process you will gain a wider view of your project and where it fits into an area of research. This can be very impressive to external examiners, who find that you can talk not only about your own work, but other ongoing research, and a knowledge of where your work fits into the bigger picture. Also, subtly, this sort of discussion makes you and your supervisor both feel more like a team, rather than a hierarchy.

c) **Move from dependence to independence** by using the supervision process to learn to be a researcher in your own right. At the start of a project you may need a lot of guidance in the topic, and in the processes of study. Supervisions may be packed with questions from you and guidance from the supervisor. During the middle stage of the project, supervisions become discussions, and towards the end – you find that *you* have become the expert in your area, demonstrating to the supervisor what you have done or discovered. A supervisor who 'makes himself redundant' by working with a student until they are a confident, independent worker, has probably done a good job. But this can only work if you play your part, and gradually take on more responsibility for the management of your own project.

5.8 Summary

The relationship between student and supervisor is a highly important one in a major project, so it is worth investing some time and study to make sure that this relationship works well for both people. As the project progresses you should expect that this relationship will change, so that at the end of the process you are a confident and independent researcher. One of the supervisor's main tasks is to help you get to that position.

It's very important for students to realise that - in a research project - their supervisor does not automatically know all the answers. In fact, a key part of the supervision process is discussion and negotiation, and from this the student will gain confidence in taking their own research decisions.

The other role that your supervisor plays is that of extra pastoral support above and beyond that which you receive from your longer-term 'academic' supervisor. It makes sense to keep them informed about any problems you are having, because the project supervisions will probably be occurring more regularly than the final-year academic ones.

Supervisors are usually full-time academics with hundreds of ongoing commitments. It's important to be aware of this when you're communicating with them or hoping that they will do something for you (such as giving you some feedback on a report). In order to maximise the benefits that you and your supervisor will get from the process, the following three things are suggested.

Managing Your Project

1. Prepare in advance for each meeting, and notify the supervisor.
2. Take an interest in the other research work that your supervisor is doing.
3. Expect to take on a more proactive approach as the project progresses, so that by the end of the process you are entirely managing your project and have become an expert in your specialist area.

In summary, your supervisor:

- Usually has more experience in running projects
- Typically knows more about the topic area, at least to begin with
- Is there for you to discuss things with, not to 'tell you the answers'
- Can help you to continually review your progress
- Needs to know about any problems sooner rather than later
- Does not have a big block of time to work on detailed projects
- Needs you as part of the team to push forward the research field
- Will not be the expert in your sub-topic by the end of the project
- Has all sorts of other commitments to deal with that you should be aware of.

SECTION 2
ORGANISING YOURSELF –
IDEAS, TOOLS & TECHNIQUES

This section contains a series of chapters covering some of the most important skills needed to navigate the solo project process. This section applies not just to the start of the project, but to the whole process and the way you organise your work in general.

- **Ch. 6 The 2-stage work process** - *understanding that your role now includes much more management and organisation than before.* You need to be both Manager and Worker, both Planner and Implementer. This chapter talks you through why this dual process is important, and why it is a distinct and necessary part of solo project work.

- **Ch. 7 Taking notes and keeping records** - *because (especially in the early stages of the project) you will be encountering masses of new material, and having lots of new ideas.* It is essential to the success of your project that you find an effective way to capture and process these ideas.

- **Ch. 8 Mind-Mapping** - *a graphical note-taking and planning technique which should be more widely taught.* Using graphical pen-and-paper or computer software, mind-mapping helps you with effective planning, note-taking, meeting planning, document development and project planning.

- **Ch. 9 Setting up a Special Interest Group (SIG)** - *because doing a solo project can be lonely work, and it is vital to set up and maximise the use of a support network.* A superb way of doing this is to gather a small group of students doing similar and related work in order to support each other.

6. THE 2-STAGE WORK PROCESS

In this chapter we identify two major functions that need to be carried out in any project; a *planning* role (the Manager) and an *execution* role (the Worker) - a 2-stage work process. In many group projects, different tasks are assigned to different people. For a solo project, there is only you, and this brings with it a whole set of challenges.

6.1 Your new dual role

Because you are now in charge of a large-scale project, it is important to recognise that you have *two* distinct roles to play.

Firstly you are a Project **Manager**. It is *you* who sets the overall direction, and monitors progress along the way. Managers generally work with a series of plans and have the job of making sure that the workers always have the right work to do, so they can make progress with minimum hassle and interruption.

However, you are *also* the **Worker**, and yet there's only one of you. If the Manager has prepared a series of plans, and is checking how things are going, it is you - the Worker - who actually gets things done. You will need to write the reports, carry out the experiments, write the computer code, run the survey, interview people, do the presentation, meet with people etc.

But why is it important to identify these two separate roles? Mainly, because both roles are vital to a project, and in my experience students often get them out of balance. The first step in re-balancing the roles is often the awareness that such a duality exists. When your inner Manager and Worker are both operating effectively the following happens:

- your project is planned, prioritised and organised effectively;

- everything gets done, ahead of schedule and to good quality;
- you feel relaxed about the whole process;
- you can communicate with others clearly about your project.

6.2 Some Doomsday scenarios

It's worth looking at some of the things that can go wrong when these two roles do not operate effectively. This is partly so you can spot and identify the symptoms if they happen to you, and partly to spur you on to make sure that this does NOT happen to you.

Scenario 1. Keen Worker. No Manager.

You wouldn't believe how often this happens. An over-keen worker just jumps right in to the project work, without a detailed plan, and assumes that just by working hard the project will be a success. Typically (and I write this from a science-computing background) the student starts writing computer code. They do this quite rightly believing that a lot of the project's final output will be in the form of code, so they assume they should just get on with it. *DOOMSDAY FACT:* Most of the hard work is likely to be wasted. Without a carefully thought-out plan with regular monitoring and communication with other people, you are likely to end up with a big piece of work that does not fit the aims of the project. In other words - you've wasted your time.

Scenario 2. Super Manager. No Worker.

Now, while this situation doesn't happen very often, it is a nasty thing when it does occur. It happens when someone gets SO caught up in all the Project Management tools that very little *progress* actually occurs. Sometimes you will find a student who has confidently produced 3 GANTT charts, 24 MindMaps, has done Risk Analysis and PERT-charts, has instituted Quality Control procedures, and technical standards, and is an expert on what *should* happen. *DOOMSDAY FACT:* Yet no actual process has been made on the project. The reason that this is rare is because a thorough Manager will usually be so overwhelmingly aware of what needs to happen, that they will *have* to get some work done to preserve their own sanity. But watch out for this, in case it happens to you. Manage your project carefully, but remember that Management is useless if nothing gets done.

Scenario 3. Ineffective or Absent Manager and Worker.

This is the worst of all. In case you're thinking "Oh no, this is me. I just *know* I'm going to be a lousy Manager and Worker", then keep reading, and the very fact that you are addressing it and reading this means that you are aware of what you need to improve and are taking steps to do just that.

Scenario 3 happens when little time and effort is given to the project. At least with Scenario 1 *something* happens, whether or not it's focussed on the correct goals! At least with Scenario 2, there is a good *plan* and eventually some actual progress may happen.

With Scenario 3 the student is fully occupied with other things, and neither Manager nor Worker does much. Life is full of interesting things at University; new friends and relationships, clubs and societies, activities, sport, visits, chilling out, etc. All of these things are great - in moderation. *DOOMSDAY FACT:* If you don't regularly work on your project you rapidly get behind, and the project can fail.

6.3 Manager and Worker roles you may know about

If you have had any contact with people in the workplace, you will probably have heard conversations about bosses and workers. Quite often this will be negative, simply because humans tend to moan about stuff at length, whilst praising things only in tiny doses. If you want more of this, please look at the wonderful Dilbert cartoons (http://dilbert.com/). Conversations are also often about the roles and personalities of bosses and how they are different from the person telling the story. This section is not about that - but more about looking at examples of a 2-stage work process in action.

6.3.1 Pulp Fiction - the Manager in action

It may seem strange to begin with a fictional example, but there's a lot to learn here. In Quentin Tarantino's Pulp Fiction (1994) there is a masterful performance of a Manager sorting out an emergency situation. Harvey Keitel plays Winston Wolfe, known in the film simply as 'The Wolf', and who is a fixer - a person who sorts out bad situations[1]. It's a violent film, and for the two main characters (played by John Travolta and Samuel L. Jackson) everything has gone wrong and there's a dead body and a lot of mess in a car and they are in deep trouble. The Wolf is called for, and while our characters fret, curse, swear and are completely ineffective, the Wolf - in contrast - asks for a cup of tea, and takes time to compliment the owner of the house. Even though time is short, he takes his time - refuses to be hurried or pushed - and gathers the facts. Over his cup of tea

---

[1] Recently the character Winston Wolfe has appeared in a series of insurance adverts to promote the ideas of being prepared and of taking rapid action in a crisis.

he devises a plan and then instructs our characters (much to their annoyance) about exactly what to do. And he saves them.

The points to take from this fictional (and warning, rather nasty in places) example are these:

- even when under the greatest pressure, slow down and take time out to plan
- over a cup of tea, work out what needs to be done
- communicate the plan simply and directly to those who will carry it out
- (and - not so much to do with this chapter - be nice, but firm, to those who are hassling you).

The differences between this and your project are:

a) *you* are going to have to carry out the work, after the plan has been calmly formed

b) hopefully there won't be any dead bodies to clear up.

6.3.2 Exam Technique

Most of you will have been through exams, some of you more recently than others. Presumably you have been coached in exam technique? One of the best pieces of advice is this:

a) take time out at the start. Read through the rubric, which will confirm how long you have got, how many questions you need to answer, and any restrictions such as "choose 1 question from 3".

b) take time out at the end. Read over what you have written. Check your working. Look for mistakes and make corrections if needed.

These two pieces of 'time out' before and after you answer the questions are a classic piece of Manager work. In the middle is the main thrust of the exam, which we can imagine as being carried out by the Worker.

You have probably felt the pressure to dive straight in and get going with the questions. After all, you only have 90 minutes and the clock is ticking. But like The Wolf, you need to refuse to be pushed, and take some of that precious time to carefully read the questions, consider which ones you are going to answer, calculate the remaining time and thus how long you have left for each question.

Just recently I have seen the results of a student who disobeyed this advice. It was not a pretty sight. He answered the first question in great detail, using up most of his time as it was a very tricky question. There was only time left to answer the second question very briefly (yet it counted equally) and only then did he see that both the other two questions on the paper were easier than the one he had wasted his time answering.

The general advice to take from this? Always take some time out at the beginning of a complex process to plan it carefully. Also take time at the end to review what's been done. (If it's complex - like your project - you'll need to also review it regularly *as you go along*). This takes up time that would otherwise be used working on the process, but now the work can be carried out in the confidence that it is the *right* work.

6.3.3 Reviewing Projects Weekly

Many time management techniques involve the notion of taking time away from your work in order to plan it effectively.

David Allen, author of Getting Things Done (Allen, 2002) says that a WEEKLY review is the key to successful management. Over many years of analysing how well (and badly) people function in the working environment, he has noticed a strong correlation between the Weekly Review and personal effectiveness. The idea is to take a few hours each week to do the following:

- gather all your 'loose ends' - empty in-trays, gather notes and scraps of paper;
- process all of these according to their function in your life (e.g. action, storage);
- review all the previous week's events;
- go through all your projects, and establish the next actions on each, which are then placed in your diary or action planner;
- preview the week ahead and do any preparation necessary.

More will be said about this in Chapter 12 – *Introduction to GTD*.

Still other time management systems emphasise a Daily review, where the next day's work is planned out.

What all of the systems have in common is that you should not just 'do stuff', but should take time out to plan what is the *right* stuff to do - THEN do it. In other words, schedule regular Manager time.

6.4 But there's only one of me

In a company where there is a real Worker and a real Manager, a physical meeting is of course possible, and communication occurs between them (verbal and written).

Things are different when both roles are carried out by you.

It is not suggested that you actually have a spoken 2-way conversation, playing both parts, but it is recommended that there is *written communication between the two roles*.

The main reason for identifying these two roles is so that you actually carry out both of them - and carry them out at different times.

6.4.1 Setting the scene for a Manager meeting

Some people find it really useful to have a certain place or set of actions that trigger them into Manager mode. Chapter 4 (section 4.7) made the suggestion that you might benefit from establishing a certain place - a Workspace - where you can make natural progress on your project. In a similar way, there may be some set of actions or locations that you can use to indicate to yourself that you are in Manager mode.

It is best to define your own, but some that have worked for other people are:

- Opening a certain 'planning book' (somewhere to write down your thoughts about the project). The type of book is up to you, but it's the fact that it's associated with planning that's important.

- Sitting in a certain place with the planning book. This could be on a favourite sofa, or armchair, or at a particular table.

- Putting on a particular piece of (or style of) music. Many people recommend Baroque music for this (see Live 365), but you could experiment. There is certainly an advantage to using music - especially with headphones - as it masks out other potentially distracting sounds, and can help you concentrate. Mostly it should be instrumental as the words of a song can disturb your thought processes.

- Having a particular drink to hand. My favourite is a nice cup of tea! Make sure it's a drink that won't impede your brain function (you know what I'm saying students!).

If you put all of the above together you should be able to create a scenario that your brain immediately recognises as requiring Manager mode. For example, you sit down on your sofa, with your planning book and a

Managing Your Project

nice cup of tea, pop on the headphones and immediately begin to review and plan your work.

6.4.2 Don't mix the Manager and Worker role

It's very important that these two roles are kept separate. You should never play both roles at the same time.

For the Manager to do a good job, the Worker must not interrupt. When you're reviewing all the to-do items in your project list, it is tempting for the Worker to run off and try to do some of them. However, this does not help you to finish your review or get a complete 'higher-level' overview of the project.

The same thing applies to the Worker. If you are sitting down to 30 minutes report writing, the Manager should not keep interrupting with thoughts of "shouldn't you be doing something else?", "what about the poster?", "what should we have for tea?". The idea is that the Manager has done such a good job that the Worker can carry out the task uninterrupted, knowing that what they are doing is EXACTLY the right thing for now.

6.4.3 Writing down the results of the Manager meeting

Clearly there needs to be a good line of communication, so that each role is not interrupted by the other. This usually means writing things down in a trusted location. One of the problems with you trying to keep Management information in your head is that it's the SAME head as the Worker, and so the roles are easily contaminated.

If, however, the Management plan is *written down* in a known and safe location, then the Worker does not have to expend energy trying to remember it, and in the process being constantly disturbed from the task at hand.

So, find a way to store the outcomes of the Management meetings. This could be a notebook especially reserved for management thoughts and plans. Or it could be an electronic organisation system. More details on different options for note taking etc. are given in the next chapter (Chapter 7 - *Taking notes and keeping records*).

Now, it's important that when you're in Worker mode you are fully able to concentrate on your specific task at hand, and not get distracted by all the other things that need doing. So, it's strongly recommended that you do not have access to the Management Notebook. If your job is to write a chapter of a report for two hours (and this has been agreed in a Manager meeting as being the most important next thing to do) then *just* write that report in your time-slot.

6.4.4 When roles collide

In real-life though you are one person, and so there are bound to be times when the two roles fight for your attention.

Here are two imaginary conversations. The first is taken from inside your head at a Manager meeting.

Conversation 1a

MANAGER: Ok, let's review the 5 sub-projects that I'm working on. Mmmm, Number 1 looks good; yes I can mark that as finished. Number 2? Let's have a look. Oh my goodness *(or words to that effect)* I was meant to get that report to my supervisor, and it's late.

WORKER: Here I am. Right - *panic!!* - you should have told me about this earlier, but I'll sit down at the wordprocessor *right now* and get on with it. <*report writing for 2 hours*>

MANAGER: < *2 hours later*> Now, where was I? Oh no, there's no time now for the rest of the Management meeting.

Let's run that conversation again, but not allow the interruption to break the Manager's flow.

Conversation 1b

MANAGER: Ok, let's review the 5 sub-projects that I'm working on. Mmmm, Number 1 looks good; yes I can mark that as finished. Number 2? Let's have a look. Oh my goodness I was meant to get that report to my supervisor, and it's late.

WORKER: Here I am. Right - *panic!!* - you should have told me . . .

MANAGER: No, sorry. Not now, we're reviewing things. OK - we've missed a deadline. Let's finish this project review, **then** we'll deal with this. <*finishes overview of projects, taking about 5 minutes*>.

Now, this missed deadline. How did that happen? I must make a note to check my To-Do list and Calendar and work out how I missed that. Ok, but what to do now? Maybe a quick email apology to the supervisor, saying that I've missed this deadline, and will get the report to him tomorrow morning.

<*At the end of the management meeting*>

Worker?

WORKER: Here I am.

Managing Your Project

MANAGER: We've got lots to do, but there's something urgent to sort out. Could you write an email to the supervisor apologising etc. After that could you write this report - but take no more than an hour; keep it short and pertinent.

WORKER: OK, I'm onto it. <*types email*>

You may not see much difference there, but in the first example the worker actually steps in and breaks up a Management meeting. Who knows whether the Manager was about to discover something MUCH more urgent and important? In the second example, the Manager notes the urgency, finishes the review task, takes a few moments to assess the problem and come up with some solutions. This is then given in a more ordered way to the Worker, saving some time in the process, and getting in the apology which is probably more important than the report.

However these potential interruptions can occur the other way round as well. Imagine this conversation in your head, in the middle of some scheduled report writing.

Conversation 2a

WORKER: Mmm, how can I express this difficult concept? Let's just start writing and see what happens.

MANAGER: Writing did you say?

WORKER: Pardon.

MANAGER: Writing? There's something else I've just thought of that we need to do. There is that research paper that needs doing by next week.

WORKER: Er, I'm trying to think of how to say . . .

MANAGER: Right. The Research paper needs to be scheduled soon. I think we need about 4 one-hour sessions to finish it off. Now, which sections are still left to write? . . . .

. . .and the scheduled writing session is completely derailed.

However, the Worker is actually allowed to boss the Manager around when there's an agreed job to be done and time has been set aside to do it. Run the conversation again, from where the interruption happened . ... .

Conversation 2b

MANAGER: Writing did you say?

WORKER: Pardon.

MANAGER: Writing? There's something else I've just thought of that we need to do. There is that research paper that needs doing by next week.

WORKER: Ok quickly write down a reminder on this pad now, then let me get on.

MANAGER: <*writes*> Finish urgent research paper.

WORKER: Happy?

MANAGER: Yes, for now.

WORKER: Right, how can I express this difficult concept? Let's just start writing and see what happens. . .

These may seem rather daft conversations to have with yourself, but this sort of discussion DOES go on inside your head, if not in words, then in the actions you take.

In Summary, allocate *plenty of regular times* for Managing the project, and during those times JUST do planning; don't try to get on with the work. Schedule also lots of working time when the goals and actions are very well described, so that you can enter Worker mode and get on with it without distractions.

6.5 Your Supervisor is NOT your Manager

One final thought on this subject is to make sure that you understand that you are your own Manager; this is not your supervisor's job.

A common trap that students fall into is that of being a 'dependent Worker', one who is relying far too much on being externally driven by their supervisor.

6.5.1 The Dependent Worker

This is a Worker who has not yet accepted that they also need to be a manager. They refuse the managerial role, and therefore constantly look to others to provide the structure that they are lacking. In Chapter 5 we examined the role of the supervision process, but the Dependent Worker does not use it properly. Instead, they pester their supervisor and insist on being told what to do, exactly how much to write, which papers to look at, how to spend their time, what is the 'correct' method, etc. So, instead of growing in confidence with their own managerial skills they become dependent on other 'gurus' or 'experts'. However, as most supervisors will tell you, the idea of the supervision process in a solo project is to turn *you* into the expert for your particular topic, and to decrease your reliance on others.

If you find yourself feeling like this, it is probably because you are so used to being told what to do that you find it hard to acknowledge that you are now in charge. What you must trust is that playing the management role is ultimately very fulfilling. It is this role which makes it become *your* project, and in the future you will look back on the solo project as one of the most rewarding growth experiences of your entire education. Students who have struggled with this transition have often described it as 'learning to grow up'.

6.5.2 When your supervisor seems like a manager

The supervisor has a responsibility to the university to make sure that you are engaging fully with your project. As part of this process they may well ask you what seem like management questions. Things like:

- "Let's take a step back; how is the whole project going?"
- "How are you progressing towards your central goal?"
- "Can you show me a Contents page and a writing plan for your final report?"
- "I'm going to suggest some changes to your Literature Survey".

All of these things may give the *impression* that the supervisor is your manager. But this is not the case. It is best to think of them as an external assessor; someone who has seen a lot of projects before and is well-placed to comment on people's progress and development. It is rather like a Head Teacher being in charge of a school (Manager) but having to respond to the probing of a school inspector (External Assessor).

Here's the thing - if your Manager is working correctly, then you should have no problem answering any of those questions or responding positively to the suggestions.

If a supervisor keeps asking these questions, they may simply be doing their job, but they may also subconsciously be hinting that the management of the project needs improving, or - at least - the Manager's work needs to be more visible.

6.6 Summary

By definition there is only one person working on a solo (or independent) project. Yes there are several roles to play. There is a fine balance to be made between Managing the project and Working on its details. Experience shows that good project progress is made when these two roles are carried out well. Too much management, and the project is just an impressive plan. Too much work (without management) could mean a lot of wasted time and effort. Too little of either role is a sure recipe for project failure.

The main Management job is to assess what needs to be done, how much time is left, and how the work should next proceed. This should be done at the start of any new complex task, and regularly throughout the project. Weekly reviews are particularly valuable. It's very useful practice to set up a routine that immediately puts your brain in Manager mode (such as a certain workspace, drink, music etc.).

Don't mix these two roles – they are meant to be kept separate. But find a way to write down the results of each Manager meeting so that your inner Worker can refer to it later, and so that you mind is free to simply focus on the task at hand. If you are in the middle of a Management session, don't let your inner Worker suddenly start in-depth tasks otherwise the managerial role has been derailed. Equally, when you are working away on a single task in an allotted time, don't let your Manager take over with worries, planning etc. Instead just write down a reminder so that it can be covered in the next management meeting, then get on with the work at hand.

Finally, remember that your supervisor is not your manager. You are the manager for your project, but this means taking responsibility for planning and monitoring the work on a day-to-day basis.

6.7 External Links

(Adams, 2000) **Dilbert**: Random Acts of Management (A Dilbert Book) Publisher: Boxtree; 2 edition (21 April 2000), ISBN-10: 0752271741, ISBN-13: 978-0752271743. See also Dilbert cartoons (http://dilbert.com/) Endless wonderful insights into all the things that can go wrong in organisations – particularly between managers and workers. Scarily, most people can identify the issues from real-life.

(Allen, 2002) Getting Things Done: How to achieve stress-free productivity, Publisher: Piatkus (24 Jan. 2002), ISBN-10: 0749922648, ISBN-13: 978-0749922641. Also available for Kindle. One of the most popular time management systems in the world.

(Live 365) http://www.live365.com/genres/baroque is a list of internet radio stations that play continuous baroque music. But actually just do a web-search for <*style*> music online inserting your own favourite style, and experiment with what works for you.

7. TAKING NOTES AND KEEPING RECORDS

A large part of research project work involves the gathering of information from many sources and the capture of ideas from yourself and others. It is very unwise to try to remember all of this information, so it's important to capture and store it in an accessible form so that you can find it when you need it.

7.1 Capture the ideas while they are fresh

When you have a good idea, it can feel so 'right' and self-evident that you believe you could never possibly forget it. But our brains are fickle, and what is interesting and important one minute can disappear the next.

Have you ever walked into a room and then wondered what it was you came in there for?

Have you ever had a *brilliant* dream but by the time you try to tell someone else it is already fading away?

The same is true with ideas that you have. You may have:

- a sudden managerial thought that will help your project
- a moment of clarity where you think of a solution to a problem
- a breakthrough, when a concept you have been struggling with becomes clear.

In those moments it is really important to capture the idea before you lose it. At the very least, just write down a summary of the idea on the nearest useful piece of paper. Now, loose leaves of paper stand a good chance of getting lost, so it makes sense to always have a Project Book to hand. This could be the same thing as the 'trusted location' recommended in the previous chapter (section 6.4.3). Most often this would be some sort of managerial notebook. You could even have a section at the back for unprocessed ideas, or just write everything down in the book in the order that it occurs to you.

It maybe that capturing the idea in computer form is more useful, and sections 7.3 & 7.4 look at this in more detail.

7.2 Summarise reading material

When you are doing your Literature Survey, or just finding out more about the project area in general, you can read a paper or a book and really feel like you have a good understanding of it. What you may not realise at the time is that your brain is going to get so full that you will not remember much detail about it in a few days, let alone weeks or months.

So, it's advisable to make notes about every paper, book, article and related web-site that you come across. Partly this will act as a catalogue of information which can turn into a Reference section later in the project, but it will also remind you of the content of the paper. As well as summarising the content of the material try to write down some of your own ideas about it, and how it is relevant to your project.

7.3 Paper versus Electronic systems

Should you get a paper notebook, or invest some time in a computer-based note-taking system?

Some people enjoy the direct physicality of pen (or pencil) on paper. They say that it helps them to think and to remember things, in a way that typing does not. For others, the opposite is true, and what flows on a keyboard can feel stumbling and messy with a pen.

It may also be useful to determine *where* you are going to be doing most of your work.

If you will be sitting in a library, getting up and down to fetch and read different books, then maybe a paper-based notebook is the easiest and most portable solution. If, on the other hand, you are doing a lot of work on a computer, looking up references and finding papers etc. online, then it might make more sense to be able to store these things electronically.

Computer-based systems can be backed up (as long as you are

methodical about it) which means that your information would still be safe if you lost your laptop, for instance. If you lose your paper-based management notebook, this is probably not backed up and is thus a serious loss.

The most important thing about your system (whether paper or computer-based) is that you use it regularly.

7.4 Computer-based note taking and storage

There are many different ways that you can take notes on your computer or mobile device. In this section we overview a few of the various methods, and in the next section I'll give you an example of the specific system I have used, as a case study.

7.4.1 The good and bad of computer note-taking

The basic principles of electronic note-taking are that you can:

- quickly type up a note, without losing the idea
- easily find and retrieve the data when you need it
- access your data when and where you need it
- back up your data so that it is safe.

If any one of the above principles is violated, the whole system becomes devalued or useless.

- If you can't type the note in **quickly** you may lose the idea. Reasons for it being slow include having to 'boot up' the computer; not being in the same place as the note-taking computer; or forgetting how to use the software.

- If you can't easily **find** your data, then you will forget what you have stored, or get frustrated when you need it, leading to a lack of trust in the system. This can happen if the system doesn't allow searching or tagging, or if your own filing method is not good enough, so you find yourself wading through endless notes, looking for some idea you are sure you stored in there somewhere.

- If you can't **access** your data when and where you need it then there is no point in having a note system. For example, if you store all your information on a computer at university, but you need to be on campus to access it, and yet you do your writing in your home office, then you can't use your notes.

- If you can't **back up** your data, then you will not feel that your notes are secure, and if you lose the device or have a system crash, then you lose all your work!

7.4.2 Types of electronic notes

It's still possible to get specialised gadgets that are 'Electronic note-takers'; little devices that often double up as calculators and dictionaries. Whilst these are great for doing crosswords on holiday, do not entrust large-scale project data to such devices. They violate nearly all of the above principles, and although highly portable, it is unlikely that you will seriously use them for note-taking work.

So, this leaves programs that you can run on your desktop computer, and those that will run on mobile devices. Typically these fall into one of the following categories:

1) **Small apps for short notes.** You can get programs for taking quick notes while you are working at your computer. In this category are 'sticky-note' apps, which allow you to put up a virtual Post-It™ on your screen. Whilst great for quick reminders, if used a lot they rapidly occupy the screen. Their purpose of being a visible reminder becomes counterproductive when your notes constantly stare at you from the screen. This is not a filing system, and the notes you can store are small.

2) **Well-established software** which can be used for notes. Word processing programs such as Microsoft Word or Wordpad (or free equivalents such as OpenOffice) or Apple's Pages are designed for large-scale documents with formatting. However, many people use them for taking notes. This can work for some people, although there comes a time when you are spending a lot of time searching through files to find the right information, or searching and scrolling within one large document to find what you need. Simpler programs such as Notepad are just text-based, and so do not have the advantages of formatting or picture storage, and also suffer the same filing/searching problems.

3) **Web-based note services.** Many new systems for taking notes online have been emerging in recent years. At the time of writing there is the new Google Keep (https://keep.google.com/) which offers a web-browser-based note taking system that is available wherever you can log in. The advantage here is that any computer system will give you access as long as it's got access to the internet. There are a number of applications in this category and it's probably best to do a web-search for "best note management software".

4) **Integrated note systems.** An integrated system is one that is not only available on the web, but also on your desktop computer and mobile

device. These are systems which are intended to be available to you wherever you are as long as you have at least one device nearby. They can take advantage of mobile system capabilities such as taking photos of what you're looking at, scanning documents, recording audio messages etc. The best ones will synchronise your notes between devices, and so your information travels with you. Examples of such systems are Evernote (which is described below), Microsoft's One Note, and many others, e.g. http://en.wikipedia.org/wiki/Comparison_of_notetaking_software.

7.5 Example of an integrated electronic note system - Evernote

The system that I have been using for the past three years is Evernote, so this is how I set it up and use it. This section is written in the first person to reflect that this is something that works for me. I don't want this to sound like some sort of sponsored push for one particular system. Other systems are available but I don't have the personal experience with them.

Firstly, though, let me tell you about how I first tried to be organised with paper only records.

7.5.1 My previous experiences of note-taking (paper-based)

When I was doing my PhD many years ago, I did the note-taking very badly. I photocopied articles and papers, and printed out any interesting material I found on the internet. I tried to read all of the articles, used a highlighter pen to note items or quotes of interest, and then filed each article in its own A4 plastic wallet so that it would clip neatly into one of a series of folders. It looked nice and neat and organised.

That's where the positives ended. In practice, I was never able to find anything without getting each paper out of its plastic wallet and searching through it. The folders eventually occupied an intimidatingly large shelf. For some bizarre reason I have kept these; maybe because they represent so much work done, and have rarely returned to them or found them useful!

7.5.2 What is Evernote?

Evernote was introduced in 2008 as a web-based note-taking service. It rapidly attracted millions of users, and has become perhaps the most prevalent note system available at the time of writing.

You can download a desktop version to your own machine (Mac or PC). But it is also available on a range of mobile platforms including iOS, Android, and Windows Phone. It's also become a bit of an industry standard, and there are many third-party Apps which use it, and can send notes to it. The two advantages of the multi-platform approach are 1) your data is usually not very far away (because it's on your workplace desktop, *and* your home computer, *and* on your mobile phone, *and* tablet), and it is synchronised across those platforms 2) forming a multi-platform back-up. There are also many different ways of capturing information and getting it into your note system. Once in the system, notes can be tagged for easy retrieval later.

Evernote's basic system is free, and holds a surprising number of notes. I started to use a lot of storage because of taking photos and scans of paper documents, and so I have subscribed to the ad-free Premium service. But many people I know find the free service meets their needs perfectly.

7.5.3 Entering Data: taking notes

There are many ways to get notes into Evernote. Here are just some of the ways I use it to capture information.

a) Typing in a note: I generally keep Evernote open on whatever computer I'm working on - Mac or PC. I click to add a note (and there are keyboard shortcuts) whenever I think of anything I might want to look at later. The good thing about this is that you can quickly record your idea, know that it's safely recorded for later, and then get straight back on with what you were doing.

For a couple of years I used Evernote as one of the key components of my Action/ToDo organising system, and I'll say more about this in Chapter 16 – *Technological Time Tricks*. If you'd like a quick overview now of how this works, check out the great videos at http://www.thesecretweapon.org/ which explains how to use Evernote with the Getting Things Done system covered in more detail in the Time Management section.

b) Storing a web-page: Evernote provides add-ons to most popular web-browsers (called a Web Clipper) so that if you come across any page of interest you can capture the whole page, or just one highlighted article on the page, or just the URL web address. This is a great way to think "I like this page, but I don't want to read it now, but nor do I want to lose it", and know that the information has been captured for later processing.

c) Storing an article to read: If you have a document (such as a PDF, or Word file) containing something you want to read later, you can save this in Evernote as an attachment. Then it is on your system, and you can search it, and read it on any device. This is great for using up spare bits of time while travelling or waiting, by reading pre-stored articles on your mobile device.

d) Emails to take action on: When I receive an email that contains an Action - something that I have to DO something about - I want to put a record of that action somewhere that I'm going to see it later. We'll discuss in later chapters on Time Management how to set up a system like this that works for you. Part of 'The Secret Weapon' (mentioned in *a)* above) is a method of using Evernote to turn emails into action records. You can Forward the email to your special private Evernote email address, and it will then appear as a note on all your devices.

e) Emails I might be interested in later: Using the same technique of forwarding to a private Evernote address you can convert emails containing some item of interest into a note. For example this might be a friend recommending a movie, an idea for your project, a recipe you'd like to try, or a funny picture or joke that you want to store for later, etc. We'll see in the next section how to make sure you file these things effectively.

f) Taking a photo: Because Evernote is also available on your mobile device, you can use its built-in camera to take a photo that you want to file away. It might be a poster for an upcoming concert, a reminder for you to sort out your room (i.e. a photo of the messy room), or the cover of a book that you'd like to buy for your project research etc.

g) Scanning a document: Again, using the camera on your tablet, laptop or phone, you can photograph a document, which is effectively the same as scanning it. This is incredibly useful. Imagine the following situations: Someone scribbles some directions in the form of a map on a bit of paper that you don't want to lose; your friend has a takeaway menu that you'd like to copy; a book in the library has 4 very useful pages, but you don't wish to borrow the whole book. By taking a photograph that immediately becomes a filed note, you have saved that information.

h) Recording a voice memo: Most laptops and portable devices will allow you to record a voice note. These can often be exported to Evernote, so that you can listen to them and process them later.

i) Drawing something on an iPad: I have a couple of drawing Apps on the iPad, which I use for sketching ideas and structures. These Apps have an export / synchronisation link with Evernote which means that any drawings I do are immediately part of my collection of notes.

There are many other ways of using it to save information, not documented here.

7.5.4 Tagging Data: organising notes

Many people just have a big stack of notes in Evernote, and they will search for them when they need them. That's ok, and the search works well, but Evernote provides two more very useful ways to organise your data.

a) Notebooks and Stacks

You can create as many Notebooks as you like, each of which can contain as many notes as you like. So you can have a category for 'Project' or 'Home' or whatever you like. This is a useful way of grouping things together so you can see all your notes together. Because of The Secret Weapon organising system mentioned earlier, you can have a special notebook called Action Pending. This could hold all your reminders and scheduled things to do, and so distinguishes it from other notebooks where ideas or useful pieces of information are stored.

b) Tagging

Evernote's masterstroke though is its ability to 'tag' each note with one or more keywords. You get to decide the keywords. The reason this is important is that most 'things to do' or 'pieces of useful information' fall into many categories. Let me give you an example to explain.

Imagine you are surfing the web and you come across a really useful gadget being advertised. You capture it using the Web Clipper and you tag it with 'Fun Gadgets' (you have to imagine that you have previously decided that's a useful tag to have, OR you can create it when you think about it). However, later on when looking through your notes, you think "My colleague Jim would really like to see this". You remember that you're meeting Jim in 2 days' time so you simply add the tag 'Jim', so that when you're with Jim this will come up (along with anything else you wanted to discuss with Jim). And then you realise that it's also quite useful for a course you are studying, so you tag it with the name of that course.

It is useful to show a list of your notes on a regular basis, ordered according to Tag. The untagged notes will float to the top of this list, and you can then apply appropriate tags so that you'll be able to find them later.

7.5.5 Retrieving Data: finding notes

The real key to good sorting and tagging is to take a few moments to think ahead to *when and where you might need* the notes.

One scenario is to sort your notes according to context, such as a particular person (e.g. your supervisor) or a specific meeting (e.g., with your Special Interest Group).

In the example above, the 'Jim' tag is useful as it groups together actions and items of interest for the next time you meet a particular person. Knowing that you have a Jim tag means that next time you think of something to discuss with Jim you can just open a new Note, type "Discuss <*interesting thing*>" and tag as 'Jim'. Then you're done and you can forget about this until the meeting with Jim. In the meeting you click on the 'Jim' tag and every action or discussion point or interesting item is displayed in a list.

Another scenario involves work that you are doing on a specific sub-project. Imagine you are gathering data on a particular topic and you're going to write a Literature Review on this subject. Over several weeks you may have tagged the following things as related to this review:

- web clippings
- articles (e.g. as PDF or Word files)
- emails discussing the issue with supervisor and colleagues
- photos you have taken of real-life related things
- scans/photos of sketches you have made.

When you click on the 'LitReview' tag, all of these notes appear in one place. Those containing articles can be clicked on and the file containing the article will open.

If you know you have put something into Evernote, but you do not know where, or maybe you did not tag it, then you can use the search function, which will find notes that contain your particular search phrase. The premium version also allows you to search within PDF files and even within scanned documents (using optical character recognition, OCR).

7.6 Summary

What is clear to you at one moment is quickly forgotten or misplaced, so it's essential that you develop a way of capturing fleeting ideas, solutions, problems etc. One way of doing this is to have a trusted notebook that is already in use for your managerial meetings. In this you can just jot down ideas as they occur to you. It should also be used to catalogue and summarise the papers and books that you read.

Decide for yourself whether a paper or electronic (computer-based) note-taking system will be better for you. Many programs can be used as ways to take and keep notes, but for a major project you ought to consider a specialised web-based or integrated note package.

Evernote has become the industry standard note management software, and is one of several programs to offer multi-platform cloud-based note storage. In practice this means you are able to capture information on any device and search/retrieve it on any device. What is meant by a 'note' is actually very varied; it could be the archetypal text-based 'idea', or equally could be a scanned restaurant menu, a concert poster, a web-page of useful information, or a voice memo. Evernote allows you to 'tag' notes with names that can be later searched for. A small amount of such organisation at the moment you capture the note, makes its retrieval much easier in the future when you need it.

What's important is that you develop your own note-taking system, otherwise you can easily get overwhelmed with information, or just lose it and not be able to locate it when you need it.

7.7 External Links

(Post-it) http://solutions.3m.co.uk/wps/portal/3M/en_GB/PostIt-EU-Global/PostIt/

Originators and manufacturers of the Post-it product range of repositionable paper-based notes and reminders.

Sticky-note apps:

- Sticky Notes 8 for Microsoft Windows:
    - http://apps.microsoft.com/windows/en-gb/app/sticky-notes-8/a691d64e-0b43-41e2-93fe-62e230551113
- Stickies for Mac:
    - http://www.macosxtips.co.uk/index_files/10-tips-for-stickies.php
- Floating Stickies for Android:
    - https://play.google.com/store/apps/details?id=genius.mohammad.floating.stickies&hl=en

Word-Processing Software:

- Microsoft Word: (for Windows, Mac, iOS, Android, etc.):
    - https://products.office.com/en-us/word
- Pages for Mac / iOS:
    - https://www.apple.com/uk/mac/pages/

Managing Your Project

- OpenOffice – open source word processing etc.:
- https://www.openoffice.org/

Web-based & Integrated Note Management systems:

- A detailed comparison (http://en.wikipedia.org/wiki/Comparison_of_notetaking_software)
- Evernote (https://evernote.com/)
- Google Keep (https://keep.google.com/)
- Microsoft OneNote (http://www.onenote.com/)

8. MIND MAPPING

This chapter is dedicated to a creative, graphical technique which can be used for taking lecture notes, managing meetings, organising your research material, and problem-solving, yet which many people have never heard about.

8.1 What is Mind Mapping?

At its simplest, a Mind Map™ is a graphical record of your ideas. It uses text in a spatial layout (and optionally colour, shading, and images) to represent relationships between topics as you think about them. This helps you to:

- remember complex topics more easily
- see relationships between topics that you weren't aware of
- make notes which group together better by topic than with linear note-taking.

Mind Mapping was made famous by Tony Buzan. In fact the phrase 'Mind Map' is a trademark of the Buzan Organisation. Various graphical text maps have been around for a while but Tony Buzan coined the phrase and made them popular in a series of books for example: (Buzan, 1974), (Buzan & Buzan, 1996) and various TV programmes.

8.2 How to make a Mind Map

Tony Buzan stresses that you should be free to develop your own style of Mind Mapping, but he has a series of suggestions that include:

- having a single central topic from which other ideas radiate
- using one (or at most a few) words on each line coming from the centre
- ideas can branch into sub-ideas, if needed
- add links to the Map as and when you need them; there is no fixed order
- where possible use colours and pictures to make the Map more distinct and memorable.

You can make a mind map anywhere - as long as you have access to pen/pencil and paper. It is nice to have lots of coloured pens available, but this is not required. Mind Mapping on paper has many advantages, including simplicity of equipment, no set-up time, and a sense of direct contact with the paper.

However, more and more people are discovering the flexibility of Mind Maps made with computer programs. Section 8.7 explains this in more detail.

8.3 Mind Maps for Note-taking

The previous chapter explained the need for managing notes, but may have left you with the assumption that a Note is just a linear piece of text. However, some notes work much better as Mind Maps.

If you have to take a lot of notes, for example in lectures, try experimenting with how you get on by:

a) taking notes by writing linearly from the top to the bottom of the page, and

b) making a Mind Map and letting the ideas grow radially from the centre of the page.

Mind Mapping also encourages the use of doodles and images to support the text. You can use arrows to show relationships between different elements of your notes. This, as well as the act of thinking and drawing, has the useful by-product of keeping you awake and engaged with the material.

Many people find that every Mind Map takes on its own patterns and visual characteristics, and because of this is instantly recognisable even years later.

8.4 Mind Maps for Paper/Chapter Summaries

One of the problems you will come across in the course of your Literature Survey is how to keep decent records of the relevant papers and book chapters that you have read. In the previous chapter I described how I didn't do a very good job of this during my own PhD, printing out every paper and copying every chapter, then going through with highlighter pen to mark those sections or comments which I thought were of particular interest. The problem was that I had to revisit all my papers and work through them again file-by-file and page-by-page every time I wanted to find something!

If you make a Mind Map of the main points of each chapter or paper, three interesting things happen:

1. You understand the paper better while you are in the process of making the Mind Map because you are focussing all the time on the key words and concepts, and their relationships to each other.

2. You can store the Mind Map as a picture file in your note-taking system; maybe even alongside the paper. The Map acts as a sort of visual index for the contents of the paper.

3. You will recognise the Mind Map even years later, and it will 'take you straight back' to when you were making it, which helps you to rapidly re-familiarise yourself with the content of the paper.

8.5 Mind Maps for Planning Talks and Reports

If you have something to present to other people, for example in a lecture or a book, it can be a daunting experience knowing how to start. One of the best ways to begin is to plan the overall process using a Mind Map.

Start in the middle of the Map with the title of the talk or the book, and gradually add branches that represent the main topics.

A little trick that works well if you are not sure that you have captured everything is to add a branch and leave it blank. This acts as a subconscious signal to your brain that says:

"What's the missing topic?

What else do I need to say?

Have I really covered everything important here?"

The good thing about Mind Mapping is that you can add things to the Map *in any order* you like, which is generally how the brain works. A typical

Managing Your Project

brainstorm session might go something like this:

> "So, what are the main topics I want to explain about Pervasive Computing?
>
> Ok, <*adds first main branch to Map*> Popular Gadgets.
>
> Secondly it's <*adds second main branch*> Miniaturisation.
>
> Oooh, I know a popular gadget that everyone will have with them <*returns to branch 1, and adds a sub-branch*> Mobile Phones.
>
> And I'd like to talk about <*adds a sub-sub branch*> Mobile Phone Operating Systems and <*adds another one*> Increasing Computing Power in Phones.
>
> Ah yes, <*adds 3rd major branch*> Connectivity. etc."

Even if you have no idea what the above topic is about, hopefully you can see how my mind was flitting about the different levels. I wasn't working hierarchically, or in order, but somehow - eventually - an order will emerge. The resulting (partial) map is shown in Figure 8.1.

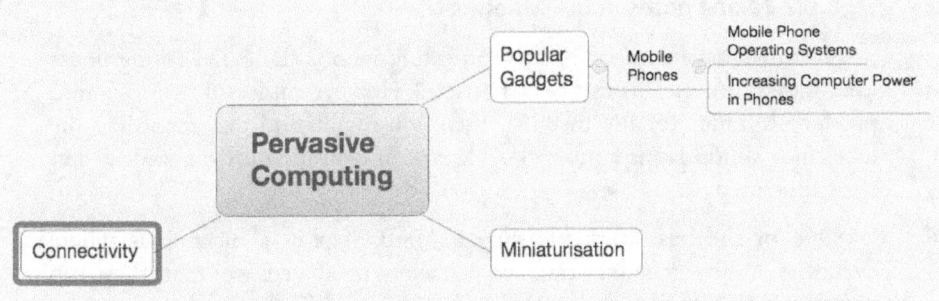

Figure 8.1 A partially completed mind map for planning a talk (produced in XMind)

At some point, the Mind Map will feel relatively complete and then it is time to move to the actual plan for the talk or book. This might be something you type up in a word processor, or it might require a slideshow presentation. Usually it is best to have the Mind Map on show as you build up your final product. Somehow the Mind Map acts as an intermediate sketchpad that allows you to build up ideas, without worrying too much about the order you had the ideas in, or the required order of the final product.

8.6 Mind Maps for taking Minutes of Meetings

Mind Maps can be really useful for handling meetings, because meetings have to be structured linearly (item by item in order) but the ideas they generate tend to be *non*-linear. This applies equally to a 2-person meeting between you and your supervisor, and to larger-scale multi-person committees and gatherings.

8.6.1 Preparing the Agenda

If you are hosting a meeting it's a really good idea to plan out the Agenda (the purpose of the meeting and the order of flow) on a Mind Map. Imagine you have a meeting coming up with your supervisor. You could open a Mind Map, and take some time to fill in the topics that would like to discuss. On the sub-branches you can start to add links, ideas, solutions etc. If you are doing this on a computer (see section 8.7 below) you can email the Map to your supervisor, which will alert them to the topics you'd like to discuss.

An Agenda that is created on a Mind Map can then also be used in the meeting itself.

8.6.2 Taking notes in the Meeting

You may have someone at your meeting who is trained at taking linear (text-based) notes. This can be very useful. However, if it is down to you to produce Minutes for the meeting, then you might find that recording the ideas in a Mind Map is a more flexible way of capturing the main ideas that were discussed.

One of the best ways of using a Mind Map in a meeting is where everyone at the meeting can see it being produced, so that they can contribute to it, add ideas, correct mistakes etc. Where there are just you and one or two other people then you can gather around a piece of paper or a computer screen and build up the Map as you have your discussion. If there are many people, then you could consider using a computer-based Mind Map and projecting the Map live at the meeting, so people can see the pattern emerging.

If you have already distributed the Agenda in Mind Map form, then it makes sense to use that as a starting-point, as people will already be familiar with the structure.

8.6.3 Distributing a Record of the Meeting

Sometimes a Mind Map is really just an intermediate stage - a stepping-stone to the final form of something. If your meeting requires formal Minutes, then you can type these up while looking at the Mind Map, which will ensure that you do not forget anything important that was raised and recorded at the meeting.

At other times the Map itself will be the best record of the meeting, because it shows more clearly the complexity of the topics discussed and their relationships. This can be particularly effective if the people in the meeting saw the Mind Map emerging as the meeting progressed, because their brains will have absorbed the structure. This means that when they see the Map again, they are transported back to the meeting and reminded about the things that were discussed and decided.

8.6.4 Continuing a Meeting

Sometimes a meeting does not conclude with everything completely sorted. Examples of this include planning for a complex event or situation, and the meeting simply runs out of time; or meetings that are part of a series of ongoing discussions, such as supervisions.

In these situations a Mind Map of the previous meeting is invaluable. In a few seconds it can remind everyone of the main points of discussion (using spatial arrangement and links and pictures and colours instead of just text). This can have the effect of taking people straight back to where they left off at the previous meeting, and the new meeting can get going as if no time has passed.

8.7 Software for Mind Mapping

Although many people like the feel of pen on paper, and it helps them to think about things freely, there are many advantages to doing Mind Mapping on computer software. These include:

- The ability to **edit** the map as you go along (e.g. to move a whole section to a different place on the map when you realise it belongs better in a different category).

- **Saving** a file, which can then be stored in your computer note-taking system (see Chapter 7 – *Taking Notes and Keeping Records*) and sent to other people for viewing on their machines. This also acts as a backup and allows you to view it in other situations, e.g. on a portable device while not near your main computer.

- The possibility of **projecting** it live to a group of people if used in a meeting.

- The overall **neatness** of a computer-generated map. This may appeal to you and indeed may be more legible.

- The ability to **export** text in the map to other formats; e.g. a block of text to go in a word processor (to write a report, or make meeting Minutes), or a picture of the mind map (to illustrate a complex topic in your Literature Survey).

- **Links** can often be added to your map, so that web suggestions include a one-click link to that website; or your own files can be indexed from the map. In this way the map becomes an active 'Index' to information in your own collection or out there in the world.

There are many different types of software available for Mind Mapping. All of the ones listed below let you do basic Mind Mapping (adding and moving branches, pictures, colours etc.) but they vary in their more advanced features.

The one I use now is *XMind* (http://www.xmind.net). This is available as a free download for Mac or PC, and also as a paid Premium version with more powerful business features. I have found that the free version is excellent as a basic Mind Mapping tool, which also includes the facility for adding links and pictures as mentioned above, but more recently I have been using the paid version. The Map files it stores can be opened on Mac or PC, which is useful if you work on different computers at different times. It also imports and exports various other Mind Map formats, so is a good general reader/viewer for computer-based Map even if they've been produced by various other software packages.

The first software I used was *Mind Manager* (https://www.mindjet.com/mindmanager/) which is a fully featured product aimed at businesses as well as educational establishments and individuals. It is a paid version only, but has a try-before-you-buy option. It is packed with features and is often considered as the most complete package available.

There are various open-source projects for Mind Mapping, the most famous of which is probably FreeMind (freemind.sourceforge.net). This is written in Java and so runs on any web-browser that is Java compatible. The interface and an example map are shown in Figure 8.2.

Managing Your Project

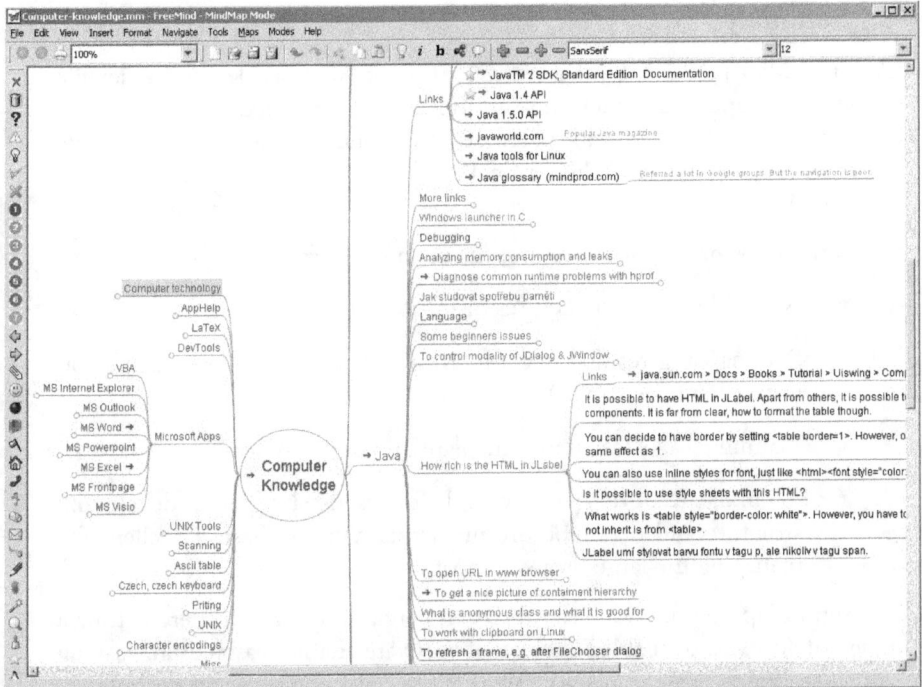

Figure 8.2: Main interface for FreeMind, with an example public-domain mind map.

Some web-pages are available for doing Mind Mapping online, for example:

http://mindmapfree.com/

The inventor of the modern Mind Map, Tony Buzan, has his own paid software, called iMindMap, which is available here https://imindmap.com/. This runs on Mac or PC, but also on various mobile platforms such as iOS, Android or via a web-browser, so it is flexible and portable.

There are several other software solutions available, but I have not tried them personally. A list is maintained on Wikipedia at the foot of this page: http://en.wikipedia.org/wiki/Mind_map.

8.8 Personal Statement

You can probably tell that I like Mind Maps. I have found them really useful over the years for creative thinking, brainstorming, taking notes, planning whole courses and individual lectures. I don't use them all the time. Sometimes, it just seems right to plan things linearly by typing in a word processor, but when this method doesn't seem to work, it just might be time to try a Mind Map.

8.9 Summary

A Mind Map is a graphical portrayal of a set of ideas. It uses a flexible layout-based approach where text and images are arranged on a page as an aide-memoire. Tony Buzan patented the concept and it's worthwhile looking at his books, and the original TV series which is now available on YouTube.

Mind Maps have many uses, but the main ones are:

- Note-taking (e.g. in lectures or meetings);
- Summarising reading (e.g. one map per chapter or paper helps you in the literature survey);
- Planning Talks (as an intermediate ideas-capture tool);
- Planning Reports (very useful for establishing and developing structure and detail, before the actual writing phase. Excellent for managing the large project report).

Mind Maps can be done simply using pen and paper, but there is now a range of software available. The use of software enables easy editing, saving and distribution, live projection so that several people can contribute, as well as easy importing of links to web-pages and other documents.

If you are not sure where to start, I would recommend one of the following:

- XMind (http://www.xmind.net/) which is free, upgradable and multi-platform
- Freemind (freemind.sourceforge.net/) which is open-source and runs in browsers, or
- MindMapFree (http://mindmapfree.com/) which is a free web-based solution.

8.10 External References

Buzan, Tony 1974. Use your head. London: BBC Books. The TV shows are now on YouTube starting from the first episode here: https://www.youtube.com/watch?v=LnYVJKxyRPM

Buzan, T. & Buzan, B., The Mind Map Book, 1996, New American Library; Reprint edition (1996), ISBN-10: 0452273226, ISBN-13: 978-0452273221.

Managing Your Project

Software

There are many ways of doing mind maps with computers. Wikipedia keeps a list here: http://en.wikipedia.org/wiki/Mind_map (see the table at the foot of the page).

A good place to start is the Think Buzan organisation http://thinkbuzan.com/ which has its own software:

- iMindMap: https://imindmap.com/

Two programs that I've used extensively are:

- XMind (https://www.xmind.net/) - free version available.
- MindManager (https://www.mindjet.com/mindmanager/).

On-line (web-based) mind mapping is available here:

- http://mindmapfree.com/

There are also several free and open-source mind mapping projects, perhaps the most well-known being:

- FreeMind (freemind.sourceforge.net/).

9. SETTING UP A SPECIAL INTEREST GROUP (SIG)

In Chapter 4 (section 4.3) we looked at the idea of setting up a team, at the start of the project, which can act as a mutual support environment.

Your supervisor's time is limited, and so ideally should be reserved for the top-level guidance that you will need on your project. A support team can work things out together, with different people having different skills, and they are more readily available - as they are working to a similar time-scale as you.

Sometimes your supervisor will have several students working on similar or related projects, and will organise a SIG for you. Most often though this is something you may have to set up for yourself. It does not need to be a big group - even just one other person working on something related can be a great source of support.

Section 4.3 listed a few of the benefits of such a support group, and these are now expanded in each of the following sections.

9.1 Your supervisor's time is limited

We took a glimpse of the role of the supervisor in Chapter 5. By now you are probably aware that there is not a great deal of time that the supervisor has available for each student. This is not a bad thing, *if* you use your supervisions well, and concentrate on the key issues that only your supervisor can advise you on. Many times students will unwittingly waste their precious supervision time by:

- being late or missing meetings;

- asking 'lazy' questions that they could have easily looked up for themselves, or asked someone else;
- expecting the supervisor to work through pages and pages of low-level detail, correcting spelling, grammar and layout, when this could have been done by someone else;
- chatting generally about things, and only getting to the 'real question' when the time is up.

I really don't know why people do this last thing; not mentioning a serious issue until it's just about too late. At best, it's just a form of Procrastination. At worst, it comes across as an attempt to manipulate the supervisor's time.

Student: blah blah blah blah *(for half an hour)*

Supervisor: Ok, great. Well, our time is up, and I've got to get to this meeting, so I'll see you same time next week.

Student: Oh, er - well - I do have this *really* serious problem . . .

What do you think the supervisor is thinking at this point?

Apparently doctors get this all the time - half an hour of moaning about life and petty issues, only to say - at the very end of the appointment - "doctor, I have found this lump".

Supervisees reading this - *please* let your supervisor know of any serious questions, concerns or problems right at the start of the supervision. If possible email ahead and alert the supervisor of any problems in advance, so that they can begin to think about solutions.

Because your supervisor is shared between many people and conflicting responsibilities, they should not be your only source of support. This is where a Special Interest Group comes in. They tend to be students working to the same timescales as you, with about the same amount of time. They also typically are looking into the same sort of things at similar times, and so become a great resource for chatting things through, helping each other, and alleviating as many problems as possible.

This way, those problems that are left over are probably at the right level to be dealt with between you and your supervisor.

9.2 Motivating each other

One of the best reasons to have a team of people working on a similar project is that you will all be going through the same sort of experiences. If you're on the same course then you'll have the same deadlines and assessment criteria. You will all be working on the same sort of project phases as you progress.

There are many activities in life when having a social dimension will help you to do things (and stick to commitments) that you might otherwise find difficult. People trying to establish a running habit find it easier if a friend calls for them, whereas when it's just you there is always the temptation not to go through with it. The same is true for research and academic studies.

If you know that - for example - you have a weekly informal meeting with other students doing similar projects, and at that meeting you ask questions and all report your progress, then you are more likely to get on with some work in the week in order to be able to report it.

9.3 Checking on each other

In a similar way, having a group of people means that you are more likely to say something like "How are you getting on with that interim report that's due for Monday?". This could be just the reminder that the other person needed to start on that report! By sharing and talking about your upcoming deadlines you can make sure that each of you is making progress.

Also, if someone is really struggling, it can really help to have someone to talk to who is going through something similar. What people in SIGs often discover is that different people have different strengths and weaknesses. For example the person who really needed some extra help organising their Literature Survey might turn out to be a great help to others in computer coding.

9.4 Proofreading and checking

We will see later in the book that it's often very hard to spot errors in your own work, so members of your SIG can provide a free service to each other to check through work or maybe proofread it. Proofreading, in theory, does not need to be done by a subject specialist, because it concerns looking for errors in grammar, syntax, spelling and - to some extent - style. However, as your reports get more specific about your topic, you can get better subject-based feedback from a group of people who are likely to understand that focus area.

Please note that proofreading and checking is NOT academic misconduct. You are not doing someone else's work *for* them, nor *generating* material for them, but instead you are spotting errors and giving feedback.

If you organise this well, you can arrange to proofread each other's work. Proofreading takes time and effort, so you have to be sure that it is worth spending time doing this. It is *very* helpful for the person whose work is being read, and hopefully they will return the favour for you. However, looking at someone else's work sometimes helps you to think about your own. Students who have done this have reported that they suddenly spotted a whole section that they had not considered incorporating in their report, and that they have subsequently gone off and written their own.

Interestingly, the process of having your work checked and analysed by other people at a similar level and working in a similar topic, is known as Peer Review. This is the basis of the methods for reviewing submissions to conferences, journal papers, and grant applications. So, working in a SIG can actually start preparing you for methods that will be used later in life.

9.5 Discussions

You can set up meetings to discuss concepts and problems. Often there are common issues to address, and this gives you a ready-made group who don't mind spending their time because everybody benefits.

It is worth being brave and trying to organise the group right from the beginning of the project. In the early days you could have general discussions about the topic that is in common to you. Later you could discuss the literature that you are finding. As the projects progress you may find the themes diverging, but you could still meet to discuss what each of you are doing.

There may emerge common problems - for example technical computing difficulties; and it can be really supportive to have a place to air these issues.

9.6 Testing things out

Many times in a project you will need to try out some ideas. This sort of thing can often happen at the beginning of a project, for example you may have a survey to carry out on your research project. Likewise, towards the end of the project you may have things that need other people's input. Perhaps you will have written a piece of software that you need to test out on some willing test subjects. Many projects produce ideas or prototypes which need testing, and this often requires a knowledgeable user-group to give you the best sort of feedback.

Your SIG will already understand the general ideas involved in your project, so they form an instant friendly and understanding group where you can get some quick and informed feedback.

Clearly you will need to be available to help other people out with their ideas as well, but (in addition to this being a necessary part of mutual support) you may learn quite a lot from how other people carry out tests, and even from the data that they collect.

9.7 Giving presentations

Some of you will have a formal requirement to do a project presentation as part of your project assessment. Later in the book Chapter 23 – *Giving Presentations* explains in detail how to plan and deliver talks to other people.

What better way at practicing your presentations than by talking to a known audience who have a vested interest in your general topic area? Even if you are not *required* to give talks, it is a really useful thing to do this with your SIG for the following reasons:

- It gives you practice at presenting (a highly useful job skill);
- The act of preparing for a presentation helps you focus and think through your topic;
- You each learn more about what the others are doing.

These can be done quite informally, for example sitting around with cups of coffee taking 5 minutes each to summarise your work progress. Or, you can create a more formal occasion. Perhaps your supervisor will book a lecture or seminar room, and you each have 10 minutes to stand up and talk with a prepared slideshow, in a mini conference.

Sometimes when you **have** to give a presentation (e.g. for an assessment or for a conference paper delivery) then you can practice your talk on your SIG, and get feedback for improving the flow and the content.

9.8 Sharing Key Literature

One of the first parts of almost every project is the gathering of key existing information about your project area. Much of the learning that takes place here is in the actual *process* of searching for and gathering the information, so you wouldn't benefit much from any short-cuts to an easy ready-made set of literature. However, during the process (and at the end) it can be really helpful to compare notes with other people who are doing the same sort of task.

Managing Your Project

It may be that because of the search methods that you have used, you have found something that your colleague has not, and vice versa. Because everyone's topic and focus is different, you would not expect or desire all Literature Surveys to cover precisely the same material, but you can learn about the process and about the key and common literature by liaising with your SIG during this time.

Chapter 19 - *The Literature Survey* covers this is much more detail.

9.9 Organising the SIG

Sometimes your supervisor will organise Special Interest Group meeting schedules, or methods for you to communicate. For example I regularly set up a schedule of meetings throughout the project period where students can meet, and where we examine and discuss the topics that are common to most research projects. As part of that process I set up some computer-based communication tools for the students to use.

You may need to do this for yourself, so why not take the initiative and think through the best ways for your particular group to communicate. Here are a few ideas that you might want to consider.

9.9.1 Email list

By gathering everyone's emails into one welcome email you automatically create a message that people can reply to. This is probably the easiest way to set up an email list. Another is to create a Group in your Contacts, which you edit to include everyone's emails. A slightly more complex one, but that can be very useful, is to create an email-based discussion group. I've been using Google Groups (https://groups.google.com), which is a free service that allows you to manage lists of people and their emails. Members send a message to the Group and it is automatically sent out to all members, according to their preferences. Some may choose to get each email relayed immediately, while others may opt for daily or weekly summaries. In addition all emails are recorded on the Google Group site, grouped by topic, and can be viewed at a later date.

9.9.2 Web Area

It can be really useful to have a single space to hold group information. Nowadays this is best done online so it can be accessed anywhere by any member of the group. Someone in the group may have their own web-space that they are willing to use (or you may get space provided by the University).

For the last five years I have use Google Sites (https://sites.google.com/) to form an easily editable web page. It gives you a free web-area that can be restricted to a limited set of viewers. There is no need to pay for the registration of a particular domain name, but your site will clearly be associated with Google sites. Each site has built-in on-line tools for editing content, uploading files, and managing who has access to what.

For my students I set up a web area that contains the following pages:

a) Welcome to the group.

b) Schedule of all our planned group meetings.

c) Resources area, where useful papers, videos, links etc. can be posted for the duration of the project.

d) Copies of the students' Presentation files (slides etc.) which are uploaded after each set of talks.

e) Link to the Google Groups page that handles email communication.

Most supervisors don't have web areas like this, so you might want to think about setting one up for your SIG.

9.9.3 Social Network site area

In the last couple of years I've noticed that students like to organise themselves using various social media sites.

A very common method is to set up a Facebook group as the coordination point for a SIG. This can work well as a way of handling discussions, which will form a 'blog'-type record for the group, as well as allowing individual chats and organising 'events'. This method tends to work well if the whole group are regular Facebook users. If someone is not regularly on Facebook they may resent being 'forced' to join, and having to remember to Log in just to get messages.

As an alternative Google+ provides similar blog-type, chat and video chat ('hangouts') facilities. The video hangouts can be recorded and kept on the site if you are happy to do that.

Twitter can work very well as a broadcasting or publicising medium when you are organising a more public event, but is probably best avoided as a way of handling highly specialised group activity that is not meant for wider dissemination.

9.9.4 Managing the Group and its Technology

Whichever technological tool you use to handle your group communications, it will need someone to champion and maintain it. Websites don't organise groups – people do – and it usually requires one person to start off the process, invite people and manage the set-up and ongoing settings on the site. Occasionally a supervisor will do this, but mostly it's down to the students. So why not let this be you? If you're not too happy with technology, you might do well to find another student who can handle the computer stuff while you drive the overall process. If nobody organises it, it probably won't happen, and you could miss out on all the benefits of having a team of people to help each other through the complex process of managing a project.

9.10 Summary

It is highly recommended that you meet regularly with people doing the same sort of work under the same timescale and expectations as you. Commonly known as a Special Interest Group (SIG) this will allow you to give each other extra support throughout the project.

Because your supervisor's time is limited, make sure that you use it well by planning carefully for each meeting, making it a priority, and discussing issues in order of importance.

The benefits of a SIG are many, but can be summarised as:

- A **social dimension** to a solo project (having a group where you share your progress is a great motivator for getting things done);
- A network of **mutual support** from people working on similar tasks and to the same deadlines (e.g. everyone has their reports to hand in at the same time and so your discussions are focussed on the most important things at each stage);
- Work checking (such as **proofreading**) by people working at a similar level as you and on a similar topic;
- A place for **discussion**. It's good to have people to talk to, not just for social reasons but to really interact with the subject area that you are all engaged in;
- A ready-made **testing** group, where products or ideas can be reviewed with a set of people who already understand the key issues, and are motivated to help each other;

- Giving **presentations** to each other, as a way of sharing ideas and rehearsing for official talks that you might be required to do;

- Sharing and discussion **literature**, so that you become mutually informed about the topic, and can discuss your findings.

There are many technological tools available nowadays to help in the organisation of group communication; from simple email lists to Google and Facebook groups, and websites. Whichever technological solution you choose, it still needs someone to start of the process and handle the technical settings – so maybe this could be you?

9.11 External Links

- **Facebook Groups** (http://howto.wired.com/wiki/Use_Facebook_Groups) are an increasingly common way for students to organise themselves via social media.

- **Google Groups** (https://groups.google.com) - a free service for hosting and managing email-based discussions with invited groups of people. Discussions are saved and accessible on a group webpage.

- **Google Sites** (https://sites.google.com/) - free web-pages, with controllable access permissions, which can give your project group a useful common area for hosting schedules, files, literature etc., without the need to pay for a domain name.

SECTION 3
TIME MANAGEMENT

Time Management is all about self-organisation, and so could just as well have been covered in the section above. However, it so important that it really does deserve its own section. Poor time management is often considered to be the biggest single reason for project failure and poor marks in higher education, and yet - as a topic - it is rarely taught.

As a student you are expected to instinctively adopt a professional attitude to managing yourself, your time and your work. But many students find that this does not come naturally, and are perpetually disorganised, feeling that this is just 'their lot' and not something which can be changed.

Quite the opposite is true, however.

Therefore this section focuses on many different aspects, skills and techniques, which could be sensibly covered by the phrase "Time Management".

Each of its chapters covers a particular topic which can be read at any time of the project, but which will be useful to read as you begin the project process:

- **Ch. 10 Time Management Techniques and Strategies** - *finding the best method for you*. This chapter gives a summary of some of the most popular systems of time management and distils them into a series of actions that you should carry out on a regular basis in order to master your time. Each person is different, so it's important to experiment until you find a methodology that suits you.

- **Ch. 11 Establishing your best times for working** - *finding out which parts of a typical day you are at your most productive, and then planning your work around this*. Even though every day is different and has its own challenges, students usually discover that their brains and bodies run to a cyclic pattern, and you can use that knowledge to your advantage when planning your work. A lot of time can be saved by avoiding fruitless working hours.

- **Ch. 12 Introduction to GTD** – *a summary of the popular and very useful Getting Things Done (GTD) methodology which has swept the business world, basically because it seems to work for lots of people.* David Allen has studied people's working habits over decades and has distilled the essence of how to best use your brain to organise and effectively carry out all the things you need to do.

- **Ch. 13 Email mastery** - *how to get to 'INBOX zero'.* Nowadays we are bombarded by incoming information, and one source which regularly gets out of control is the email inbox. Many people in the professional world use a few relatively simple techniques, carried out regularly, in order to keep their email inbox empty. Those with thousands of emails in their inbox often don't even realise there is a problem, or that 'zero' is even possible. However, once you have seen this in action, and realised how it kick-starts your organisation system, you'll probably never want to go back to your old ways.

- **Ch. 14 Calendars, Time-tracking and reminders** – *looking at best practice in managing your schedule and commitments.* Early on in higher education your time management consists mainly of getting to the right place at the right time. But now, you need to be generating your own deadlines and internal commitments. This chapter explains the most effective methodologies for using a calendar or planner, and explains why you really should use one.

- **Ch. 15 Project and Action Lists** – *because most 'To-Do' lists have their limitations.* In this chapter we examine how to best keep track of all the higher-level commitments in your life – using the generic term *Projects*. There are methodologies for converting these into working weekly and daily action lists, which are much more effective than a simple To-Do list.

- **Ch. 16 Technological Time Tricks** - *using modern technology to help you manage your time and your work.* The previous chapters focus on the methodology behind time management, which works just as well on paper as with electronic gadgets. This chapter, distilled from my own experience and that of my students, explains some of the best ways to use technologies (computer, gadgets and various Apps and software) to build an effective management system. It's not for everyone, and you may well be a 'paper person', but read this to find out if this would suit you. For those people it suits, it can be a life changer and they never look back.

10. TIME MANAGEMENT TECHNIQUES AND STRATEGIES

Time Management is one of those things which is talked about often, published about even more, and about which almost everyone feels inadequate. Yet there are things that everyone can do to improve their productivity and their effective use of time. In this chapter we will look at some of the different theories of time management and summarise what appears to be the most common advice. I will mix this in with my own experience of my quest to find 'the perfect system' and countless chats with students who have really struggled with this issue, yet have overcome it and even flourished.

10.1 Introduction to Time Management

Let's consider in some depth the issue of how to manage your own time in the context of a major solo project. You have been put in charge of a large block of time, and you need to use it wisely. This whole section discusses some well-tried advice for making the most of the time that you have available, and for balancing your work commitments with the rest of your life.

The most important thing to acknowledge is that you cannot actually *manage* time! The phrase "Time Management" is therefore a bit of a misnomer, because time just moves on regardless of what you do. Better phrases would be "Time Awareness" or "Self-Management", as the only thing we can really do with time is to acknowledge that it happens, and react accordingly. It is rather as if you were a canoeist, battling to stay afloat in turbulent water, and claiming that you were doing "River Management". In reality the river is just 'happening' and there is nothing you can do to manage or control it. However, you *can* deal with the tiny part of the river that you are in momentary contact with. You can control how you respond to the river, and you can use your oars and the angle of your body to prevent yourself from being thrown onto the rocks, or submerged, which is what might happen if you did nothing.

Similarly, time moves on, and the only part of it we have any contact with is the present moment. Yes, we can review what's gone (the past), and plan for what's coming up (the future), but the actions we take now (the present) are the only things we can really control. So Time Management - in essence - is about managing the actions we take from moment to moment, weighing up what has happened and pointing ourselves in the direction of what we want to achieve.

This is why the central question of all time management systems is "what is the right thing to do now?". We will return to that question later in the chapter, but first let us consider again your changing managerial role as you take on a solo project. We'll do this by looking at 'Reactive time management' (which is what most students are initially driven by) and seeing how this needs to change to 'Proactive time management' during a solo project.

10.2 Reactive time management

Typically students are driven by their timetable; the schedule of lectures, tutorials, lessons, supervisions, practical sessions and exams which are produced for you by your place of learning. Your experience of this will differ according to which course or institution you are enrolled with.

Some courses are lightly loaded, with only a few scheduled sessions per week. These tend to give you some practice in time management skills as your main task may be, for example, to prepare for a seminar in three weeks' time. If you are used to this type of course, you will probably be comfortable with the concept of setting your own schedule. Your biggest problem will be in coming to terms with just how *much* needs to be done for a solo project, and realising that you will need to generate all the actions and deadlines yourself.

Other courses, in dramatic contrast, schedule every hour of the working day with taught sessions, laboratories, back-up courses, and supervisions. In addition to this they often have a high assessment factor, with many continuous assignments active at any one point, and several courses to revise for examination. Students on this type of course may *feel* as if they are practising intensive time management, because they are constantly aware of how much there is to do and how little unscheduled time they have to do it in. However, they are typically in for a shock when they come to the solo project, as this frantic structure disappears. All of a sudden, there is no daily scheduling prepared for you; only an empty calendar and one big deadline at the end of the project. The good news is that you will be used to intensive work and handling many different tasks, so many of the techniques that follow may seem familiar. This will help you to create your own detailed schedule to fill the empty calendar.

10.3 Proactive time management

Now that you are the Manager for a solo project, you are solely responsible for deciding what you do every month, every week and every day. You will have many different tasks (or threads of activity) to do, but you need to *define* them all. You will have been given a final deadline (and possibly some interim deadlines) but there is a lot of time between now and then. Like our imaginary canoeist, if we do nothing we will drift with the flow and capsize or hit the rocks. Instead, we need to be *proactive* at every stage. Then, you can learn to use the power of the river's flow to take you where you want to go. The more you practise, the better you can steer yourself in the correct direction, and handle the turbulent flow. So it is with time management.

From Chapter 6 - *The 2-Stage Work Process* you will be aware of how important it is to plan thoroughly, so that you can switch off your Manager mode, and act as the Worker for set periods of time to actually make the project move along.

So the three main skills of proactive time management are:

- to know what has happened so far,
- to identify what needs to be done, and,
- to organise the upcoming tasks so that your Worker handles them effectively.

These three skills could be referred to as Review, Plan, and Organise. Look out for them throughout the rest of the time management chapters. In the next section we examine some basic time management techniques, which will give you the methods for carrying out your reviewing, planning and organising.

10.4 Methods of time management

If you go to a bookstore and look in the self-help or business section, or if you look at an online seller such as Amazon and search for "Time

Management", you will see a huge array of books on this topic, many of them bestsellers.

Many books have been written on this subject, and each has a particular flavour. Some assume you are a high-powered executive with secretaries and personal assistants at your service (e.g. Godefroy & Clark, 1991). These often focus on how to delegate tasks effectively to other people. As a student you do not have this luxury, but the job of a Manager is to delegate well-thought-out tasks to a Worker. It's just that both jobs now fall to you. Other books are written for people busy trying to manage conflicting life goals such as looking after children and carrying out a career (e.g. Morgenstern, 2004 or McGee-Cooper, 1994). You may fall into this category and so may find such books worth reading. In short, there is now a wide range of books (and audio programmes on tape or CD) available, each with its own target audience and favoured methodology.

You might need to experiment with a few books to find the right one for you. For example the first book I read on the subject was the abovementioned (Godefroy & Clark, 1991). I found this really helpful, with loads of ideas on how to organise work and do things better. But a colleague of mine just could not get on with it, finding it too prescriptive, and instead much preferred *Organising for the Creative Person* (Lehmkuhl & Lamping, 1994).

Very little has been written for the student, and less still regarding this very important final phase of your course - the project. So how do you go about choosing a method?

The most important thing to realise is that *almost any method is better than no method*. Anything that gets you thinking about your priorities and tasks, and discusses how to handle deadlines, appointments and discretionary time will help you to improve your skills. However, the most common (and somewhat ironic) cry is "I don't have any time to study time management"! Whilst this may appear to be a perfectly logical response, it is rather like someone who has fallen in the sea telling the lifeboat crew to go away, saying "I am too busy trying to stay afloat to be rescued". Time management techniques are the rescue team which can help you escape from either having too much to do, or not knowing how to handle your time.

Different time management methods suit different personalities and job roles. Your preferred method may well change as you change job, or as you develop as a person. The rest of this chapter takes a look at what these techniques all have in common, and then adds some specific advice that will be helpful for you in your dual role as a manager-worker.

10.5 Main principles of time management

Having looked at numerous time management books and courses over the past twenty years, there are a certain set of principles which seem to be in common to almost all of them.

Most time management methods encourage you to do the following five things:

- Get your life goals established
- Know what you're committed to
- Define what needs to be done to make this happen
- Prioritise these according to importance and urgency
- Learn to control the 'new stuff' coming into your life

Let us look at each of these in turn.

10.5.1 Get your life goals established

It is really important that you take time to think about what you want to achieve in life, and what your priorities are. We will assume that part of your life's ambition is to successfully complete your current course (if not – then stop reading now, and go and do some serious top-level thinking). A major part of achieving this goal is to carry out your solo project effectively. So this book will *assume* that you want to do well in your project, and that is what we will concentrate on. However, you may wish to look at some of the reading material referred to in the links at the end of this chapter to help you look at your life goals in some more detail.

10.5.2 Know what you're committed to

Before you can prioritise or schedule your tasks, you first need to establish what jobs you have to do. If you have ever felt compelled to write down a list of what you needed to do (a 'To Do' list) then you were probably trying to get some control over the sense of internal panic that hits everyone when they feel they have too much to do, or they realise that what they have to do has not been properly defined yet.

A 'To Do' list is a reasonable way of helping you capture the fleeting information that bubbles up inside your head, but it is not very effective as a time management tool. The main problem is that your brain will 'throw' things at the list without any apparent order or relationship.

In Chapter 15 - *Project and Action Lists* we will see how the concepts of a To Do list can be extended into something much more reliable; well thought-out records of your major projects and their next actions. The main idea is to get all of your commitments and plans out of your head and into some sort of system that you will see often enough for you to make effective management decisions about what to do next.

10.5.3 Define what needs to be done to make this happen

Given that you have identified those things in life that you are committed to, most time management systems give you some techniques for making sure that those things happen.

At the most basic level, it seems that the human brain is not very good at seeing 'the big picture' at the same time as it is looking at very specific details. Therefore we need tools and techniques to help us externalise our thought processes. You need to do most of your planning and thinking at Manager level, so that your Worker does not have to think about anything else other than the task in hand.

The specific tool we mention later in Chapter 15 - *Project and Action Lists* is the Action List. This is like a highly specialised To Do list, but one that has been managed effectively, so that your Worker can trust it as being reliable and accurate.

10.5.4 Prioritise these according to importance and urgency

Once you have a list of actions that need doing, you should consider their relative priorities. Which one is most important to do at this moment in time? This also requires knowledge of relative timing. Which ones are *due by a certain date* and can only be done in advance of that date? Which ones can only be done *after* another action is completed? Which ones are actually *optional*?

Once the relative priorities and timings are sorted, these can be marked on the Action List, or entered into the *Calendar* and *Daily Planner* (the other two Tools for Time Management which will be discussed later in more detail).

10.5.5 Learn to control the 'new stuff' coming into your life

The final issue that most time management methods urge you to deal with concerns the inputs to your life. The theory goes that once you acknowledge just how much you are already committed to it will be easier to deflect any new unwanted inputs. Inputs come in the guise of requests such as "Ah hello, I was wondering if you could help me . . .", as well as information that needs processing, in the form of e-mail, post, phone calls, voicemail and interruptions (by others and by yourself).

You owe it to yourself to learn when it is appropriate to say "no" to a new task. Once you have completed your Project list, which shows all the active commitments in your life, you will be able to say in all honesty "I cannot take on that task with my current level of commitments". If you really have to take on the new task (because it is essential to your goals, or somebody more senior insists) then you have every right to reconsider your Project list, and see what project currently on the list can be cancelled, or delayed. You can even give this back to the senior person, saying "If I have to do this, could you help me by relaxing the deadline on another project, or cancelling one of these?" It may help to show them your Project list so that they can appreciate the extent of your current commitments.

You can deal with the new information which constantly streams into your life by becoming an expert at removing things as fast as possible. David Allen urges (and I can support this personally) keeping your e-mail Inbox empty! To many people this is counterintuitive, but it is a fantastic way of really knowing what is new and unprocessed, and of being clear about the purpose of anything that you decide to keep. We cover this in detail in *Chapter 13 - Email Mastery.*

10.6 Creating time with the 80:20 rule

Most of the time management books quote the 80:20 rule. It appears in various guises, but its basic claim is revolutionary:

80% of a task is typically completed in just 20% of the time allocated to it

The implications of this are astounding. If it is true, it means that most of us could carry out the majority of our work in one fifth of the time! It also implies that the remaining 80% of the time is spent refining, adjusting and only making small improvements (or possibly just wasting time unproductively). It is certainly worth challenging yourself to work more effectively, and create more free time for you to spend as you wish.

Let's take an example; imagine you had the large task of writing up a five chapter report. Most people would naturally allocate several weeks for this. But *what if* you only had one week? Well, you would have to write one chapter per day. Is that even possible? Certainly. The chapter might be shorter than before, and more focussed, but is that necessarily bad? Might it be better for the reader? But let's push the analogy further. How much of each day do you actually wish to spend working on it? You may wish to allocate certain key times (e.g. one hour in the morning) for planning, and sketching out the structure. Then, let's say you have 3 hours working time left in the day. You divide up the number of sections in the chapter by the time you have available, and that's how long your Worker has to do the writing. Later, when in Worker mode, you can then scope the writing accordingly, perhaps writing a given section in 20 minutes. When you are under such time pressure, just ask yourself "what is essential to cover in this section?", then take 20 minutes to do it.

While we're challenging ourselves, let's imagine you only had 2 days to write the whole report. Think it through. Could you do it? What changes would you have to make? Would you actually have to work harder? Everyone assumes the answer is 'yes', but you could instead trade off the level of detail of what you write, and be happy with shorter sections, and less time for fine-tuning and revision.

Please note that this is NOT an excuse for leaving your report until a few days before the deadline! It's an example of how we should challenge our assumptions about how much time something will take. Later, in Chapter 27 - *Perfectionism* we will watch out for the trap of always needing more time, never finishing and ironically never getting any satisfaction or 'closure' on a piece of work. Giving yourself a strict deadline is an effective tool for counteracting the problem of perfectionism.

10.7 Tools of time management

Now that we have looked at some of the common issues of time management, we will examine a set of four tools which will help you to manage your work, and will enable the Manager and Worker to communicate effectively. The tools are:

- a Calendar
- a Project list
- an Action list
- a Daily planner

This book gives you some specific examples of how to use these tools. Throughout the explanations you are encouraged to customise the entire process to suit your own temperament and preferences. Be aware that for effective time management you need to know:

Managing Your Project

1. What events are already planned in your life (here called the **Calendar**)
2. What things you're committed to (here called the **Project list**)
3. What has to happen to carry out those commitments (here called the **Action list**)
4. What needs to happen today (here called the **Daily planner**).

As long as these functions take place, it doesn't really matter what you call them. However, over the years I have noticed that many students *own* a diary or a computer organiser, yet do not *use* them to carry out those functions effectively. In other words - just having an organiser doesn't make you organised; just owning a diary doesn't (by itself) sort out your time problems.

So over the next several chapters we will describe a system that works well, using the tools mentioned above. This will help to get you very organised, but as you read about it keep thinking if there are better ways for you to achieve the same functionality.

10.8 Time Management self-diagnosis

To start the process of considering where your strong and weak points are regarding managing your time, think about the following questions, and write down your answers in no more than a paragraph.

1. What would you say is your worst time management or organisational problem?

2. Do you already know what the solution is?

3. How do you keep/note/track appointments (lectures, meetings, visits to friends etc.)?

4. Do you feel better working with gadgets/computers or on paper?

5. Which two hours of a typical day are you at your best - most alert and able to carry out tasks with keenness, energy and inventiveness? (Actually many people have 2 such slots; do you?)

6. Barring your typical sleep times, which 2-3 hours of a typical day are your most sluggish and unproductive?

7. How many emails do you have in your INBOX, and how 'in control' of your email do you feel?

8. Do you think you are fully aware of all the responsibilities that you

have, tasks to do etc? or alternatively are you afraid that you are missing loads of things?

9. When you become aware of a task or receive a new commitment (such as an assignment) how do you process it? What, essentially, is your system for getting things done?

10. How do you feel about answering these questions? (Do you feel terrified, intimidated, judged, or alternatively interested, intrigued, or confident?).

The act of answering these questions will help you relate more to the following chapters.

10.9 Summary

One of the biggest growth opportunities that students have during a solo project is to gain practice at managing their response to time. Although we cannot control time itself, we can learn to organise our response to it by planning and prioritising. One of the first major shifts that students typically need to make is from 'reactive' to 'proactive' time management. In other words, a good project manager is not driven entirely by externally set pressures and deadlines (such as timetables and assignments), but learns to plan out the whole process in much more detail to an internally set rhythm.

Much has been written about time management, and different books make different assumptions about their readership. However, start with the summary of techniques described in this book, because almost any method is better than no method at all.

Most time management methods agree that you should do the following five things:

- Get your life goals established;
- Know what you're committed to;
- Define what needs to be done to make this happen;
- Prioritise these according to importance and urgency;
- Learn to control the 'new stuff' coming into your life.

Many systems quote the 80:20 rule, which challenges how much time you really need to do each task by suggesting that 80% of any task's effectiveness is achieved in the first 20% of time spent on it. Most assume

Managing Your Project

that you need some form of the following:

- a Calendar (where you record your commitment to timed events)
- a Project list (which stores commitments of things to do)
- an Action list (for each project, a breakdown of required tasks)
- a Daily planner (a place which integrates the above commitments for one day).

10.10 External Links

(Godefroy & Clark, 1991) *The Complete Time Management System* by Christian H. Godefroy and John Clark. Published by Piatkus Books 1991. ISBN 10: 0749910445, ISBN 13: 9780749910440

(Lehmkuhl & Lamping, 1994) *Organizing for the Creative Person: Right-Brain Styles for Conquering Clutter, Mastering Time, and Reaching Your Goals* by Dorothy Lehmkuhl & Dolores Lamping. Published by Harmony (1994). ISBN-10: 0517881640, ISBN-13: 978-0517881644

(McGee-Cooper, 1994) *Time Management for Unmanageable People: The Guilt-Free Way to Organize, Energize, and Maximize Your Life* by Anne Mcgee-Cooper. Published by Bantam (1994). ISBN 10: 0553370715, ISBN 13: 9780553370713

(Morgenstern, 2004) *Time Management from the Inside Out* by Julie Morgenstern. Publisher: Owl Books (NY); 2 edition (2004). ISBN-10: 0805075909, ISBN-13: 978-0805075908

11. ESTABLISHING YOUR BEST TIMES FOR WORKING

One of the best ways to improve your use of time is to allocate the most appropriate tasks to particular times. For example, if you know that you are always tired and sluggish after lunch, that probably isn't the best time to allocate an hour of creative thinking in front of a computer screen in a stuffy room, as you probably won't stay awake for long. Instead you should find a better part of the day for important and brain-intensive tasks.

People often describe themselves as 'morning people' (often known as "larks") or 'night people' (or "owls"). I've found, from talking to students over many years, that life is often more complicated than that.

11.1 Daily Rhythms

You probably already have a good idea of when you do your best work. If you are a morning person, even though you might struggle with getting up like the next person, you will probably have a couple of hours of creative flow after breakfast. On the other hand, if you are a night owl, you will likely work most effectively late into the evening. For some of you *both* morning and evening will be good, but you will probably have an afternoon 'slump'.

Figure 11.1 illustrates a typical pattern of daily energy levels, but everyone is different. It is essential that you establish what *your* peak working times are (as there may be more than one) during a typical day. Conversely, you should have an honest appraisal of when you are useless (often this is in the few hours after lunch, or in the early evening).

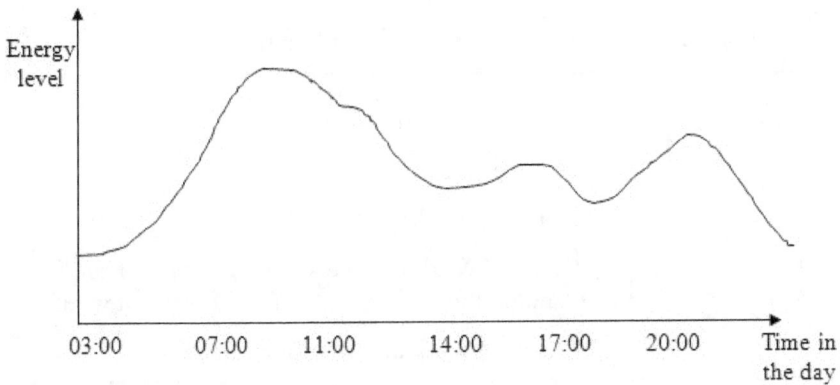

Figure 11.1 Typical daily energy levels

11.2 Allocating tasks to appropriate times

Now that you have some idea of your varying energy levels during the day, you can allocate activities accordingly.

1. Your very best times should be given to your managerial tasks, as this is when you need to be most mentally alert. When these duties are complete, allocate the remainder of your peak time to your inner Worker for making progress on special or creative tasks. Many people regularly use up this peak time by watching television, reading the paper, checking email, browsing the internet, or chatting to friends on social media. There is nothing wrong with these activities in themselves, but in order to maximise your productivity you really should not do them in your peak working time.

2. Give your good-to-moderate times to your Worker, as in this mode you only have one thing to focus on, but you do need a reasonable level of concentration.

3. Give your least attentive, lowest energy times to non-critical activities – preferably resting or having fun. If you have so much to do that you simply *must* work during these times, make sure that you allocate activities with a low mental load (see Figure 11.2).

Energy level	Typical activities to allocate
Peak	Setting aims and objectives Managerial Review Planning the day Creative Work (e.g. creating a Contents Page for a report or planning the outline structure of a piece of work) Checking work before submitting it
Moderate	Writing large chunks of text Reading reference material Checking and responding to e-mail, post, etc. Meetings with supervisor, colleagues etc. De-bugging computer code
Low	Fun activities Non-critical meetings with people (as having other people present will provide stimulation to counteract tiredness). Walking to collect things (e.g. books from library), as exercise helps invigorate a tired mind and body. 'Paper-shifting' tasks which do not require much thought (such as working through a set of hand-written questionnaires and typing them into a computer) Consuming media, chatting, relaxing.

Figure 11.2 Allocation of activities to times of differing energy levels

You may be amazed at the difference that you can make to your effectiveness just by allocating the appropriate tasks to the right times. Most people gradually discover a 'magic time' when they can get through an immense amount of work. Guard that time protectively against interruptions, and use it well to make progress on your most important tasks. As an added bonus, you may find that you complete your work faster, and that you gain lots of extra time. This feature is further enhanced by the 80:20 rule we considered in the previous chapter. When you are at your peak mental alertness, you can often instinctively select the part of the work that will make the most progress for you - in other words you have enough brainpower to begin to master the 80:20 rule.

11.3 Longer-time Rhythms

Whilst it is the Daily rhythm that can give you the most effective productivity boost when you allocate tasks correctly to it, there are other rhythms that you should be aware of.

11.3.1 Weekly

Many people notice that their week has a mood and energy pattern associated with it. Radio stations are always brewing up to the weekend as if it is the only time when you can have a good time. The phrase (and the TV show) 'Thank God it's Friday' highlights this. Various studies show that people are happier at weekends. Certainly parties and later sleeping patterns create a different feel for the weekend, and of course there is nothing wrong with having a change and a rest each week.

People talk about the Monday blues, with the return to work, although some believe that Tuesday is the worst, particularly if partying to excess at the weekend and coming down from natural and chemical highs. However, many of these weekly moods appear to be a *response* to the working week, and maybe working too hard in the week, thus creating the idea that only the weekend is worth living for. This seems a real shame, and it's worth doing everything you can to make sure that the work that you are doing each day has a purpose that you agree with, and preferably that you enjoy.

Interestingly, many time management studies show that it is good to establish a weekly rhythm, mainly in the context of taking some time off to Review what you are doing. The idea of the **Weekly Review** has been mentioned already in section 6.3.3, which looked at the roles of the Manager and the Worker, and it will be covered in more detail in the next chapter (Chapter 12 – *Introduction to GTD*). The basic idea is that one week is a practical amount of time to plan for. In other words if you have long-term goals, it's worth reviewing them once per week to see if there are any actions you can take during the next week to move those goals onwards.

Diaries often are arranged in weekly chunks, and the fact that the days of the week cycle every seven days gives us a structure to plan work around. Universities and working places have timetables that repeat on a weekly basis, so there is a natural structure to your work that is imposed on you by your commitments.

So, to fit in with these cyclic weekly structures it is highly recommended that you have a weekly planning session that allocates the tasks for the following week, taking into account the typical flow of activities through that week and your recurring weekly energy levels.

11.3.2 Monthly

Many studies have shown that both women AND men have hormonal cycles which vary on a roughly monthly basis (see links at the end of this chapter). It seems that not only does the moon control the world's tides, but responses in animals and humans are evident too. Many workers will attest to the fact that the lunar cycle affects things. It is a common observation with schoolteachers that after a particular difficult or disruptive day they find out at night that it's a full moon. And it's even worse if a full moon occurs on a windy day!

But what does this mean in terms of allocating work to particular times? Mainly, this is about your energy & engagement levels. If you acknowledge that there are times of the month when you will feel less motivated, more distracted, less able to complete work, and that THIS WILL PASS, you are equipped to cope better. If you *know* what your cycle is, and it has a predictable time, then you can plan work around this. For example if you know you're in a slump, but experience tells you that in 3 days' time you will be much better, then you can allocate intensive or challenging tasks for later. Note well - you can ONLY do this if you leave enough time for planning. If you leave things until the last minute then you have to complete the work however stressed, unmotivated, unhealthy or moody you may feel at the time.

So, to cope with a monthly cycle, you need to have a good long-term planning strategy that gives you flexibility to cope with a few 'down' days.

11.3.3 Annual

We live our lives with the annual fluctuation of the seasons. Whether we like it or not these changes in climate and sunshine levels affect our moods, our health and our ability to work. Many people can pinpoint times in the year when people seem to be struck down by disease (e.g. flu season). People's moods tend to be lifted by a sunny day, and equally are depressed by several days of poor weather.

Managing Your Project

Some people are affected severely on an annual cycle, with conditions such as SAD (Seasonal Affective Disorder). Symptoms are described on the SADA website (http://www.sada.org.uk/) as:

- Depression
- Sleep Problems
- Lethargy
- Overeating
- Loss of Concentration
- Social Problems
- Anxiety
- Loss of Libido
- Mood Changes.

Clearly these are going to affect a person's ability to work effectively. Luckily there are many treatments, sometimes very simple ones such as light-boxes, which can alleviate the symptoms, and which may be worth investigating if you feel that you suffer from the "Winter Blues". This affects many students, because around the world the majority of academic studies take place clustered around autumn and winter.

However, even if you do not have extreme symptoms, there are going to be things you can do to lift your spirits, mood and body chemistry during 'the hibernation season'. These include all the standard advice (that's very easy to list, but much harder to do consistently) such as:

- eating well,
- taking regular exercise
- getting enough sleep
- taking breaks in your work
- getting outdoors often, if your tasks are usually indoors.

11.4 Summary

Everyone has varying levels of energy and effectiveness. It's vital that you establish what is your default Daily rhythm. Identify those parts of a typical day when you are at your best. Allocate your most important and creative tasks to those times – your managerial / planning / evaluation duties. Protect this time and make it work for you.

Equally, be honest about those periods of the days when you are typically most sluggish. To those times allocate less critical tasks, and make sure you use these slots for any media consumption (TV, recreational reading) or social interaction (via technology or people). The interaction helps to keep you awake. Make sure that you keep these activities away from your peak time.

The bulk of your work can be done in the times between these peaks and slumps. Remember to monitor your energy levels and to take breaks when you need to.

We also live in a world with many cues for a Weekly cycle, based on the recurrent activities that occur on certain days. Many time management systems recommend using the week as a very convenient batch of time for planning a set of activities that get you towards your goals and deadlines.

There are also longer-term cycles, such as monthly and annual, which can affect the quality of your work. It's worth paying attention to these if they seriously disturb what you can do and when, because then it is possible to plan around them.

In summary, it is good practice to regularly plan activities - customised to your own moods and energy levels - according to the time of day, day of the week, and maybe monthly or annual cycles. Good planning is the best way of maximising the effectiveness of your peak times, and minimising the effect of your slumps.

11.5 External Links

Interesting reading about Daily Cycles and what tasks to allocate to different times:

http://productivelifeconcepts.com/use-your-energy-cycle-to-be-more-productive-successful-and-happy/

Discussion about monthly cycles in men as well as women

http://uk.answers.yahoo.com/question/index?qid=20071011055849AAb3Bsn

http://www.medicinenet.com/script/main/art.asp?articlekey=53725

Seasonal Affective Disorder Association (SADA) website (http://www.sada.org.uk/)

12. INTRODUCTION TO GTD

Overview

Getting Things Done (GTD) is a methodology of time and project management developed by David Allen over many years. His first book on the subject "Getting things Done - the art of stress-free productivity" (Allen, 2002) was published over a decade ago and has inspired millions of people to organise their time better.

It's certainly not for everyone, but it deserves its own chapter because of its influence, and because I can personally vouch for it as a bit of a life-changing experience for me and for many of the people I have introduced it to. For several years now I have found that the Getting Things Done methodology is a great way of keeping on top of a busy and complex home life. But I have been constantly searching for the best way of physically and technically implementing this system. In Chapter 16 – *Technological Time Tricks* I'll tell you how I'm currently doing this, and I'll keep this chapter up-to-date, as it does develop and change over time.

However, in this chapter, we'll look at the main principles of GTD, and the sort of practices you need to adopt if you're going to use it. It's important to understand that David Allen describes himself as the laziest person on the planet, and that his systems help you achieve the most outcomes with the minimum possible effort. When you first hear about it, like many time management systems, it actually sounds like *more* work to do, which is not what you want to hear if you already feel overworked.

12.1 Outline of GTD

To get the full benefit of the GTD system and to appreciate some of its subtleties, you should consider reading David Allen's book (Allen, 2002), or listening to one of his recorded seminars e.g. (Nightingale-Conant, 2008), or reading what people around the world are doing with GTD (Allen, 2015), (Mann, 2015). Links for each of these are given at the end of this chapter.

For starters though, here is a summary of the main steps that you need to rigorously follow if you are to benefit from GTD. The system only works if you do all of them, regularly. That is why it's not for everyone. It takes quite a bit of effort to set up. Certain people (me included) have found that effort incredibly rewarding, as you can feel your life getting sorted, and your world getting more organised as you do it. For others, it just all seems like too much hard work and organisation, and it's just not how they want to run their life. I don't know which of these you are, but read the following summaries and see if you feel like giving it a go.

So, the main steps of GTD can be summarised like this:

1. **Get everything out of your head**, your bag, your email inbox, your answerphone etc. into one place where you can think about each item in turn.

2. Work out **which of the above things are Actionable** and either:

    A) **do it right now** if, and only if, it will take less than 2 minutes to do this

    B) **schedule** this to be done at a specific time on your calendar

    C) add it to one of several **Context Lists**, such as @Computer, @Phone etc.

    D) decide that this is bigger than a single action, and thus constitutes a **Project**

3. Once a week do a **Weekly Review** where you look at all your Projects and work out the next moving steps on each one.

4. When working, **look regularly at your Calendar and Context Lists** to find the next most appropriate thing to do.

That's a gross simplification of the methodology, and some people would rather concentrate on the *principles* behind it rather than the workflow as above.

These are things like:

- Empty your head, don't hold onto anything there
- Instead write it down or store it externally

Managing Your Project

- you MUST be able to trust that you will see that stored information
- see it and review it as often as you need to keep in control
- spend some time *managing* the system and some time *doing* stuff

Let's look at each of the Steps outlined above, and then review the principles.

12.2 Getting everything out of your head

It is important that you use tools such as a Diary, Action lists and Project lists (covered in more detail in the following chapters), and are not tempted by the alternative of using your memory as a complete Time Management tool. Around the world the following scenario regularly takes place when a supervisor is arranging the next meeting with his or her student:

Supervisor: (looking at calendar on the computer) Er, how about 10.15 next Friday?

Student: (not looking anywhere) Yes – that's fine.

Supervisor: (knowing how complicated life is) Are you sure that's ok?

Student: Yes – no problem.

Supervisor: (knowing how bad his own memory is) Aren't you going to write that down?

Student: No, that's fine. I just keep it up here (points to head). See you next week.

<1 week later>

Supervisor: (Getting on with work in office, waiting for student who never turned up)

Student: (Sitting in another lecture which they hadn't written down, and now completely unaware that they're missing their supervision).

Your brain is bad at remembering *when* things should happen (as compared to a calendar whose only job in life is to store reminders of events). It is awful at remembering *what* to work on as it is clouded by emotion and energy levels, neither of which is completely predictable. However when you are looking at a pre-prepared Action List, you can use your emotions and current energy states to *choose* the most appropriate action from your list. It is bad for your psychological state of mind to have lots of 'actions' (unresolved activity) stored in your brain.

Andy Hunt

However, this is how a lot of people live their lives.

So, the GTD system is really a formalised way to clear out your brain-space, so that two things happen:

a) Your brain is freed up for important things like making decisions and getting work done, and

b) Your commitments are stored externally, which allows you to sort and prioritise them more effectively.

So, David Allen recommends (and I endorse this from years of getting mentally cluttered) a regular 'brain dump'. The idea is that you sit down with a pen and paper and write down the things that are "on your mind". You can write anything you like, but you're mainly looking to capture commitments or ideas whose only existence at the moment is in your head. This can take a while to get started and what comes out can appear very unorganised. Here's an example of a mental conversation you might have during a brain dump . . .

"Ok. Got my pen and paper. Now - what's on my mind? Well it's obviously that piece I need to sing at tonight's Karaoke. I really don't know the tune and it's going to be very embarrassing if I mess it up. But, what else is up here in my head?

Ah - I need more tea bags.

Anything else?

Batteries for the torch. OK, this is like a shopping list.

OMG - the Research Assignment!! It's due this week and I haven't started yet. Ok, (panic) I'll need to read the assignment, reschedule everything. There's no way I can do the Karaoke party. Well - at least I don't need to practice. How did I forget that?!

I wonder if there's anything else I've forg . . . .

Mum's birthday! That's next week and I've got to get something and post it, which means doing it today. Right after this I'll make a list.

Add Birthday Present to the list.

Ok, what else? Er, I think that's it.

Ah, there is that reading list I'm meant to be going through before Monday.

Oh no, what's the time? - OMG !!! I've just missed a meeting with my supervisor!!"

Managing Your Project

Obviously this is contrived, and probably doesn't describe *your* life, but notice how all of this 'stuff' has been lurking around in this person's brain, and they've been not aware consciously that there are these unsorted commitments. However, their subconscious brain clearly was holding on to them. But the subconscious brain clearly isn't a good time-planner. Did you notice how the items appear in what seems to be a very non-prioritised order? It's like they are "locked in there somewhere". So all of these things - all of your commitments - need to be externalised - somewhere that you can see them all, evaluate them, review them, schedule them and take action on them. As a by-product this can remove stress by taking the responsibility away from your subconscious brain to hold on to all of these things.

But GTD is not just about emptying your *brain*. There are all sorts of things that you may have in your life that you need to take action on, but they are not yet properly acknowledged as *actions* to be taken. These may be sitting in some of the following places:

- your email INBOX (this is such a common place for unacknowledged actions to pile up that there's a whole chapter coming up on how to sort this out)
- your voicemail
- that little pile of letters, papers and various unsorted things that grows up by your door
- bits of paper written and thrown into your bag
- action items scribbled on a meeting agenda when you were in a meeting
- things written in this week's (or last week's) diary page.

The idea is that - at least once per week - you 'empty' all of these places where input is gathering in your life, and you list them. Often at this point you can get rid of the original piece of paper, because you were simply using it as a crude physical reminder that there was something to be done.

And so, in summary, the first phase of the GTD system is:

"Get everything out of your head, your bag, your email inbox, your answer phone etc. into one place where you can think about each one in turn."

12.3 Work out which things are Actionable and process these into an external system

The above step helps you to *gather* all the raw information that's been sitting inside your head and in notebooks and email etc.

Now you need to know how to *Process* these things, and specifically to determine which of these things are 'Actionable'.

There are usually several categories of things that you have collected (e.g. that pile of stuff on a table somewhere). These can be split up as follows:

1) **useless** items; which should be thrown away

2) **information** items; which you may want to store for later

3) **pending** items; which should be stored somewhere until the right time

4) **Actionable** items; which need doing or scheduling

5) items you need to **review** because you don't yet know what to do with them.

Most 'piles' (and by that I mean physical piles such as in-trays, as well as electronic piles like email) build up because we don't take the time to Process what is in them. David Allen calls these piles "Huh stacks". We half-heartedly set out to get the pile sorted out, pick up the first item, go "Huh" and put it back in the pile unsorted. No progress, and now we feel bad! He says that the piles build up because they represent a whole set of little decisions that haven't been made, and these decisions masquerade as a threatening pile, which we try to ignore for ages, and which makes us feel bad every time we pass it.

Lots of people agree that the solution is to go through *every item in turn* and decide which of the above categories it represents. That way you face each little decision, one at a time, and you deconstruct the threat.

Let's think a bit more about each of the categories, then we'll return to the process of sorting them.

12.3.1 Useless items; which should be thrown away

You might wonder why you would have a pile of useless items. It's precisely because you haven't yet sorted them, so you don't yet know what is useful or otherwise. In this category go things like junk mail. However it's not really junk unless it's useless to you. For example a piece of junk mail about the latest computer offers could be of interest if you need a new computer, in which case you might decide that this brochure is Actionable. Other things in this category can only be put there once you've processed them. For example a letter from your bank could be explaining that you are overdrawn and there are some big charges coming your way if you don't sort it (urgent Actionable) or it might be offering a loan or a new card when you don't need it (junk/Useless).

12.3.2 Informational items; which you may want to store for later

If you have decided that an item is NOT useless then the next step is to decide *why* it is useful to you. If there is no immediate action to be taken then it is probably an Informational item. For example it might be a menu from a local takeaway; you're not wanting to eat right now, but you want to put it somewhere for later. Or it could be the local news leaflet, which contains numbers for local tradespeople. These are the sorts of thing that some people pin to a noticeboard in their house, or you might have a special drawer where you put these things. The most important thing is that you ONLY put things here that are Informational. Do not mix up Actionable or junk materials, otherwise it becomes another 'Huh' stack. To be clear, you can put something in your Informational location *if* you can say the following about it "I *might* need this one day, but nothing in my plans will fail if I don't see this again".

12.3.3 Pending items; should be stored somewhere until the right time

This sort of item really does deserve to be in a pile because it's waiting for something to happen. However, it's often really in the pile because what it's waiting for is simply your decision about what it is. So, if you've got rid of the Useless stuff, and have separated out the Informational material, then you are left with things that are important to you which need to be done. Pending items are tricky because you can't do them yet. Here are some examples to make it clear that there are a few types of Pending item.

a) You've invited a group of friends to see if they want to have a weekend away. In the pile is a copy of your invite letter and one reply. You are waiting for 3 more replies. You don't want to plan the accommodation unless it's worthwhile and enough people can come. In this case there are actually two decisions to make. Firstly, what is your minimum number of people you need positive replies from for the weekend to be viable? And secondly, when do you need to make a decision on this? It's really important that you have a cut-off date for every Pending action, so that this date goes in your diary and reminds you to make a decision. Equally if all the replies come in quickly then you can go ahead with the decision at that point.

b) A brochure comes through your door containing local events information. You decide rapidly that this is not junk, and that there is an Action on you to get tickets for one of the concerts. BUT tickets are not available until April 15th, and so you place it back in the 'Huh' pile. But you will forget this and miss the concert. Instead you should put an action reminder in your diary for April 15th, along with information about what the concert is and how to book. If it's simple to book (e.g. Concert title and a phone number), then write that information in your diary (next to the reminder) and you have just converted your original item to Junk! It's now useless to you and can be thrown away UNLESS you think there might be other events of interest, in which case you've converted it to Informational, in which case you need to file it somewhere.

So, you need two things:

1. a diary or calendar in which you place the deadline for the decision, and
2. a place to store the Pending items while you're waiting.

Do you also see that it is simply your *decisions* that determine which category these items are in, and that the category can change about the item as you process it? It is the lack of small decisions that explains why they are currently all lumped together in a pile.

12.3.4 Actionable items; need doing or scheduling

Sometimes you will pick up something off your pile and will immediately know that it is an action, or that it has an action associated with it. Such things might be:

- a bill which needs paying
- a report from a friend which you said you would proofread
- a brochure from a holiday company that you need to call in order to book a room
- a letter that you want to reply to

etc.

However, sometimes the Action might be *implied* by the item you have put in the pile. For example you might have put a birthday card in the pile because it reminded you that you need to buy a birthday present for a family member. It may have been obvious to you when you put the card on the pile, but now (after a while) you find that you need to do some re-thinking to discover why you put it there.

Once you have cleared out the junk, the Informational and the Waiting items what you have left is stuff that you need to take Action on. David Allen strongly recommends that unless the action can be handled really quickly you do NOT do it now, but you put it in that Actionable pile. This is because you are currently in 'sorting and decision' mode. If you keep stopping to take action on some of the things you find, you will lose your flow and focus and the pile will remain unsorted. Another way of looking at this is this; how do you know that if you stop sorting - to do an action - there isn't a much more urgent and important one waiting for you in the pile? In fact, Allen advises to get ALL your 'piles' sorted out first before you start doing actions. This means getting your paper, your email, your head, etc. all sorted, and then move on to an Action Processing stage. This stage is described below.

12.3.5 Review items; because you don't know what to do with them yet

If you do all the above processing, there really shouldn't be anything left at all. However life is never as clean as theory and there are bound to be several things that don't appear to fit into the above categories. Typically you will find yourself saying things like "I just don't know what to do with this" (usually in a whingey voice!). Right, this is where you need to be ruthless. Your job now is to MAKE it fit into one of the above categories. Allen says that the only reason it's in this undecided no-man's-land is that you haven't yet answered a question about it. As a reminder, here are the questions you need to ask about this item. Pick it up and look at it (as if you are interrogating a suspect) and ask:

"What ARE you?"

"Why should I not just throw you away right now?"

The sort of replies you typically get from an 'undecided' item are things like:

"I don't want to decide about you yet"

"If I throw this away I might find I need it later"

"I don't really know what to do about this"

These are valid replies, but if you start with the premise that everything is junk, information, pending or actionable then all you have to do is to hold firm and force it into one of those categories. Your reasoning might go something like this;

> This is a really interesting advert. It might be useful for a project that I might do later, but I haven't really got an action on it now. Let's just check that. Do I want to start an *action* on this, e.g. Launch a new Project to look into this thing? i.e., is this a timely reminder to get going on something?"

If YES, put it in the **Actionable** pile. If NO, then carry on the thought conversation as follows:

> "Am I *waiting* for something else to happen before I can decide on this? Something that I can schedule in my diary or put in a waiting folder?"

If YES (e.g. It's an idea for a holiday but you haven't yet met up with the friend you want to go on holiday with) then this is a **Pending** item, so treat it like case 3, above. If NO, then there's one more decision to make.

> "Can I get this information relatively easily from somewhere else if and when I need it?"

If NO, then you've got a reasonably unique piece of information here that is of interest to you, so you have just categorised this as **Informational**.

If YES, for example something that's always on display somewhere else or on the Internet or known by people that you know, then there's no reason to hold on to this anymore and it is effectively **Junk** to you and can be thrown away. Yes really - those of you who love holding onto things 'just in case' - if this is not a direct action, nor are you waiting for something, nor is it the only easy way of getting that information, then it is useless from an informational point of view.

Of course, you might be holding on to something simply because you LIKE it, e.g. A nice letter from family or a friend, a thank you note, a piece of art from the children etc. You do not NEED to throw it away, but you do need to throw it out of this pile, because it's nothing to do with your planning or actions.

Be very careful about using this 'Review' pile at all, because it can be used to defer making a decision about what an item actually is. If it's in your pile, and it's not Junk, and it's not just Informational, and it's not obviously Pending and it hasn't got an obvious Action, then it means that you have some sort of attachment to this item that needs thinking about.

Managing Your Project

If it helps you sort through the pile quickly then by all means put things on a Review pile, but know that at the end of the process this pile needs to disappear, so it is only to be used as a temporary resting place while you are sorting.

When you come to sort through this pile later, you need to allocate each item to one of the remaining categories. If you REALLY are struggling to define what this item is, then it is an Action! Why? Because the next action is to decide what this item is. So put it on the Action pile.

More on this in the next section (12.3.6).

12.3.6 Processing each item into one of four categories

Now that we have an idea of what sort of things may be in each of the above categories, we can make some progress by Processing each item in turn and deciding which category it is. By definition this gets rid of category 5 (Review items). This is the time when you *decide* if something is Useless, Informational, Pending or Actionable. No exceptions.

The advice is to pick up each item, and you are not allowed to put it down until you have decided what category it's in. David Allen suggests you ask the rather obvious question "What IS this?". It's actually a great question because as well as helping you focus on the item, it also implies that you're asking "What is this to ME?".

I've found that another really good question to ask of EVERY item is this:

> *"Why should I not just throw you away?"*.

This is good because the *default* process here is to get rid of junk. Only if you can come up with a jolly good reason to keep it does it stay - BUT you still have to know what it IS, and which of the categories it belongs to.

Here's an example conversation you might have with yourself as you sort through your pile of paper.

> *"Ok, here we go.*
>
> <Picks up first item - an envelope. Opens it>.
>
> *What IS this? A holiday offer? Ah that IS junk mail. In the recycling. One down. Next.*
>
> <Picks up another envelope. Opens it>
>
> *What is this? Ah a bill. Boo. Would like it to be junk, but it's not. I need to pay this so it's Actionable.* <Puts it into an Actionable pile>. *Next.*

119

Andy Hunt

<Picks up a scrap of paper. All it has on it is a phone number>

What IS this? A phone number, yes, but whose? Er, really can't remember. Ok, Why should I not just throw you away? Because I only write down numbers that I want to call back. Ah, yes, I remember now that meeting I had in the library. This is the chap who can help me with my computer. That's an Action then, 'cos I need to call him to get it fixed. <Puts it into the Actionable pile>. *Ok, Next.*

<Picks up a colourful brochure>

What's this? Ah, yes, a concert series at the local hall. Why shouldn't I just throw it away? Well, I think I deserve a musical treat now and again. Is this an action? Well - it could be if I choose to go, but - d'you know what? - it's just information for now. I'll file it <Puts it on the information pile>. *Hey this isn't so bad. Next.*

<Picks up a folder>

What's this? Oh dear! This is Jim's essay I said I'd proofread for him. Whoops; how long has this been here? Ok - this is an Action and an urgent one. Call Jim to apologise, and then - schedule it to do as a priority if he can still take my input. <Puts on Actionable pile>"

And so it goes on until every item has been processed.

At the end of this process we should have:

1) A pile of **useless** items to throw away or recycle

2) A pile of things to file away for **information**

3) Some **pending** items which are stored in a known location for later, with a note in a Calendar of when you need to chase this up

4) Items which need **Action**!

12.3.7 Processing each non-Action

The **Junk** items need to be disposed of, so do that straightaway. You'll feel good. Take it to the recycle bin, or dispose as you can. If you're really lucky your pile will have disappeared, or at least reduced to a few items.

The **Informational** items need to be stored somewhere. Chapter 7 – *Taking Notes and keeping records* has lots of ideas about saving notes in paper and electronic systems. If you're using paper, you might want to have a place (a drawer, a noticeboard, or a file-folder) where these items can sit

Managing Your Project

until you need them.

The **Pending** items (as described above in 12.3.3) need to be stored somewhere until the allocated time arrives for processing them (which is to be written in your diary or calendar as a reminder). You can use similar techniques to that just described for Informational items - but make sure you use a *different* drawer, folder, or electronic location. Now you've got these categories separated, don't be tempted to mix them up again.

12.3.8 Processing each Action

Once you have sorted everything into these different piles, removed the Junk, and filed the Pending and Informational, it's then really important to change gear, and sort out the Action pile.

The wonderful thing that's different about your Action pile from the pile you first started with is that it ONLY contains Actions. In other words, each time you pick up an item on this pile you *know* you've already committed yourself to doing something, and you simply need to process that action into your organising system.

GTD suggests four different things you can do with an Action:

A) Do it *right now* if, and only if, it will take less than 2 minutes to do

B) *Schedule* this to be done at a specific time on your calendar

C) Add it to one of several *Context Lists*, such as @Computer, @Phone etc.

D) Decide that this is bigger than a single action, and thus constitutes a *Project*

Now, we'll examine each one of these in turn.

A) Do it right now if, and only if, it will take less than 2 minutes to do

This is the fantastic "Two minute" rule. You have to make a snap decision about whether you can get this item done within 2 minutes. If you can, then get on and do it right now.

Examples of this sort of immediate action include:

- sending a short email

- leaving a phone message for someone

- fetching a book and leaving it by the door so that you take it out with you when you leave.

Try not to get distracted while you're speeding through that action. For example don't start responding to other emails. The idea is to get back to sorting out actions as quickly as possible.

Just as important is the opposite side of the rule: if it's going to take *more* than 2 minutes then do NOT do it now, but *schedule* it for later.

The reason that the rule works is that if it's a short action, then you do it and it's gone - and you get the buzz of an easy win. Equally, if it's going to take longer than the 2 minutes, then you have to think about when and where and how to do this. That is described in the next 3 sections.

B) Schedule this to be done at a specific time on your calendar

If your action needs to be done at a *particular* time, then make an entry in your calendar as a reminder for you to do it then.

Here are some reasons why you might need to wait for a particular time:

- You need to talk to a colleague but they are away on holiday for two weeks, so you schedule a reminder for this action when they are back.

- You are waiting for some information or product to become available, and you have a date for this.

- You decide for strategic reasons that you want to wait a certain amount of time before taking action. This might be because you need time to think about the action before you do it, or could be because you're very busy with other more urgent things and you want to 'park' this safely in the future so that you will be reminded to think about it later.

If you have still have some paper associated with this action, then you need to find a place to store it. This could be - for simplicity - a single file or folder containing things that you've scheduled for later.

Or, you could scan the information and store it in your electronic note system.

Managing Your Project

C) Add it to one of several Context Lists

One of the masterstrokes of GTD is the idea that actions are associated with 'contexts', in other words - the places and situations where you can actually DO the action. Following on from that idea is the suggestion that you write down your action-reminders on lists for where/how the action will be carried out.

Rather than having one big To-Do list you have several lists. These lists are different for everyone but my main ones are:

@Computer - any computer or laptop connected to the internet will do for these tasks

@Office - I need to be physically at my office to do these

@Phone - any phone will let me carry out these actions

@Home - I specifically need to be in my house for these.

You can invent your *own* contexts, and each one will have a list.

Some people have 'people-based' contexts, such as @Boss (which is a list actions that can only be dealt with when you're with your boss).

The way these are used in practice is as follows; if you get some discretionary time, or there is unallocated time on your calendar, you get to choose which task you do according to which contexts are available. For example if you are in the office you could do anything from @Office, @Computer or @Phone, but not @Home and maybe not @Boss if your boss is not there.

More detail on the use of these contexts is given in Chapter 15 – *Project and Action Lists*.

D) Decide that this is bigger than a single action, and thus constitutes a Project

The sort of actions that you put on your Context lists above should be 'unit' actions. In other words you should be able to visualise yourself doing and completing these actions in a certain place. If you cannot do this, it may be because you are thinking about something much bigger, or with multiple steps, or which will take a lot longer.

This is probably best classified as a **'Project'**.

A Project is a multi-part task that can be split up into a number of different steps.

Let's look at two example Projects, one which appears in response to an unexpected event and just needs to be sorted quickly, and one which is very much expected and takes place over a longer time-scale.

a) Research a new printer.

If your printer breaks at home, you will probably want to replace it. Imagine you can't do this straightaway so you want to organise your actions.

Some of you would put this down as a single @Computer action. When you come to do it, you sit down at the computer, log in to your favourite on-line retailer and order the most popular printer that you can afford. That's a single action, carried out in one context like this: @Computer: Research and buy printer online.

However, others of you would want or need to make this into a multi-step project. What if you don't know how much money you have available for this and you need to phone your bank? Perhaps you share a house with a group of fellow students and you have an idea that you could all contribute to a common printer and share it. Your new project might begin to look like this:

Project - research new printer

1) @Phone: Call bank to establish balance

2) @Home: Chat to people sharing the house about if they wish to share printer and thus contribute to the purchase

3) @Computer: Go online and find best deals

4) @Home: Decide democratically which printer is best

5) @Computer: Go on-line again and order printer

6) @Home: Gather everyone's monetary contributions.

b) Write Thesis

Clearly, if you are doing a Masters or PhD/DPhil course, writing your thesis is one of the largest and most complex tasks that you are going to encounter. For that reason alone it is worth having a Project created especially for this - and you then get to review it weekly (see section 12.4). The earlier in the process that you can create a Project for this, the more it will become part of your weekly focus, and the more likely you are to make progress with it, rather than leaving the write-up until the end.

Now, because this is such a large and long-term exercise, it will probably 'spawn' a whole series of sub-projects. It is up to you how you handle this.

Managing Your Project

Some people put all the details of the sub-projects within the master project. However, there is an alternative that GTD followers would probably do. Let's say you're currently working on Chapter 2 of your thesis. You could have one Project called 'Write Thesis' and another separate Project called 'Research and Write Chapter 2'. They are both reviewed weekly for their next Actions, and those Actions are written into the appropriate places in your context links.

Examples of what might go in the two Projects are as follows:

Project - Write Thesis

@Supervisor: Discuss thesis chapter structure and writing schedule

@Computer: Type up Contents page

@Computer: Decide which sub-projects to open (e.g. 'Research & Write Chapter 2')

@Home: Look through reading material in files. Useful for literature review?

@University: Visit Print Unit to find out about printing & binding costs and deadlines

etc.

Project - Research and Write Chapter 2

@Computer: Expand Contents page for Chapter 2 into full detailed subtitles

@Home: Read through gather information in filing cabinet and type up the relevant stuff for the literature review.

@Supervisor: Agree a deadline for Chapter 2 to be delivered to Supervisor for comment and proofreading.

@Computer: Schedule writing sessions in calendar for each subsection of chapter

etc.

The difference between the two Projects is that 'Research and Write Chapter 2' is of a shorter duration. The moment you have finished writing Chapter 2 there is no longer any need to have a weekly review of this project so you can remove it from your list. In contrast, 'Write Thesis' will probably be there from the very start to the very end of the degree.

12.4 The Weekly Review

One of the core concepts of GTD is the idea of a Weekly Review. Once a week you look at all your Projects and work out the next *moving steps* on each one. David Allen has found by experimentation that a week is a suitable length of time to plan for. Of course you can make plans for the year or even longer ahead, but they don't tend to contain much working detail. Equally, you can (and are encouraged to) make Daily plans, but these tend to be quite 'fast-moving' and driven by more immediate pressures. Planning for a week, in contrast, tends to give a good balance of the immediate versus the long-term.

Many people have come up with ideas about exactly what should be done in a Weekly Review. The truth is that it varies from person to person, and indeed from week to week depending on how busy you are and how many things you are trying to 'juggle. So here are a few ideas of what could be done in a Weekly Review. Remember the idea is to put aside some time (typically 1 or 2 hours) where you take stock of all your commitments and plans.

- Give yourself time and space to empty your head of commitments and reminders which you may be carrying around mentally (as described in section 12.2)
- Check you have no unfinished business from the previous week by looking at the calendar of events from the week just gone by.
- Sort out all incoming information (as in 12.3)
- Empty your email and voicemail INBOXes (more detail on that in Chapter 13 – *Email Mastery*)
- Work methodically through each one of your Projects, asking:
    - have I completed any of these actions? (and if so mark them off or remove them)
    - does this project have any NEW actions? (add them)
    - are the next actions stored in Context Lists? (if not, add).
- Ask yourself if there are any NEW Projects to launch (e.g. you've finished Chapter 2, and now need to start work on Chapter 3 so it needs its own new Project)
- Review the Calendar for the upcoming week and see if anything needs doing in preparation (e.g., a meeting for which you need to read a document).

Managing Your Project

So, a Weekly Review is like the powerhouse of your organisational system. It helps you to capture all your loose ends and the commitments that you've gathered in the week, and to carefully review all your current larger-scale commitments and make a detailed plan for the upcoming week. In other words it is the bridge between your longer-term, higher-level plans, and your day-to-day detailed Unit Actions that you need to carry out over the next week.

12.5 Calendar and Context Lists

When you are working throughout the week, GTD requires that you look regularly at your Calendar and Context Lists to find the next most appropriate thing to do. If you are still trying to remember every detail and task then the system isn't working properly and you won't feel the benefit of a mind free to concentrate on each current task in hand.

The Calendar should hold those commitments that are tied to certain days. These include meetings, supervisions, deadlines for work, as well as any information you wish to see on a certain day (such as 'Jim back from holiday').

As a rule you should give priority to the things on the Calendar, because they are only happening on those days and cannot be put off. Anything which is discretional, and can be done on a variety of days, is often best omitted from the Calendar, and instead should appear on your Context Lists.

The Context Lists hold all your low-level tasks that can be done in a certain 'context'. For example, the @Computer list contains all those things which can be done when you are seated at a computer. If you are using an electronic system, such as the Evernote system described in section 7.5, you can 'tag' each task with several different contexts (specifically see "7.5.4 Tagging Data: organising notes"). As an example, if you had to phone someone while you were at your computer you might tag the task "Call Person X" as @Computer AND @Phone.

The idea is that when you are in a certain context (e.g. at work and at a computer) there are:

- certain tasks that you can only do there (e.g. look on the internet for a new printer and compare it with a folder in your physical filing cabinet)
- some tasks that you *could* do elsewhere (e.g. make a phone call)
- several tasks that you *cannot* do here (e.g. mow your lawns at home).

You can arrange your Context Lists so that they help you to *filter* all your existing commitments by context. It's often best to prioritise those tasks which can *only* be done in your current context, then fill your remaining time with any tasks which *could* be done in that context.

12.6 Keeping the system up to date

As well as completing date-specific tasks from the Calendar and context-specific tasks from the Context Lists, you need to keep the GTD system up to date.

This can mean:

- processing emails as they come in
- capturing any new ideas in the system to be processed later
- ticking off or removing completed tasks
- making sure that your Context Lists are up to date
- processing any incoming paperwork
- organising anything else which is a new commitment.

Whilst these activities can be done in a Weekly Review, most people find that life moves so fast and generates new commitments so rapidly that you need to keep the system up to date at least once a day and maybe several times.

GTD is a wonderful system for organising your life and work, but it is like a garden and needs constant work to keep it 'weed free and watered'. If you would like to capture all your commitments in one place, and free your head up to think about things and do work (rather than remembering all your complex commitments), *and you are willing to work at keeping it up to date* - then GTD may well be the system for you.

12.7 Summary

Getting Things Done (by David Allen) is one of the most popular time management systems in the world. It's not for everyone but I have found it transforming for my own work, and that of students who have been struggling with chaotic and out of control self-management.

In summary, the methodology involves applying a series of steps regularly and reliably.

Managing Your Project

1. Get everything out of your head into a place where it can be processed.
2. Decide – one item at a time – whether it is Actionable. If so, either a) do it now if less than 2 minutes; b) schedule it to a later time on a Calendar; c) add it to a Context list such as @Computer; d) make it a Project.
3. Do a Weekly Review where you identify and schedule next actions for each Project.
4. Work through your Calendar and Context lists regularly to decide your daily work.

However, behind that workflow are several principles:

- Get things out of your head (as human memory is not a great reminder tool)
- Write it or store it in a trusted place
- Review it as often as you need to keep in control
- Spend some time *managing* the system and some time *doing* stuff.

Many people describe GTD as a life-changing system, which finally gave them control over their complex lives and work commitments. But it does require consistent and regular 'maintenance' to keep it up to date. It really doesn't work if you do it half-heartedly as your brain can never really trust that your system is complete.

The rest of this chapter helps you to think about how to use this system in practice; sorting through piles while really working out what is meant by Actionable, Pending, Informational and Junk. Whether or not the GTD system is ultimately suited to you and your way or working, it is worth giving it a try if you currently don't have a reliable way of storing and retrieving all your tasks, goals, commitments and information.

12.8 External Links

(Allen, 2002) Getting Things Done: How to achieve stress-free productivity, Publisher: Piatkus 2002, ISBN-10: 0749922648, ISBN-13: 978-0749922641. Also available for Kindle. One of the most popular time management systems in the world.

(Allen, 2015) http://gettingthingsdone.com/   The David Allen homepage.

(Mann, 2015) A website dedicated to helping people share best working habits and practices. http://www.43folders.com/topics/getting-things-done

(Nightingale Conant, 2008) Getting Things Done with Work-Life Balance (7CD set plus Workbook) http://www.nightingale.com/getting-things-done.html

13. EMAIL MASTERY - HOW TO GET TO INBOX ZERO

One of the most impressive benefits of the GTD ("Getting Things Done") system is that it enables people to get control of their email Inbox. If carried out systematically this can result in ZERO emails in your Inbox several times a day, and a reassurance that every email has been processed correctly.

This chapter explains how to achieve this apparently amazing feat. I can personally assure you that it's not only entirely feasible, but it feels very good and gives a sense of control in a chaotic world. I've been regularly pruning my Inbox to ZERO several times a day for the last 8 years.

13.1 Inbox overload

Ever since the introduction of email several decades ago people - as a rule - have not known what to do with incoming messages. Consequently they pile up in the Inbox and eventually become unmanageable.

The effect of this can range from mild inconvenience (where it takes you a long time to sort through messages to find the one you want) to total dysfunction (where you miss lectures and assignments because your Inbox is in chaos and nothing is sorted or properly acted on).

Some email systems actively encourage you to *keep* all your messages, forming an ever-increasing archive of material. The claim is that - using the built-in search tools - you can quickly find what you're looking for. The problem with this is that you do not go looking for something that you've forgotten about or never even noticed in the first place.

13.2 The methodology for sorting emails

It would be really helpful if you could have read Chapter 12 before continuing, as this will give you a background to the GTD system, and some terminology about sorting incoming paper that we can use again here.

The theory goes that there are only 4 types of email:

- Junk
- Informational
- Pending
- Actionable.

The idea for clearing your email Inbox to ZERO messages goes like this, in outline:

Work through your emails from the latest to the earliest as follows:

1. As you identify **Junk** messages just DELETE them.

2. As you identify **Informational** messages (ones with no action, but containing information you might like in the future) MOVE them into a Folder or Archive.

3. If you identify **Pending** messages (those for which you are awaiting a reply) MOVE them into a special @Waiting folder.

4. If an email demands an **Action** of you MOVE it into an @Action folder.

At the end of this process your Inbox should be empty, and you will have:

a) several emails in an @Action folder which require some action by you.

b) some emails in an @Waiting folder, which will need chasing-up at some point in the future - maybe at the Weekly Review.

c) lots of emails Archived or stored in folders for future information.

At this point you still need to process the @Action folder, but we will deal with that in section 13.4.

For now, let's look at each of the email categories in more detail, so that you learn to recognise and process them more easily.

13.3 Identifying the email categories

The faster you become at quickly working out what an email really is, the faster you can get your Inbox to ZERO.

13.3.1 Junk

Some truly 'Junk' email will have already been removed for you by your email program's Spam filter. It's probably worth checking through the 'Spam bin' every now and again in case a valuable email has accidentally been sorted into there.

Occasionally Junk email makes it through your filters, and messages offering you performance-enhancing drugs; cheap loans; millions of pounds in offshore investments; requests to enter your password to reactivate your 'closed' account; will be sitting there in your Inbox. Don't get mad - just press DELETE. Enjoy their destruction.

However, learn to be very liberal with your use of the word 'Junk'. Redefine it as meaning any message that you don't need to do anything with or want to keep. Here are some things which you could easily redefine as 'Junk' and so just delete:

- any message not intended for you and which you declare is not *needed* by you
- messages from a company you have dealt with, amounting to adverts you don't want
- messages copied to you 'for information' which isn't relevant to you
- any message that tells you something you already know, or which is already in your planning system
- emails from a newsfeed that you've subscribed to that you are too busy to read and don't want to save for later.

Basically, look at every message and ask yourself "Why is this not Junk, and therefore why should I not just DELETE it?".

13.3.2 Informational

Section 12.3.2 describes paper-based informational items as "I might need this one day, but nothing in my plans will fail if I don't see this again". So these would be emails that contain information that you wish to keep for later reference, but you don't want to take any action on.

These could be:

- a record of some interaction with a person that you want to keep, but that doesn't have an immediate Action associated with it.
- some ideas for a project that you are working on that you might want to refer to in the future.
- menus from restaurants you may like to visit
- products you like the look of but don't want to commit to buying right now
- articles from a newsfeed that you might like to read one day but doesn't appear to contain any immediately relevant material for your projects.

So, these should be filed away for potential future use.

Some people (including myself) like to 'Tag' the information as it's being filed (and many email clients such as Gmail allow this). This allows the information to be tagged in multiple virtual 'folders'. For example, a restaurant menu might be tagged with 'Food', 'Restaurants', and 'Night out ideas', and thus can be easily found when any one of these tags is clicked on in the future.

I take this a stage further and have hierarchical tags. So I have 'top-level' tags such as Teaching, Research, Home etc., and within each of those is a series of sub-tags for each project or lecture course or supervisee etc.

Others prefer a quicker approach, which is to simply 'Archive' informational emails. The idea is this - if you know this isn't an Action, then it's information and can be put in one big Archive folder, because you can search for it when you need it. This works for many people, but personally I like the discipline of tagging an email as I'm filing it, as I guess it makes me consciously aware of *why* I'm filing it rather than deleting it.

13.3.3 Pending

This can be a huge category for emails, particularly if you are in charge of people, or are working with people on different projects. Pending messages are ones that are awaiting a response from another person or an external event.

A really common type of email is created when you send a request message to someone and you want to track the reply, because you really

Managing Your Project

need an answer. So you send an email to the person with a copy to yourself. What most people do is to leave this reminder (along with all their other reminders, and the junk, and the information, and the actions) lurking around in their Inbox.

These emails should be immediately moved into a special folder (or tagged with the label) @Waiting. David Allen suggests this title; and the @ symbol forces it to the top of the alphabetic list of tags or folders. If you like you can also tag it with a label related to its final resting place. As an example, if you are sending a message to your supervisor and you need an answer, then you might send off a message with a copy to yourself. The copy arrives almost instantly in your Inbox so immediately tag it as '@Waiting' and 'Supervisions', then remove the automatic tag for 'Inbox'. This has the effect of removing it from your Inbox, denoting that there a reply you're Waiting for, and marking it as relating to supervisions. Once a week - at your Weekly Review - you can look through your @Waiting folder and see if you have had replies from people. If your supervisor has replied to the above message you can 'untag' it from @Waiting and it will still be tagged as 'Supervisions' and so it is automatically filed for you.

13.3.4 Actions

An Action email is any message that you have to (or want to) do something about. This is a source of confusion for many people, because they do not take a little time to think what the Action really is.

Sometimes it's quite obvious that it's an Action and exactly what is required.

e.g., you receive an email from your supervisor saying *"I have not received your initial report. If you can email me an electronic copy by 1pm today then it won't be marked as late and I can read it on the train this afternoon".*

You now have an URGENT Action to find a report and send it to your supervisor.

Sometimes it is less obvious what the Action actually is and whether it even applies to you. Imagine that you receive a long and complicated message from the student rep about the staff-student liaison meeting. It doesn't seem as though this is an Action message, but buried in the report is a request for people to do some paid proofreading. As you have decided that this would be an interesting thing to do and you might earn a bit of money, you decide that you will contact the student rep and offer your services. At this point you might decide to send a short email to the student rep. If this was the only thing of relevance in the email you can now file it or delete it.

If you hadn't yet read the message, then the Action might simply be 'Read this to see if there are any actions buried in here'.

You have to be very careful not to come across an Action and get so wrapped up in it that you stop your sorting. This might sound counterintuitive, as surely processing an Action is good? Well, not if there is a much more important one still waiting to be sorted! One of the best ways to stop you *doing* Actions *until* you've finished the sorting is to have a folder or tag labelled @Action. Again, the @ sign floats this folder to the very top of the alphabetical list, so it is easy to drag an email message from the Inbox into this folder as soon as you identify that it's an Action.

13.4 An Empty Inbox

At the end of the above process, you will move or delete your last email and will stare at an empty Inbox. This is the fabled Inbox ZERO.

Take a few moments to bask in the glory of a job well done. You have deleted the irrelevant emails; you have filed the ones you might refer to in the future; you have 'parked' in @Waiting those messages awaiting a reply; and you have put all those that need Action together in the @Action folder.

Some email programs feel sorry for you that you have no messages and will immediately suggest you join more social networks so that you can fill your Inbox again! Don't be tempted, as it will fill up perfectly happily by itself. In fact, it might even happen as you are watching. Your first reaction to a new message might be "How dare you clutter up my empty Inbox!" Test yourself - see how fast you can identify what sort of email this new message is.

The two other things we need to do to complete this process are:

1) Decide *when* you're going to clear the Inbox again

2) Process the Actions that we've identified.

For 1), you need to decide (based on your job / course) how often you are likely to need to process your Inbox. We recommend to our students that this needs to be at least once a day. Some people are happier doing this 4 times a day. Others schedule some email processing time in their Calendars, or between meetings - to keep up to date. The more you practice the above sorting technique, the faster and more automatic it will become.

13.5 Processing the @Action folder

Once you have finished processing your Inbox as above, it is good practice to sort out everything in the @Action folder.

The idea is to EMPTY this folder as well (and you'd thought it was hard enough emptying the Inbox). Remember that at the moment this is just effectively a list of messages that contain Actions – you haven't yet processed the Actions into your organising system.

Work from the most recent message, looking at each message and decide:

- Exactly what is the required Action here? and
- Will it take me less than 2 minutes to just do it?

If the Action takes less than 2 minutes, then do it now. David Allen and the GTD system have come to the conclusion that 2 minutes is a good cut-off point. If it's a short Action then it would take longer to organise it into your time management system than it would to just get it done.

However, if the Action will take you longer than 2 minutes, then you should NOT do it now, as this will distract you from the sorting process.

So, what do you do to an email that contains an Action that you now think will take you more than 2 minutes to do?

This is where you need to have an organised system in place so that you do not forget this Action, but put it somewhere that will remind you when and where to do it.

In section 7.5 (and specifically in subsection 7.5.3d) I describe how for a few years I used Evernote (as part of 'The Secret Weapon' methodology) to forward any email I want to take action on. Nowadays I use *ToDoIst*, an app that also allows emails to be created as Actions. As you do this it is a good idea to change the email subject to be something that tells you what to do. For example the original email subject might be "Notes for Staff-Student Liaison meeting" but can you see how it would be better to edit the subject to be the title of the Action, such as "Contact student rep about proofreading jobs". That will make a lot more sense when you look at the list of tasks later.

If you do not use Evernote or a task manager such as ToDoist, then you must make sure that this action email is not forgotten. You COULD keep it in the @Action folder but this would mean having to look in that folder every time you needed to know what email Actions you had still to do. Or you could put a note in your To-Do list, or straight onto your context lists.

However, you often need the original email so there needs to be a place to hold this. Many people move the email from the @Action folder into another folder called something like @Processed_Actions or @Action_Support. This is only done if you have put a *reminder* about this email somewhere visible in your planning system. You need to move it out of the @Action folder so that you can empty this and know that you have now not only emptied your Inbox, but have processed every Action that was in there.

13.6 Summary

Many people have a problem with a dysfunctional email Inbox – sometimes with thousands of unsorted messages. But there is a methodology which, if followed regularly, can reduce your Inbox to zero and keep it there, and in the process put you back in control.

The methodology can be summarised as follows. Work through your emails from the latest to the earliest as follows:

1. As you identify **Junk** messages just DELETE them.

2. As you identify **Informational** messages (ones with no action, but containing information you might like in the future) MOVE them into a Folder or Archive.

3. If you identify **Pending** messages (those for which you are awaiting a reply) MOVE them into a special @Waiting folder.

4. If an email demands an **Action** of you MOVE it into an @Action folder.

Once this sorting process has been done you will have an empty Inbox, but you will still need to sort through the @Action folder. The best practice here is to empty that folder as well, by making a note of the action to be done (e.g. in a task manager app, or To-Do list, or straight onto you context lists) then moving each message into a special folder for processed actions.

13.7 External Links

(Dachis, 2003) How I went from 1000 emails to Inbox zero, by Adam Dachis http://lifehacker.com/5984417/how-i-went-from-1000-emails-to-inbox-zero-and-stayed-there-with-mailstrom

(Fox, 2013) "5 Tricks to Finally Achieve Inbox Zero", by Zoe Fox http://mashable.com/2013/10/10/inbox-zero/

Managing Your Project

Evernote: https://evernote.com/

(see also Chapter 16 – Technological Time Tricks)

ToDoist: https://en.todoist.com/

(see also Chapter 16 – Technological Time Tricks)

14. CALENDARS, TIME-TRACKING & REMINDERS

In Chapter 10 we saw that the 4 basic tools of Time Management were:

- a Calendar
- a Project list
- an Action list
- a Daily planner

This chapter focuses on the Calendar, which is where you keep a record of those events which are tied to a specific date. We will look at the advantages and disadvantages of different types of Calendar, and review some of the best practice in their usage.

14.1 Just *Having* a Calendar is not enough

This is a surprising observation that happens so often, that we need to acknowledge it - just in case it happens to you (or a friend).

Many people think that just by owning a Calendar that somehow they are organised.

So often a student has said "It's ok, I've got a Calendar on my phone" as they fail to enter the appointment into it.

Equally, some people invest a lot in a beautiful leather-bound diary/organiser, only for it to languish on a shelf, dusty and unused.

Let's get this straight - the Calendar is just like a posh piece of paper - it stores information that you enter and you use. The real work is done by

Managing Your Project

you, but some of the memory load is taken off your brain by having a single place where all timed or day-specific events or information are stored.

14.2 Why do I need a Calendar? I remember everything!

A calendar is any system that holds details of appointments you have in the future. This could be:

- a paper-based diary (although many people use diaries as notebooks, and as ways to record the past rather than plan for the future),
- a special paper-based organiser (either bound or loose leaf)
- a program on your computer
- an app on your mobile phone or tablet
- a chart or poster on your wall where you write events.

Too many people simply try to remember all their appointments. There are two main problems with trying to run a Calendar in your head:

1) It's not very good; you tend to forget things; or be late; or turn up on the wrong day because you forgot that it's "every Tuesday, *except* in week 3".

2) It occupies a good deal of brainpower, which could be better used for something else. Once you have attended an event, you don't need the reminder of it anymore, yet your 'head storage' is partly still configured to remember that appointment.

Over the years I have come across many students who try to remember everything - every lecture, meeting, supervision, tutorial, party, coffee meeting, project briefing and assignment deadline. A few handle it well and seem to have no problems with this system. However, the majority manage ok *up to a certain point*, then their system starts to break down, and they start to miss meetings or deadlines for handing in work. Many at this point seem to cling doggedly to this way of doing things out of some sort of sense of pride (*"I am a clever person. I've always managed to remember everything and I'm not going to be defeated now"*). The reality is that University challenges and fills your memory like never before. My advice would be to let go - delegate the task of remembering your appointments to a mechanical gadget or piece of paper that doesn't have all your other problems and course content to worry about.

By the way – you should be careful if you spot this tendency in other people. For example, imagine you are leading a group of students and you are organising the next meeting. You say "Are we ok to meet next Tuesday at 11am?" and you watch as various people open their planners, or write things down on paper pads, or fumble for their electronic calendars. Beware the person who just answers, "Yes that's fine" without reference to anything else. They MIGHT be one of a very rare set of people who do remember everything, but they are much more likely to belong to the much more common bunch of people who THINK they remember everything, but do not. You may not see them next Tuesday, because when they walk out of the room their minds will quickly move to something else and next Tuesday becomes a distant memory.

A Calendar is an excellent and essential management tool. Your inner Manager needs to have a clear view of what is coming up over different timescales:

- Over the lifetime of the project (see Chapter 20 – *Successful project planning*)
- This month
- This week
- Today.

Every time you have a new appointment, enter it into your calendar. Regular meetings and supervisions should go in there, as should any social commitments. Also put in there anything you wish to be reminded about: e.g. project deadlines that you have set, events going on that you don't want to miss, things which really need to be done on or by a particular day.

However, your inner Worker should only be concerned with the commitments for 'today' or in the near future, and for this reason it is advisable to also use a special reduced calendar known as the Daily Planner (see section 15.4).

14.3 Dangers of Multiple Calendars

Be very careful if there are *multiple* calendars in your life! These very easily become unsynchronised, and you may not know the true state of your appointments and commitments.

Some people *try* to be good with appointments and so write them down all over the place - some engagements in a pocket diary; others on a phone calendar; some on bits of paper - placed on the fridge and maybe a noticeboard; others on a wall calendar shared with other people in the same house. They think, "I must be organised because I have a diary and a noticeboard" and yet they keep missing meetings and end up coming to the misguided conclusion that "time management doesn't work for me".

It is best if you have *one* calendar, which becomes your *single* point of entry and reference. Ideally, carry this around with you everywhere, so that whenever you're planning a meeting you can see when you are free, and immediately enter the new appointment. There is no room for confusion this way. If you need to make an appointment somewhere that you don't have your diary, write it down on a bit of paper and then transfer this into your diary as soon as you get home.

The other advantage is that when you plan your day, you only need to look in one place to be sure that you are looking at all the commitments for that day.

14.4 Comparison of Paper and Electronic Calendars

A common question asked by people who are setting up a calendar system is whether it should be paper-based or electronic.

Here are the advantages and disadvantages of both:

Advantages of Paper-based Calendars

- Essentially these are **simple** books (often called a Diary or Planner), which don't need batteries or charging, and are easily carried around.
- **Access time** is quick - when making an appointment you take out the diary, flip to the right page, and write it down.
- Some people **think better** when writing. The physical act of hand-eye coordination engages their brain better than typing.

Disadvantages of Paper-based Calendars

- There is **no backup**! This is by far the biggest disadvantage of paper. We have seen how you have to have ONE diary otherwise the system does not work effectively. With paper, this means having one physical book. If you use a calendar properly, it will become essential to you in your planning and your daily operation. If you lose it - you lose all that data and planning thought and time.

This is a serious disadvantage.

- You **need a pen**! It's amazing how often you don't have a working one to hand when you need to write something important.
- You often **run out of space**. If a paper diary is small (ideal for carrying around) then - by definition - there isn't really much space for writing. This can lead to a cluttered and unreadable diary, and worse - to you not entering (or not being able) to enter new appointments, commitments and ideas.

Advantages of Electronic Calendars

- There are **electronic calendars everywhere** nowadays - on mobile devices such as phones and tablets, and on every computer, so they are easily available.
- Online calendars mean that you can have **several ways of accessing your data** (phone, tablet, program on home computer, via a web-page on any computer etc.) but it is the SAME data. This is a great advantage and gives you the impression of having several diaries, but actually you always see the same, coordinated, information.
- Most electronic calendars allow you to set **reminders**, and because these are active systems that come with you, they can remind you (with a beep) about upcoming appointments or things you need to remember on a particular day.

Disadvantages of Electronic Calendars

- Some people just **don't like 'gadgets'**. As you are probably reading this on some sort of electronic device, this probably doesn't apply to you. However, with a bit of practice, almost anything can become easy to use.
- Some calendars can **take a while to access**. For example if you're sitting in a meeting and everyone says "ok then, before we finish, are we ok to meet at 2pm next Tuesday", the paper-based people will say "hold on, let's have a quick look - yes, ok". However, if you at this point need to take out your laptop computer, wait for it to boot up, navigate to the calendar program, discover there's no wireless internet in the room etc. you are going to hold up the proceedings. This is why it's really important - if you're going

electronic - that you have a portable version of this calendar readily available for quick time-based decisions like this.

On balance, I would strongly recommend an electronic system, because of the backup of data, and the flexibility to use the data alongside all your other computer tools. However, it is worth investing a good deal of time:

- **getting used to the operation of the system**. Just as in the Wild West, people would practice being 'quick on the draw' since the first to fire their weapon usually stayed alive; so should you practice to be quick on the draw with your calendar. Practice getting the gadget out, launching the calendar, getting to the right date, and entering data, so that you can do this at least as quickly as with your paper-based calendar.

- **ensuring your calendar is available across multiple devices**. Ideally set up a system that allows you to enter and view data on your mobile phone or tablet, but then as soon as you're next at your desktop or laptop computer you can seamlessly see and edit the same data. A few examples are shown in the next section.

- **making sure your data is backed-up**. Most modern systems are set to synchronise automatically between multiple devices. Other systems require you to carry out a synchronisation process.

14.5 Programs and Apps

If you decide to have an electronic (computer-based) calendar, you may be wondering which one to choose. There are many systems out there, and different institutions have their own preferences - and you indeed may already have your own.

At the end of this chapter is a reference section with some links to calendar and planner system that you may wish to investigate.

Often, the best practice is to find out what you already have available on your computer and devices, and learn how to use that effectively.

14.5.1 Electronic calendar principles

Whichever system you use, make sure that it gives you the following properties:

- Available on several devices, with easy (or seamless)

synchronisation;

- Available on some gadget that travels with you, so you have ready access to your appointments and can quickly add new ones without making other people wait;
- Editable on a larger-screen (e.g. desktop/laptop computer) so that you can see 'the big picture' when you are doing your planning.

The next section describes my individual set-up, just to give you an idea on how this can work in practice.

14.5.2 My set-up

I'm writing this bit in the first person because I'd like to tell you specifically about what I do right now. It's only one way of many, but it works for me and you may want to try it out if you don't already have a preference. (I've used many other systems before, and I'm sure I'll use others in the future; so this is just an example).

My Calendar is based around Google Calendar (https://www.google.com/calendar/).

I have set up a series of individual 'calendars', each coded with its own colour (such as Red for Teaching, Light Blue for Exercise, Yellow for Travel etc.). As a default, all of these appear on the same Google Calendar screen. Because Google holds the data on its servers, it is available to me anywhere that there is a web connection (which there usually is at home or at the University, or even by mobile data on my phone).

My university has adopted Google Mail and Calendar as standard, so this an added bonus, as my teaching timetable and other events are stored on their own calendar streams, and can be linked in and viewed alongside my own personal calendars.

Where possible I use a desktop computer (sometimes Mac, sometimes PC, depending on where I'm working) in a standard web-browser to view and edit my calendar. While I'm working at a computer, one tab of the browser is always open on my calendar so I can see my appointments and other commitments when I need to.

Now, I'm not always at a desktop computer. Sometimes I'm working remotely on a laptop computer, and I just use the calendar in the same way via a web browser. Quite often though, I am out and about - or in meetings - and I have with me only a portable device. Sometimes I'll have my iPad with me, and I have an app downloaded (there are *many* available) which

Managing Your Project

can access my Google Calendar. It's called CalenGoo (http://www.calengoo.com/docs/). I've set it up to synchronise with all my Google Calendars, so I am viewing the same information on whatever device I use. I find this works just a little better for me than the built-in iOS calendar (CalenGoo suits my need to rapidly flip through several weeks of appointments just using 'swiping' gestures).

Finally, when I'm travelling I still have access to my calendars via my phone. This happens to be an Android phone, and I use two apps here. This is unusual as I actually recommend using just one per device, but both apps are pointing at the same data, so really what I have is one calendar with a choice of views. The Google Calendar app has a lovely, simple and colourful interface (and is available for Android and iOS), but quite often I appreciate the extra features and functionality of Business Calendar Pro (http://www.businesscalendar.de/). Both apps allow me to view my calendar, for example in a meeting to see if I am available on another date.

Some people I know LOVE their phones so much that they are using them seamlessly, all the time, and it would probably make sense for them to make their phone the core of their calendar system (but make sure that it adheres to the principles in section 14.5.1 above).

14.6 How Calendars link with GTD

Chapter 12 introduced the Getting Things Done methodology for time management and organisation. One of its essential features is the use of a Calendar.

When you have 'captured' your outstanding tasks (from your head, your Inbox, your paper notes etc.) you then *organise* them according to the type of task. If it's a specific time-based event then it should be recorded in your Calendar. The sorts of information best stored there are:

- **Appointments** (specific meetings or actions which should be done at a fixed time, e.g. "Meet Mike for Lunch at 12 noon on Tuesday in Cafe Noir", "Collect children from school at 3.30pm", "Board of Studies Meeting, 2pm in room HG21".
- **Allocated Time** (not a commitment involving other people, but one which you schedule at a fixed time to ensure that a particular task gets done, e.g. "Tue: 2-4 Visit Library to work on Literature Survey", "Fri 6-8 Catch-up phone-calls with family".
- **Deadlines and Notifications** (reminders to you of other things happening in the world which might affect you, e.g. "Fri 12 noon

Initial Report due in at Dept. Office [DEADLINE]", "Mon morning: Supervisor returns from conference [NOTIFICATION]"

- **Day Events** (most calendars have a space dedicated to events that happen on a certain day, but not at a specific time. You can use these as reminders or notifications for information you want to see on that day, e.g., "Tue Feb 4th: Tim's Birthday", "Fri Apr 6th: email Special Interest Group", "Sat Dec 8th: Concert in Central Hall").

The overriding reason for using a Calendar is to empty your head of appointments, and thus free your brain from the onerous task of remembering hundreds of little bits of information. However, the cost for this working correctly is as follows:

- you must use your Calendar for **all events and appointments**. Don't keep some "in your head" because your brain will no longer have a single place to look. Every appointment, deadline, event & notification must go in your Calendar.

- you must use the Calendar **EVERY day**. There is really no point at all in trusting an external system if you do not look at it daily to retrieve the information you have entrusted to it.

In many years of helping people get organised I've often come across those who say that a Calendar "just doesn't work for them" and that they're "better just to remember things". On further examination, it turns out that they entered only a few appointments in their diary, and then only looked at it occasionally. In other words the system was not complete or operational.

This would be as silly as carefully putting all your cash in a wallet, then going shopping without it and blaming "money management and wallets" for your lack of ability to buy something.

See section 12.5 for more information about the difference between Calendars and Context Lists (which are task-lists NOT tied to a specific time).

14.7 Using Calendars as Tickler notifications

Many offices, and indeed Time Management systems (including GTD), recommend the use of 'Tickler Files' (so called because they are designed to 'tickle' your mind, i.e., remind you of things to do on certain days). Traditionally these are sets of moveable folders into which you can place documents that you don't need until a specific day (e.g., your Car Tax forms to be placed on the day you set aside to renew it, or a finished paper assignment which cannot be handed in until next Friday).

The idea is that rather than having loads of piles of paper cluttering your room and your desk and potentially getting lost, you are freshly reminded of each document only on the day that you require it.

Again, for this system to work properly, you must build in the discipline of looking at the folder for every day.

Personally, I do not use such a Tickler File system, and this is because the majority of my work is computer-based. My work is stored in electronic files, so what I need is simply a *reminder* on a certain day to access that file.

So I use the "All Day Events" part of my Calendar to store such reminders.

You may wish to do the same - and when you are processing something that cannot be done until a particular day, then enter an All Day Event into your Calendar - and (because you can add notes, explanatory text, to all electronic appointments) make a note of WHERE to find the file, and WHAT exactly you should be doing with it).

14.8 How much to put in your Calendar?

There is an ongoing debate amongst Time Management practitioners about how much of your Calendar you should fill with tasks that you want to do.

Clearly your Calendar needs to contain a full record of every meeting or time-based event that you want to keep track of. We have also seen that it's a good place for time-based reminders, such as notifications of birthdays or someone's return from holiday, or upcoming deadlines.

However, it's important to think about what you do (or don't do) with the *gaps* between appointments. Some people suggest that if you have a list of priorities to accomplish then the only way is to *schedule* a *specific* time to do each task. For example if your list contains "Complete Biology assignment" and "Go to shops to buy new phone" then you should use your Calendar to block out time for these priorities. For example you might schedule an hour on Tuesday morning for finishing the Biology work, then use the remaining free two hours to shop for a phone in town, arriving back in time for your scheduled supervision at 1pm.

One advantage of this approach is that your Calendar becomes a master time-planner, giving structure to your days and helping you allocate definite times for your priorities.

Other people and methodologies, including the GTD system mentioned earlier, claim that life isn't that simple, and that scheduling up your 'gap time' allows for no flexibility. In fact, the GTD system recommends making several 'Context' lists (e.g. one for at your office computer, one for home, one for shopping, etc.). The idea is that when you have some free time (or a gap in your Calendar schedule) then you glance at your lists for the most appropriate task to do in your current situation with your current energy levels. This approach tends to help you feel in charge of the day moment-by-moment, and more able to respond to things which occur that were not on your list.

So, this choice of methodology is very much up to you. Personally I use a mix of the two. I follow David Allen's advice, and generally only use my Calendar for what he calls the "Hard Landscape" - the fixed, unmoveable events; and for all my other tasks they are laid out in context and project lists (more in the next chapter). However, when I feel that I am getting behind with a particular important task, I allocate some time on the Calendar for getting it done. This acts as a reminder not to schedule a meeting or some other activity in that slot and instead focus on a specific important or urgent task.

14.9 Best practice in appointment planning

When you are scheduling an appointment in your Calendar, it's important to consider allocating some *extra* time before and after it.

Things you could consider include:

- Do you need travel time to get to and from the meeting? How long will that take?

- Are there things you should prepare for in advance of the meeting? How long will you need? When is it best to do this?

- Is this a meeting you can mentally 'walk away' from, or do you need some time to gather your thoughts or do some follow-up work?

If you've answered 'yes' to any of the above points, then it is worth scheduling that time in to the Calendar, so that you reserve the appropriate thinking, planning, transit and debriefing time.

Imagine, for example, that you have a Supervision scheduled for one hour on Thursday at 11am. A friend emails and wants to meet you for a chat. You might be tempted to say "meet you at 12" because that is the next available time in your Calendar. However, from experience you might know these things:

- Sometimes the supervision can over-run.

Managing Your Project

- Occasionally, after the supervision, you need to arrange things with the other students present.
- It takes at least 10 minutes to walk from the supervisor's office to where you want to meet your friend.

Might it be better to arrange to meet your friend at 12.30? This allows you to absorb any over-run, keep managed with your fellow students, and have a leisurely stroll to meet your friend for lunch.

Try to apply this thought to the scheduling of all your appointments. Allow yourself some space in your Calendar for these things, rather than scheduling it wall-to-wall, and life will feel less stressed.

14.10 Thinking backwards from an event

One of the best things you can do with your Calendar is to think carefully about every event you enter into it - in case there are *other* things that you need to put in as well.

We have already seen (in the previous section, 14.9) how it is often good to plan in extra time before and after an event to allow for transit, preparation & debriefing. In a similar way, many of the events you enter into your Calendar will end up demanding more of your time than just the event itself - and it is good practice to also schedule those extra time-reminders into the Calendar.

What are these 'other things' associated with an event?

Consider an assignment deadline. Imagine it is currently September 7th and an important assignment is announced, whose deadline is October 25th. Let us consider some of the different ways that people can choose to handle this new information, in order of effectiveness:

- Some people just file this assignment paper into a desk drawer, or even shove it under the bed, hoping somehow it will go away. This sounds crazy but many people, especially students, actually *do* this. Most of these people 'discover' the assignment with a day or two to go (from hearing others talk about it) or they miss it altogether.
- A smaller number of people pin the assignment to a noticeboard, so at least it is on display. However, when you see the same thing every day you tend to go numb to it, and it's just a noticeboard, and the assignment is forgotten. This is better than being stuck out of sight, but notice that nothing is yet committed to.

- Others put a note of the deadline in their diary or Calendar, but haven't learned to look at it every day, so often miss the deadline. Putting it in a diary is a good step, but only if it is regularly checked as a way of planning each day's work.

- Still others use a diary, and use it every day, and indeed put in the assignment deadline for October 25th. So far, so good, but sadly their diary is a "Week-View" and it's filled with information so they only get a reminder when they turn to the week beginning October 21st. They see the deadline and now only have 4 days to work on it. However, at least they *saw* it and *did something* about it, but wouldn't it be better to get some more advanced reminders of the deadline?

- A few people will enter the October 25th deadline into their Calendar, but will also enter a series of reminders as follows. On October 21st they enter a 'day event' saying "Finalise assignment – due on Friday" in red ink. On October 14th they enter a similar day event saying "1 week til assignment due - do final proofreading", and on October 7th "2 weeks til assignment - main writing", and on September 30th "3 weeks til assignment - complete all research reading", etc. In this way - because they use their Calendar daily they will see regular reminders, and will gradually work towards the assignment. This is a huge leap in effectiveness and it does not take very long to do.

- A *very* few people (and this could be you after reading all this book's chapters on time management) pick up the assignment and do the following:

    o Read it through immediately a couple of times and make detailed notes about what it involves;

    o Establish what reading and research needs to be done;

    o Think about who needs to be contacted;

    o Decide what production or computer work is involved and when and where that can be done;

    o Work out the best order of tasks so that the production of the whole assignment flows correctly;

    o Create a Project name (see next chapter) for this assignment and add this to the list of projects which are reviewed weekly;

    o Assign a time for each of these project stages and enter each of them into the Calendar;

Managing Your Project

        o Work out the very Next Action (again see next chapter), which will get the assignment started and rapidly making progress.

Compare the first and last strategies: a) sliding it under the bed, hoping that it will magically disappear, versus b) immediately creating a detailed project plan that is split into manageable chunks and will be reviewed daily and weekly.

Needless to say, the final strategy is the most effective of all, but - as you can see - it demands a commitment to deal with things as soon as they arrive, and to consider in detail the implications, and then to write all of these things down in Calendars, Project and Action Lists, and to review these daily and weekly. It's not as bad as you think it's going to be! What's more, you get the reward of peace of mind, knowing that things are under control and will get done, as opposed to the bed-filer's gnawing sense of dis-ease that there is "something I'm meant to have done".

14.11 Summary

A Calendar is an essential part of a time management system, which stores your time-based commitments and thus relieves your brain of this task. Do not try to remember every appointment because at some stage your system will let you down.

Use *only one* calendar, so that it contains a single up-to-date record of all your commitments. Multiple calendars rapidly become dysfunctional and can undermine your entire time management system. It doesn't matter if this is a paper or electronic system as long as it works for you. Paper is quick and needs no batteries, but there is no automatic backup if you lose your diary. Electronic systems are flexible (and nowadays distributed across multiple devices) but you should make sure you can use each device speedily for entering and retrieving appointments.

In your Calendar, you should enter ALL your appointments, deadlines, time-specific notifications, and personally allocated time for tasks. Then make sure you refer to it EVERY day. It only becomes a trusted system if every time-based commitment is entered, and you see it often enough to use that information reliably.

There is an ongoing debate about how much of your Calendar you should fill up with *non*-time specific activities. The GTD system recommends keeping such flexible commitments away from the Calendar and instead storing them in Context lists. However, in practice it is sometimes helpful to use the Calendar to 'block out' some time to work on a high-priority or urgent project.

When you're scheduling an appointment, ask yourself whether you also need to allocate some time beforehand in order to prepare for the meeting, and likewise whether any time needs blocking out afterwards (e.g. to allow over-run, follow-up arrangements, or transit time to your next appointment). This can help to create a bit of 'space' in your diary when life gets busy.

When a new major commitment comes into your life (such as an assignment) it is worth investing time immediately to analyse what is required, breaking it down into manageable stages, and entering interim deadlines and reminders into your Calendar.

14.12 External References

Google Calendar (https://www.google.com/calendar/).

Microsoft Outlook Calendar:

see https://www.youtube.com/watch?v=gP7gKvxujIA

Sunrise Calendar: (cross-platform)

> https://calendar.sunrise.am/

iOS Apps

The built-in iCal Calendar app is fine for many people.

CalenGoo: my currently preferred calendar app for my iPad:

> http://www.calengoo.com/docs/

> https://itunes.apple.com/gb/app/calengoo-for-google-calendar/id300370871?mt=8

Android Apps

Google Calendar app:

> https://play.google.com/store/apps/details?id=com.google.android.calendar&hl=en_GB

Business Calendar Pro:

> http://www.businesscalendar.de/

http://www.businesscalendar.de/

15. PROJECT AND ACTION LISTS

In the previous chapters in this section, we have looked at various methodologies of time management, and at some of the tools and techniques that people use to implement them. In Chapter 14, we studied the correct use of a Calendar, which is vital for capturing all the events that are 'fixed' in time, such as appointment and deadlines. However, that leaves a big list of activities which need to be done, but not at a particular time. Most people instinctively write occasional 'To-Do' lists to try to capture this information.

In this chapter we will see how the concept of a To-Do list can be extended into something much more reliable; well thought-out Project and Action lists.

15.1 The Limitations of a To-Do list

A typical To-Do list might look like this:

- ☐ Mend puncture
- ☐ Shopping
- ☐ History assignment
- ☐ Call Jack
- ☐ Tea, Sugar, Milk
- ☐ Start project
- ☐ Set TV recording timer
- ☐ Torch batteries

You may instantly feel better having made such a list, because you have got things off your mind and onto paper. This is a good thing, and is one of the central tenets of David Allen's *Getting Things Done* (Allen, 2002) methodology. Allen also acknowledges that such lists on their own are very unhelpful for planning and organising. Let's consider five aspects of the above list to determine why this is;

1. How do you know that the list contains **all** the things you need to do? If you're not sure, then how could you trust it as a basis for planning what to do next? There will always be a nagging doubt that you might need to be doing something *else* more important.

2. The **order** of the list was simply the order your brain thought of the items. It is highly improbable that it is ordered in a sensible way. Is mending the puncture somehow more important than the history assignment, and even more so than starting the project?

3. Some of the items might **relate** to each other, if only they were to be re-organised. Maybe 'Tea, Sugar and Milk' and 'Torch batteries' are part of a higher-level task called 'Shopping'.

4. The list gives you no clue on absolute or relative **timings**. What things need to be done by a particular time? What things ought to be done *before* other things? Maybe the puncture really does need mending before you can go shopping or hand in the assignment. But perhaps the TV timer needs setting in the next hour if you are not to miss that special programme? Perhaps the History assignment should be completed before you start on the project, and this needs to happen before next Tuesday.

5. The **actions** are not well defined, and exist at many different levels. What exactly do you have to do to 'start project'? (Such vague list items are often the cause of procrastination; you don't start the project, because you haven't yet thought out in detail what that really means). Presumably, 'torch batteries' refers to buying some more, but unless this gets transferred to a shopping list which you have with you when you are shopping, the batteries are likely to remain unbought.

15.2 Project Lists

The typical To-Do list (which many people, and some software organisers, regard as the only planning tool) is highly limited. To move beyond the 'brain-dump' level of a typical To-Do list, you will need to address the five issues listed above.

Managing Your Project

To address the first point (does your list contain all your commitments?) you should take some time to establish the tasks that are in your life. The following questions might be useful to prompt you:

- What things in life need *doing by you*?
- What things have you embarked upon that you need to *complete*?
- What tasks have you *promised* other people that you would do?
- What would you *like* to do, but haven't done anything about yet?

It can take quite a long time to fully capture all these commitments, but it's amazing how many of them you can gather in just 15 minutes of quiet with a pen and paper. Let your mind remind you of all the commitments it is holding on to subconsciously, and write them down.

One of the best ways of getting a handle on all the different commitments in your life is the *Project List*, and we will now deal with this specifically.

To address issues 2 to 5, you will need to organise the raw responses to the above questions by re-ordering them, spotting relationships between them, considering their relative and absolute timing, and ultimately determining the actions which you will need to carry out later when you're in 'Work' mode rather than 'Manage' mode.

Whilst the Calendar holds all your scheduled appointments and deadlines, it is not a complete record of what you have to do in your life. It is vitally important that you have a trusted list of *all* the tasks, projects, commitments and threads of activity that belong to you.

Earlier in this chapter, we criticised the To-Do list as being a rather raw 'brain-dump' that needed much further processing before it became useful for planning purposes.

Let's consider again the questions raised above:
- **What things in life need doing by you?** What are the things - currently stored only in your head - that you are committed to? What things are you aware of that you haven't started work on yet? What things are you avoiding thinking about because they are scary? These are the sort of items that your subconscious knows about and wakes you in the middle of the night to remind you that they are still there.

- **What things have you embarked upon that you need to complete?** It's sometimes easy to do the first step but then not follow through with actions. Strangely enough it's towards the end that progress can often slow down. You can often spot these items as piles of paper 'filed' around a room or desk. Ask yourself what exactly would count as 'complete', and what would be the next action to get you to that state.

- **What tasks have you promised other people that you would do?** Think about the people in your life - friends, colleagues, tutors, etc. and note down any commitments that you have to any of them. By thinking about the people in your life, you will often remember something that you have said you would do but have not yet taken action on.

- **What would you *like* to do, but haven't done anything about yet?** Most people have a list of things that they would like to do, but life is so busy that they remain purely as dreams. If you take the time to think about them and write them down, then you can weigh them up against your other commitments, and think about what actions you would need to take to make them happen.

If you have spent some time answering these questions, you may now have a long list of incomplete projects which you can look at in one place.

It might look something like this:

- History assignment
- Choir rehearsals
- Major solo project
    - Literature survey
    - Initial report
    - Prepare aims & objectives for supervision
- Prepare for Auntie Eve's visit
- Decorate the spare room
- End of term report
- etc.

Managing Your Project

Notice how you instinctively split 'Major solo project' into three *sub-projects*. Each of the sub-projects probably should be an entity in its own right on your Project list, but it is good to see that the three components are part of a bigger plan.

Many people have forty or more of these commitments. However, when you first start making a list you may only be able to think of a few, but gradually things will pop into your head, and you can update the list as you go along.

There are many more tasks that are so ingrained into your life that you do not even consider putting them on this list:

- Eat regularly: (includes cooking and washing up)

- Wash and keep clean

- Travel regularly to a place of work or study

- Wash and dry clothes

- Tidy the house

- Weekly exercise.

Whilst these are part of your life, and they take up time and energy, they probably do not need to go on the Project list as long as you do most of them automatically. The Project List is for things that you *want reminding about regularly*.

The Project list gives you a visual handle on all the different parts of your life where you have commitments. You should update it regularly, delete completed projects from it, and add new ones to it. The GTD methodology recommends doing this as part of a Weekly Review.

Figure 15.1 is an expansion of the To-Do list (from the start of section 15.1) into a five-column table, with many more details added, which are discussed below.

Please note that there may be better ways for you to store this information (for example in a more graphical form such as a Mind-map, described in Chapter 8, or a series of pieces of paper - one for each project - in a folder). Whatever form you choose, the important thing is you are *not* relying on your head to store all this information.

Project List

Project	Outcome	Deadline	Next Actions	Deadline
History assignment	Report written, proofread and submitted	May 4th	Write last chapter	Apr 20th
			Check references in library	Apr 23rd
			Proofread report	Apr 30th
			Final printout	May 2nd
			Take to Departmental Office	May 3rd
Choir rehearsals	Concert successfully given	August 10th	Choose music	Apr 19th
			Get music from library	Apr 23rd
			Put in folders	Apr 24th
			Create rehearsal schedule	Apr 26th
			Phone choir members	Apr 26th
Solo project: Literature survey	Good mark for literature survey	May 10th	Complete internet search	Apr 22nd
			Check journal section in library	Apr 23rd
			Write plan for contents page	Apr 25th
Solo project: Initial report	Hand in initial report promptly	May 2nd	Read report specification	Apr 25th
			Sketch basic sections	Apr 27th
Solo project: Prepare aims & objectives for supervision	Establish aims for project, and agree them with supervisor	April 30th	Brainstorm aims	Apr 22nd
			Type up aims &objectives	Apr 24th
			Read them to Jim for feedback	Apr 25th
			Email to supervisor in advance of meeting	Apr 27th
Prepare for Auntie Eve's visit	Auntie has nice time staying here	July 15th	Phone bus company (enquire about cheap tickets)	May 3rd
			Decorate room (see next project)	July 12th
Decorate the spare room	Room comfortable before Auntie Eve arrives	July 12th	Select colour scheme	May 5th
			Buy paint	May 7th
			Invite friends for painting party	May 10th

Figure 15.1 Example Project List

Managing Your Project

1. In the first column is the project title, e.g. *History assignment* (this is often taken directly from your expanded To-Do list).

2. In the second column put a short description of the *intended outcome*. In other words, when this stated outcome becomes true you will know that you have completed this project. Sometimes this may be the same as the title, but it is really helpful to be descriptive and specific here. For example if you are learning to swim you may simply have the project title "Swimming", but the intended outcome is "confidently swim two lengths, and float for two minutes".

3. The third column contains a deadline for this activity. Most time management systems stress the importance of setting deadlines. Either put in the deadline that you have been given, or estimate by when this thing really needs to be completed. For example, you want to be able to swim before June because that is when you are going on holiday.

4. The fourth column is for the *next actions* on the project (described in more detail below).

5. The final column contains the individual deadlines for each 'next action'. This might be one step too far for some people, but as a rule, it is good to get some idea of *when* you are going to address each sub-task.

The 'next action' column encourages you to turn each project into set of actions that you can carry out without any further planning. You really do not need to identify *all* the actions needed to complete the project, but rather just the *next* one or two. If possible, give each of these actions a deadline (working backwards from the final deadline and allowing time for slippage) so that you can get them all done in good time.

In summary, what you are doing with the Project List is acknowledging all the commitments in your life, and then breaking them down into the next one or two concrete actions which need to be taken to keep them moving. You should experiment with different formats, until you find something that works for you.

15.3 Action Lists

An Action List is simply a reminder of the tasks (generated above at the project planning level) that need to be carried out. This is used as the list of instructions that advises you which day-to-day activities need to be carried out.

Action Lists are more useful if you order them to suit your life, and to reflect the various priorities and relationships between them. Therefore you might want to group actions together that can be done in a particular *context*. For example, you could put under one heading all the things that you can do at your desk and/or computer (*@Computer*). Under another heading might come all the things you can do when you are in the library (*@Library*).

This method of grouping tasks into context is just an extension of what you do when you make a shopping list. What you are effectively doing when writing a shopping list is bringing together a series of outstanding actions (get sugar, get milk etc.) into one list that is uniquely useful *at the shop*. You do not put "complete history project" on your shopping list, because there is little use in seeing that when you are at the shop! The same principle applies to your other contexts, such as "*@Computer*". So, establish the main areas of your life where you need lists of actions.

If we take the above example Project List, and carry out this process, it might start to look something like Figure 15.2 (overleaf).

Notice the following features of the example Action List.

- The **deadlines** are listed along with the action. This is so that you are aware of the relative urgency of each action. In fact, the actions are arranged in date order within each category. You do not have to do it like this, but it gives you some sense of which tasks need completing before others. You may prefer to mark up deadlines in a different way, e.g. [by Friday], or [ideally during week 6] - whatever you are most comfortable and familiar with.

- The **titles** of each action have been changed so that it makes sense in the new context. Where "Write last chapter" had made perfect sense as a row of the Project table called 'History Assignment', when it is isolated under the 'Desk' heading on the Action List, it requires a reminder that this is about the history assignment, so it becomes "Write last chapter (history assignment)". Likewise "Check References in Library" (on the Project List) turns into a Library Action entry called "Check references for history assignment".

Action List

Desk / Computer

Write last chapter (history assignment)	Apr 20th
Complete internet search (lit. survey)	Apr 22nd
Type up project aims & objectives	Apr 24th
Read Aims & Objective to Jim	Apr 25th
Write plan for lit. survey contents page	Apr 25th
Email supervisor re: aims & objectives	Apr 27th

Library

Get choir music	Apr 23rd
Check references for history assignment	Apr 23rd
Check journal section for lit. survey	Apr 23rd

Home

Put Choir Music in folders	Apr 24th
Select colour scheme for spare room	May 5th

Phone-calls

Bus company (cheap tickets for A. Eve)	May 3rd
Invite friends for painting party	May 10th

Anywhere

Choose Music (choir)	Apr 19th
Brainstorm project aims & objectives	Apr 22nd
Read initial report specification	Apr 25th
Sketch basic sections of initial report	Apr 27th
Proofread history report	Apr 30th

Shopping

Paint for spare room	May 7th

Figure 15.2 Example Action List

- The category 'Anywhere' refers to those paper-based tasks that could be done at home or on the bus, etc. in that they just need reading and possibly marking up with a pen.

- Not all the actions from the Project List are brought across. Some are so date-specific that they should be entered directly onto your Calendar, to ensure that they are done on a certain time on a given day. For example the History assignment's "Take to Departmental Office" would become a calendar/diary entry called "Take History Assignment to Dept. Office".

The changing of context, mentioned above, can take some getting used to. Have you ever done something like this? You and Jim are arranging to meet for lunch. You say "let's meet here next Monday at noon". You don't want to forget this so you hurriedly get your diary out, flip to the following Monday and write "meet here Monday at noon" because those are the words still ringing around your head. When next Monday arrives, you look at your diary and see "meet here Monday at noon". But *who* were you meant to meet? And *where* exactly is 'here'? What you should have written was "12:00 – meet Jim for lunch in Library snack bar". In general, when you write a note to yourself (or compose an entry in your time management system) you need to use words and information that will be useful to you *when you wish to look at it*. This is one of those things that looks stupid or obvious when you read about it, and yet all round the world millions of diaries are filled with badly phrased entries that are confusing to understand.

15.4 The Daily Planner

Even though the Action List has broken down all the complex tasks of your life into a series of simpler actions to be carried out, it is still rather distracting to see all of these on a day-to-day basis. The Action Lists include reminders of many things which do not necessarily have to be done 'today', and maybe many which you cannot do today (e.g. if you are not near the library, or meeting with your supervisor). Therefore, some people like to produce a Daily Planner, which incorporates the Calendar Events for the day, and the actions that *have to be* carried out, and those which *could be*.

Other people see the Daily Planner as an unnecessary step; as all the information you need is on the Calendar and in the Action List(s). You must choose for yourself whether or not to use it. The biggest advantage of preparing the Daily Planner is that it gives you a managerial review at the

Managing Your Project

end of one day, or the start of the next. It is a common experience to come to the end of each day and find that planning the next day's work is a very good way of 'closing' today's working time, leaving yourself mentally free for the evening.

Figure 15.3 contains an example Daily Planner, showing a hypothetical day in the life of someone who owns the Project and Actions lists above.

Daily Planner

Date: **Monday April 20th**	**Action List**
	Desk/Computer
08:00	*Write last chapter (history assignment) Apr 20th*
08:30	
09:00	Complete internet search (lit. survey) Apr 22nd
09:30	
10:00 Supervision	**Home**
10:30 -	Put Choir Music in folders Apr 24th
11:00	
11:30	**Library**
12:00 meet Jim for lunch	Get choir music Apr 23rd
(Library snack bar)	Check references for history assignment
13:00	Apr 23rd
13:30	Check journal section for lit. survey
14:00	Apr 23rd
14:30	
15:00	**Anywhere**
15:30	*Choose Music (choir) Apr 19th*
16:00	Brainstorm project aims & objectives Apr 22nd
16:30	
17:00	**Shopping**
Evening:	
	Incoming

Figure 15.3 Example Daily Planner

Let's examine some of its features:

- There are not many appointments for this day, so it's up to you to select which tasks to do and when. This gives you some operational flexibility and choice throughout the day. Two of the actions are marked in *red & italics* as they are overdue or are due today.

- Some people prefer to mark up their Daily Planner with specific times in which they plan to do their actions (e.g. putting 08:30-10:00 "Write last chapter"). There are advantages and disadvantages to this approach, and we discussed some of these in section 14.8 - *How much to put in your Calendar?* The advantage of doing this is that you will probably use that allocated time for that purpose (which may be good for your chapter-writing task as it really does need to be done today). The disadvantage is that you block out all your time in advance, which makes it difficult to be more flexible in your approach to time, as things can change on an hour-by-hour basis. Also, if you schedule a fixed time, you are quite likely to spend that amount of time doing it. This can be a good or a bad thing, depending on the accuracy of your estimation of the time the task will take.

- There is a space in the bottom-right corner marked "Incoming". This is where you write down anything which needs to be processed by your time management system. It could be an action you have just said 'yes' to (but has not yet been put onto the Action List, or turned into a more complex task and entered into the Project List), or an idea to investigate, or a date to put in your Calendar which is not yet to hand. In other words "Incoming" is a section where you can write down anything which needs to be seen and processed later when you're in 'Management Mode'.

15.5 Summary

Although a Calendar is an excellent place to keep your fixed-time commitments such as appointments and day-specific reminders, it is not suitable for storing the big list of activities that you *need* to do – but not at a *particular* time. Many people instinctively write To-Do lists as a way of capturing these other tasks, but they tend to be unordered, vague, and incomplete. Therefore, we need to extend and enhance the concept of a To-Do list into something more useful as a way to organise your life and work.

Managing Your Project

A Project List is a record of all the things in your life that you want reminding about regularly so that you make progress on them. A Project is a task that contains many sub-tasks. Projects can relate to your main job or topic of study, but also promises made to people, social commitments, house-tasks and chores, and longer-term plans etc. Give each project a title, a deadline, and a list of the next major sub-tasks (possibly with their own deadlines). Update the Project List every week – at your Weekly Review – and check to see the progress of all projects and their subtasks, deleting projects if complete, and adding any new commitments that have come into your life over the past week.

You can use the Project List each week to create a series of context-based Action Lists. Each of these lists contains the actions that make sense within a particular situation (context). Examples of such contexts are:

- "At the shop" (*@Shop*, which is what you're familiar with as a shopping list),
- "At any computer" (*@Computer*),
- "Phone-calls using any phone" (*@Phone*),
- "Only do-able in my office" (*@Office*),
- "When I'm next with my Supervisor" (*@Supervisor*), or
- "When I'm next in the library" (*@Library*).

Best practice is to make your own context lists, and to have them with you in those contexts, so that you can use them to select the most appropriate thing to do from your commitments.

Some people really appreciate creating a Daily Planner, which brings together the Calendar commitments and the relevant context-based tasks depending on what is possible for that day. Other people find they are fine with their Calendar, Project List and Action Lists.

15.6 External Links

(Allen, 2002) Getting Things Done: How to achieve stress-free productivity, Publisher: Piatkus 2002, ISBN-10: 0749922648, ISBN-13: 978-0749922641. Also available for Kindle.

16. TECHNOLOGICAL TIME TRICKS

In this chapter we take a few moments to consider how technology can help in the process of personal management. The idea is not to recommend a specific system, but to give some options for you to consider when setting up your own way of working.

But first, let's start by considering whether you are a 'paper person' or someone who really works well with technology. Earlier - in section 14.4 - we considered the specific choice of whether or not your Calendar should be held on paper or electronically.

16.1 Paper or computer

Each of the main time management tools (Calendar, Project list, Action list and Daily Planner) can be purely paper-based, or they can be computerised, or can consist of a combination of both. This is something which you need to work out for yourself. Some people love using computers so much that they will be much better organised if they can use computers to hold all their lists and appointments. Others are much more comfortable with paper lists. Here are the basic issues you will have to consider when making a decision to use paper or computer.

- Computers are good for backing up information, but only if you have a system that works and you back-up regularly. However, if you lost your paper diary/planner, how would you get the information back?

- Some people actually *think* better and more fluently with a screen, mouse & keyboard, and others with a pen & paper.

- Portable computers can allow you to take a lot of information around with you, but they still tend to be slower than paper & pen (or voice recording) for inputting or recalling information. However, this difference is narrowing as interfaces and processing speeds improve.

It's important to realise that no technology (paper or electronic) will "get you organised". Your personal organisation is purely about what you *do* and the effectiveness of how you do it. Nevertheless, technology can help to provide the right tools to make the whole process a lot easier. (A person determined to eat a tin of food will eventually find a way in, but it is a whole lot easier if they have a can opener!).

16.2 Principles of using Electronic Time Management tools

Whichever system you settle on, here is a checklist of what it must offer you, in order for it to work effectively as a time and project management system.

- **Appointments**: you need to be able to enter time-based commitments quickly and easily. You must be either reminded of these appointments, or look at the upcoming events, often enough so that you do not miss anything (this is usually *at least* daily).

- **Lists** for:

- **Actions**: Easily accessible Context-based lists of things you are committed to do.

- **Projects**: Every commitment that involves multiple Actions, or long-term goals, needs to be stored on a Project list, along with any other materials or information associated with that Project.

- **Storage**: A filing system for information that is not a scheduled Action, but that you might need in the future.

However, it is vital to understand that an organisational system is only as good:

- as the information you put in it, and

- the regularity that information is retrieved from it.

No electronic system will sort through all your incoming material (paper, email or stored in your head) and sort it according to whether it is

Actionable, Schedulable, Fileable, part of a bigger Project, or indeed Deletable. Only you, acting reliably and responsively, will give the right inputs to the system. Only you, acting regularly with discipline, will look at the results of this organisation and decide what to do next, then actually do it.

The real purpose of an electronic organisational system is to act as a buffer for actions that you want to do but cannot do immediately.

16.3 Summary of a Working System

For two years I used a variation of the GTD implementation called TSW (The Secret Weapon; http://www.thesecretweapon.org/). This is a combination of an email system along with Evernote. I use Gmail (actually 2 accounts - one for home and another for work). The basic idea is that your Communications are handled within Gmail, but that your Actions are handled within Evernote. Many people try to handle their Actions via their email Inbox and this rarely works effectively.

Recently I have changed system, and this is explained in section 16.3.5. However, I got two good years of organisation out of the original system, and many people love it, so it's still worth explaining in detail. I still use Gmail and Evernote, but now Evernote is for my *non-Action* storage.

If you've not come across Evernote, it is a free, cross-platform note-taking and organising system (with an option of a Premium upgrade that I took because I wanted the freedom to throw loads of images and scans into it). Evernote is explained in more detail in sections 7.5.2 to 7.5.5).

16.3.1 Use of Evernote for Organising

Evernote has 3 attributes that make it really good for the type of organisation demanded by the GTD methodology.

1) **It is superbly cross-platform.** There are native Windows and Mac versions to run on your workstation or laptop, but it can also run in a web-browser; and there are mobile versions for iOS, Android, Windows Phone etc. So, basically, if you are someone who uses technology, you will be able to get at your data almost anywhere, as long as there is a phone or tablet or computer nearby. All the data is seamlessly synchronised across all your devices.

2) **You can throw notes at it from a wide variety of sources**, which means that you can capture new inputs very effectively. You can launch a new note from any place on your computer via a keyboard shortcut;

you can send an email to your Evernote address and it appears later in your Evernote 'Inbox'. You can make audio recordings and take pictures and document scans from your mobile device. If you find something interesting on the internet you can use a special 'web-clipper' to grab the page or the article, and it's there for you later on any device.

3) **It allows Multiple Tags**, so that each piece of data can be labelled (and later found) by a variety of contexts. This means that you can tag the Urgency of each note, the People associated with it, the Project to which it belongs, and the Context in which you're most likely to get it done (@Computer, @Shops etc.)

16.3.2 Use of different devices and screen sizes

I like to be able to check my emails regularly, and to get to 'Inbox Zero' at least once per day. I carry round with me a phone (Android operating system), which allows me to access each of my email accounts from a single Gmail app. Checking email on such a device is great, and it has the added advantage that if I'm away from a Wi-Fi zone (such as home and work) then the phone data still allows me to get access to my emails. The phone also has a front-page 'widget' for my Calendar, showing my next event.

If I'm moving around more locally (e.g., between different rooms in the University) I carry a tablet device (currently an iPad Mini). This allows more screen and interaction space and is much better for displaying a Calendar (e.g., for setting appointments in meetings), and it's easier to cope with emails - especially when typing replies – than a phone.

Personally I have found that portable devices with smaller screens are fine for *checking* email and sending quick replies, but they are not very helpful for *organising* as you tend to be able to only see one thing at a time. Also I do not appear to be equipped with the modern 'teenage thumbs' which appear to allow amazingly speedy typing. I'm just much more comfortable with a conventional QWERTY keyboard.

16.3.3 My process for Organising Emails

For my organising I find a desktop computer with two screens to be most helpful. On the left screen I put my 'incoming' information (such as emails and notes) and on the right screen I put my 'organisational' information (such as Evernote, or maybe a document I'm editing). I've found this to give a reliable 'flow' of information from left to right. A laptop computer will do, but you've usually got a single screen and it's smaller.

So, on my left screen I open GMail in a web browser, and look at just one account at a time, let's say my Work account. On the right screen is Evernote.

I work down my list of emails, starting with the most recent. Remember the methodology (described in detail in Chapter 13 – *Email Mastery*) is to identify each email as one of 4 types:

- Junk
- Information
- Pending
- Actionable.

1. Junk messages are easy - I just DELETE them.

2. Messages with no action, but that contain information I might like in the future, need to be stored. If I want to keep the email trail I simply MOVE them into a Gmail Folder. If however the information is just the content of the email (e.g. a scanned takeaway menu sent by a friend) I FORWARD the message to Evernote. This will appear as an Evernote note which I can file accordingly. I then DELETE the email.

3. If a message is Pending (awaiting a reply from someone) I MOVE it into a special @Waiting folder.

4. All that is now left are Actionable emails.

If I'm working on a portable device (or maybe don't have much time) I might MOVE the message to my @Action folder, but that will mean I have to remember to process it later, so the following is what I try to do whenever possible, and definitely when I'm in 'organising mode' at my desktop computer. The act of later processing that folder is described in section 13.5.

If the Action can be done in less than 2 minutes I will do it, then DELETE the email. (An example of this might be a colleague who asks me to send her a document). Sometimes an action might involve putting an event on my Calendar (for example if I'm setting up a meeting). I have this open in another window on the right-screen. (Details of my Calendar setup are given in section 14.5.2).

Managing Your Project

If it's going to take more than 2 minutes I FORWARD the message to Evernote. As I do this I take care to change the Subject Line to something meaningful. For example, the original subject line might have said "Minutes from Course Review Sept 14th". As I forward it to Evernote I might change this to "Read Course Review Minutes and check for Actions". Evernote can then help me to remember what action I need to do.

Because Evernote is open in the right-hand Window, I see the message arrive and then I 'Tag' it with appropriate Tags that I have already set up. For instance this one might be tagged as '2-Next' (i.e. second priority') but also 'Course_Review'. I use tags to help me produce lists of information and show only those notes. My top 3 tags are '1-Now' (for my top, urgent priorities), '2-Next' (as above, for second priorities) and '@Project' (which shows my Project List as a series of notes, one for each Project).

Using the above system I ensure that my email Inbox is NOT the place where I keep my Actions. I think that's the reason that most people, whose Inboxes are out of control, lose their Inbox as a functioning message notification system. Instead it tends to become a huge stack of rather threatening information, actions and waiting-fors, all hidden randomly in a pile of junk.

16.3.4 Reviewing and using the system

Every day I try to find time to process my email Inbox down to zero messages. It doesn't always work, and sometimes I *want* to see a few email messages in my Inbox for the day while I'm working on them. However, once a day, everything is moved out of there and put in its place.

Also each day I use Evernote to show a list of activities that I have prioritised as most urgent and important. These are the ones tagged as '1-Now', and so a click on that tag shows that list of tasks. To be honest I don't *like* looking at that list as it represents all the commitments I have to myself and to others that are all rather pushing. But - and here's the clue - I look at it *often enough*. When life is really busy, and the day is heavily scheduled, I will try to have a quick look at the list, basically asking "is there anything on this list (of my own top priorities) that I need to make space for today?" However, the list really comes into its own when I have a more flexible day with blocks of free time. Then I take the time to read through the list and choose the activity to work on that seems to make the best use of the time I've got right now, or which is nagging me so much that I just want to get it done.

Completed activities are deleted from Evernote.

Andy Hunt

I try to complete a Weekly Review once a week, usually on a Sunday. I'm so likely to forget this that I have a weekly-recurring reminder in my Calendar!

I even have a note in Evernote called 'Weekly Review'. It contains a ticklist reminder of all the sort of things that I like to review if I've got time. I include it below to show you the sort of things I try and do to regain control and perspective over the week. I open this up in another Evernote window and work my way through it, ticking things off as I go. The real aim of carrying out this review is to feel reassured that what I'm working on during the week really IS what I SHOULD be working on.

WEEKLY REVIEW

Goal:
- To **capture** all new events, ideas & commitments into a single system
- To **review** priorities on all major projects
- To **set up** week-ahead commitments & to-dos

Part 1: capture all new events, ideas & commitments

Email Zero
- ❏ Empty **Work** email to zero
- ❏ Empty **Home** email to zero
- ❏ Ensure all **Actions** are sent to **Evernote**
- ❏ Check **@Waiting and @Action_Support** folders are up-to-date

Physical INBOXes
- ❏ Open and process all **Post** and Bills etc.
- ❏ Empty **Bag** and Pockets for **Notes** and **Paper Actions**
- ❏ Tidy Desk and 'own' / 'delegate' anything that shouldn't be there

Calendar Review
- ❏ Look over last week of the **Calendar** for any follow-up needed

Evernote 'INBOX'
- ❏ Go through **Evernote's Action List** and Tag every note appropriately

Managing Your Project

Part 2: review priorities on all major projects

Projects Review

Remember the aim is to keep the cogs moving and unstick any next actions.

If **stuck** - see notes at end.

Open up an Evernote window with a list of all top-level projects:

Action notes with the Tag **@Project** ()
- ❏ For each Project - review **project** status and spawn new Actions (with Tags).

Tasks without Projects
- ❏ Look through Tag-list to find any tasks not yet assigned to projects
  - ❏ Should they be **part of an existing project?**
  - ❏ Does it deserve a **new project?**

Part 3: set up week-ahead commitments & to-dos

Revisit Values
- ❏ Open & read **Mission Statement** note - focus on long-term aims
- ❏ Open & read **Values** note - Use as a filter to plan this week's activities
- ❏ Open & read Sharpen the Saw note - Anything which needs to happen this week? *(N.B. This comes from (Covey, 1989))*.

Preview Calendar
- ❏ Look ahead to **next week** (and further). Any **actions / prep** needed?

Re-order Time Priorities
- ❏ Work through **time Tags** (from 1-Now to 6- waiting) updating each To-Do as needed

Exercise set-up
- ❏ Book **Badminton** for the week
- ❏ Decide when I'm going to **run**

Andy Hunt

Home Tasks
- ❏ Choose **Podcasts** for the week
   < List of regular family & home actions goes here >

Other Tasks
- ❏ Back up USB stick
- ❏ Back up Hard-Disk
- ❏ Remove Checkmarks from this list !!

If Stuck on a Project
- If (complex / difficult / uncomfortable)
  - break into easy steps
  - get help in
  - delegate
- If not truly committed
  - park in Someday (if not, Delete and move on)
- If too low a priority c.f. other stuff
  - consider if I *want* to do this, and if so find a simple, exciting thing to start the cogs moving.

The specific items in this review probably won't suit you, but it may give you a good idea of what sort of things you would like to have in your *own* review.

Every now and again I get a feeling that the Projects I'm reviewing each week aren't covering ALL the commitments that I have. At times like this I do a 'brain-dump' to paper to try and capture some of the things in my head that are not yet in my system. At complex times, such as a few weeks before the start of my teaching term when all my courses need to be reviewed and updated, I make a Mind-Map of all the activities to be done using XMind.

My system is not a permanent solution, and I update it regularly. I think it's a feature of anyone who tries to get organised that you periodically review and update the very system itself. Over the years I have moved from paper lists and diaries, via a Palm Pilot with its To-Do lists, via Outlook, to Google and more recently Evernote, and now including *Todoist*.

Managing Your Project

16.3.5 Update to my system using Todoist

Recently I have changed system. I still use Gmail and Evernote, but now Evernote is for my *non*-Action storage only. I found a new system for the Actions that is cross-platform, works with Gmail, and helps me deal with fast-moving actions more seamlessly than with Evernote.

It's called Todoist (https://en.**todoist**.com/).

It works well with the GTD system because it allows you to sort tasks into Projects (which can have sub-tasks) *and* you can Tag tasks with one or more Contexts (such as @Computer or @Supervisor). Tasks can have dates, which makes it easy to show a list of tasks due today or tomorrow, labelled and coloured by Project. It works seamlessly across any web-browser, operating system or tablet or phone.

My methodology has not changed from that described above, apart from now when I'm sorting emails – Actions go to Todoist, and information goes to Evernote. ToDoist has a Gmail plug-in that allows you to turn an email into a task with a single click. This is really useful. Later, when you see the task, you click on it and the original email comes up, along with any attachments.

Only after making this change did I discover that there are other people who have made the same discovery as me, e.g. https://nebulous.wordpress.com/2014/12/04/gtd_evernote_todoist/.

16.4 Alternative Technological Solutions

What's described above is simply one way of keeping organised. Many people have come up with very different solutions to essentially the same problem, so let's take a very brief look at those now. The GTD company provides purchasable guides full of ideas on how to specifically set up some of these systems for implementing GTD.

16.4.1 Microsoft Outlook & IBM Notes

These two programs have been around for years, and so have attracted a huge group of followers. IBM Notes used to be called Lotus Notes. Outlook is a very commonly installed program, particularly on work PCs, and so it is a natural choice for many. Its best feature is that it integrates email, calendar and task lists in one place, and these can be moved around easily (e.g. dragging an email onto a task list, or dragging a task onto a specific time on the Calendar).

Because it is so widespread, there are many programs / apps on portable devices that can be set up to synchronise with the data. This is very important if you are not to be limited to all your data residing in one place (e.g. on your desktop computer).

From a functional point of view IBM Notes is similar to Outlook in that it provides ready access to an integrated Calendar, To-do list, email and note-taking environment. It's not a system I've ever used so I can't give a personal review of it.

16.4.2 Omnifocus

Omnifocus (https://www.omnigroup.com/omnifocus) is a productivity management suite of programs which shares data between your desktop Mac and your portable iDevices. It's been designed with GTD in mind, and focuses on projects, lists, categories, and regular review. Many people I know love the iPad version as they feel it gives them a strong sense of easy access to their projects and tasks from a single place. A few others say that it is rather complicated. That debate may come down to whether you want your system to handle the GTD methodology for you, or whether you prefer your tools to be 'dumb' and it's *you* who is handling and running the methodology. Remember that you can - if you like - run a GTD system on paper; so it's worth looking into what this system can offer you. It costs a significant amount and is Mac / iPhone / iPad only.

16.4.3 Things

There are many debates on the web about which is best - Things or Omnifocus. Things (http://culturedcode.com/things/) is another Apple-only list manager whose tagging features lend themselves to handling multiple projects and context lists. People often say that Things is simpler to use, and Omnifocus offers more flexible and powerful features.

16.4.4 Other List-managers & GTD Apps

This is not meant to be an exhaustive list, and certainly not a reasoned product-by-product comparison (there are plenty of those on the web; just search for something like "best gtd app" or more specific such as "Omnifocus v Things"). Products are being invented and updated all the time, and as tablet computers become more widespread, software is being updated to give people portable, synchronised and quick touch-access to their organisational data.

Here are a just a few of the other programs and Apps that you might want to investigate when you are setting up a system.

- Remember the Milk (http://www.rememberthemilk.com/) is a To-do list manager and reminder system which is very popular, and synchronises across your portable devices, but also has a web-page where you can access your data from any computer.

- Rescue Time (https://www.rescuetime.com/) is time-tracker software that helps you to analyse and review how you spend your time when on your computer. Many time management systems recommend finding out how you currently spend your time, so that you can identify common time-wasting patterns, and build up knowledge of how long it takes you to complete common tasks.

- As we've seen in Chapter 8 – Mind Mapping many people think visually and spatially, and the idea of lists does not always appeal. Several mind-mapping tools exist, both paid and free, and some of these include:

    o XMind (http://www.xmind.net/)

    o MindManager (http://www.mindjet.com/mindmanager/)

    o MindNode (http://mindnode.com/)

    o FreeMind (http://freemind.sourceforge.net/)

16.5 Be willing to experiment

My current system has evolved to suit my needs as I have refined, over the years, how I like to work, and as technology (new devices and software) have been developed.

A common mistake is to think that just getting some sort of technological solution will 'get you organised'. We modern humans seem to have developed the ability to think that buying something will sort our problems out. We reason "I need to get fit, so first I need a gym membership, a lovely pair of running shoes, some night gear, a heart monitor etc.", and sadly so often these things just sit there gathering dust. What gets you fit is having a plan and *doing something* about it regularly.

What really matters is that you do *something* to get yourself organised, and you input *all* your commitments to it and *monitor* it regularly (daily and weekly).

So before you buy a technological solution, first try to sort out how you want to get organised, and maybe do this initially on paper. Work out your Projects, Commitments, Tasks, Appointments etc. and try to identify how technology would help you handle this better.

Be willing to try a system, and then review it. Many people change their organisational technology regularly. You may lose the familiar ease of use, but if you find something better, or if you just get bored of your current system, then why not?

All of the tools and techniques will be much more effective if you customise them for your own purposes. Design, print and copy your own forms based on the ideas discussed in the previous chapters, and start using them on a regular basis. It will probably take several weeks of refinement before they are truly suited to your needs, but most people find an increased sense of confidence and competence when they begin to use such a system.

Good luck in finding something that works for you. If you're confused after reading here about all the technological options, why not re-read Chapter 12 – *Introduction to GTD* and determine what the underlying mental reasons for organisation really are.

16.6 Summary

Deduce for yourself if you are someone who works better with paper and pen **or** with computers and technology. If it's with paper and pen then this chapter probably isn't for you, but it's still worth a read to get some ideas about what a technological system can offer.

Whichever type of system you opt for it must be able to cope with:

- Appointments: All time-based commitments, easily entered and visible.
- Lists for:
    - Actions: Easily accessible Context-based lists of things you are committed to do.
    - Projects: Every commitment that involves multiple Actions.
- Storage: A filing system for information that you might need in the future.

In this chapter I've described the details of my own system, not because it is the 'right' way of doing things, but just because sometimes it's good to see what other people do. You'll also notice that I update the system itself every so often as new technologies become available, and as my commitments and responsibilities alter.

I spent a couple of years working with The Secret Weapon. This uses an email system (I use Gmail) coupled with a single destination (Evernote) to move emails to when they contain information or actions. More recently I have started using Todoist as the task organiser to store all my actions, while I retain Evernote as the place for all other information. However, there are many other options for technological solutions; full-screen software such as Outlook and IBM Notes, cross-platform apps such as Remember the Milk, and the Apple-only Omnifocus or Things.

You'll need to spend some time choosing a system, setting it up, and getting used to it. You'll also need to trust it with all your serious information and commitments, and review it daily and weekly. This can take some time at first, but is a necessary investment if you're going to have a professionally organised workflow.

16.7 External Links

(Covey, 1989) Stephen R. Covey, Seven Habits of Highly Effective People: Powerful Lessons in Personal Change, Simon & Schuster Ltd; Reprinted Edition (4 Jan 2004), ISBN-10: 0684858398, ISBN-13: 978-0684858395

Evernote (https://evernote.com/) - a multi-platform note management system.

Todoist (https://en.**todoist**.com/)- a multi-platform task/action management system.

TSW (The Secret Weapon; http://www.thesecretweapon.org/). This is a combination of an email system along with Evernote. Or see this link for a discussion on how to use it with Todoist: https://nebulous.wordpress.com/2014/12/04/gtd_evernote_todoist/.

GTD company purchasable guides (https://gettingthingsdone.com/store/home.php?cat=263) - ideas on how to specifically set up Google, Evernote, iPhones etc. for implementing GTD.

Microsoft Outlook - http://www.microsoft.com/en-gb/outlook-com/

IBM Notes (formerly Lotus Notes) http://www-03.ibm.com/software/products/en/ibmnotes

Andy Hunt

Omnifocus (https://www.omnigroup.com/omnifocus) Apple-only.

Things (http://culturedcode.com/things/) is another Apple-only list manager

Remember the Milk (http://www.rememberthemilk.com/)

Rescue Time (https://www.rescuetime.com/) is time-tracker software. Popular Mind-mapping tools include:

- XMind (http://www.xmind.net/)
- MindManager (http://www.mindjet.com/mindmanager/)
- MindNode (http://mindnode.com/)
- FreeMind (http://freemind.sourceforge.net/)

SECTION 4
PLANNING, WRITING, THINKING

This section brings together some of the key project-oriented information that you'll need as you progress through the project. Some of these chapters are best read right at the start of the project, but can also be useful if you are approaching this later on.

- **Ch. 17 Title, Aims & Objectives** - *how to set and develop the main goals of the project.* This chapter looks in some detail about how to encapsulate what you really want to do in a series of vital project elements that drill down into more detail. This helps you not only to focus effectively but to communicate clearly about your work.

- **Ch. 18 The Project Proposal** - *many departments require that you write an initial report after several weeks of work, and for good reason.* It establishes the basis for the project, acts as a 'contract' between you and your supervisor, gives you valuable feedback, and works as a starting-point for the all-important final report.

- **Ch. 19 Literature Survey** - *often an integral part of any research report, the Literature Survey is your statement of what is already 'out there'.* This chapter gives you hints and advice about writing about other people's work, and how to make it lay the foundations for what you are going to do in your own project.

- **Ch. 20 Successful Project Planning** - *although this whole book is about helping you carry out a successful project, there are various tools and techniques which help you manage the project in a professional way.* This chapter takes you through these techniques and explains a method of devising Work Packages for all the major sections of your project. This also has the advantage of introducing you to a popular planning method, often used in research grants and industrial organisations.

- **Ch. 21 Detailed Time and Project Planning** – *specific tools and techniques for managing time and uncertainty in projects.* For many people GANTT charts and other timing diagrams are what they think of when considering the words 'Project Management'. Graphical time-plans are indeed an important part of project planning and they are covered in this chapter. However, the rest of the book shows that they are just part of a much bigger self-organisational task that needs to be done, which is why time-charts on their own are rarely effective.

17. TITLE, AIMS AND OBJECTIVES

Setting and refining your project's aims and objectives isn't just a formal exercise; it can be the very essence of bringing a project out of your head and into the real world. In this chapter, we discuss how to form the project title, how to define aims, objectives, and a hierarchy of tasks, all of which will act as a guideline to the rest of your project. Along the way we'll meet several ideas for generating and managing creative ideas, and then communicating them to others in a clearly written proposal.

17.1 Setting the overall focus

The opposite of having a clear focus is being vague about what you are doing. Imagine for a moment that you were going on a car journey. How many of you would set out on such a journey without knowing where you were going? How would you know where to turn the wheel on a moment by moment basis? Yet this is what many students do, and they sustain this state for an amazingly long time by keeping 'busy' – which is analogous to driving around very fast without establishing where you are heading. Pushing this analogy a bit further – would it not be rather strange to stop and ask directions:

Driver: "Excuse me, I'm lost",

Police Officer: "Ok, where are you going?",

Driver: "I've no idea, but you're the expert, so tell me how to get there".

Even though this is a rather ludicrous conversation, many students expect their supervisor to play the role of the police officer. Run the conversation again, once the goal has been set, and see how differently it turns out:

Driver: "Excuse me, I'm lost",

Police Officer: "Ok, where are you going?",

Driver: "I need to find a supermarket, but I'm new to the area".

Police Officer: "Well, I think there are two main ones you could go to. I'd suggest going over the bridge to the next village. Turn right onto the ring-road and you'll find a superstore on your left. If you get lost, ask again for directions at the shop in the village . . . ."

In other words, once you have set your goal you can ask for help, people can respond positively to you, and you can then work at getting there.

So, you need to determine *what your subject area is*, and you should develop some idea of *what you're trying to achieve*.

As soon as possible practice explaining your topic and goal to as many people as will listen to you. If a friend (who is not studying your subject) asks you about your project, try to reply using everyday words. Sometimes this can help to cement the ideas in your own mind, and to help you feel comfortable with your project. However, you should also have some deep and detailed discussions with people who are more familiar with your subject area. This should be the topic of an early conversation with your Supervisor, or another member of staff who understands the subject, or indeed your fellow students who have trained with you up to this point, but are now doing other projects.

At this early stage you should allow yourself permission to dream. Rather than restricting yourself by saying "I've only got 4 months, and I'm new to the subject; what can I *possibly* do in that time?", think more like this: "If my resources were unlimited, what would I like to achieve in an ideal project?". Permit yourself to think of a breakthrough in your particular area. Try to visualise what a great outcome for your project might be. A really good test of a worthwhile project is to ask "In what ways might the world be different when I have completed this project?"

After a session of dreaming, you will of course need to come back to reality, and ask questions such as:

- How many hours in total do I have for this project?

- How much training do I need before I can really start making progress?

Managing Your Project

- How much equipment and support are available in my Department?

If you alternate your thinking between vision (dreaming) and realism, you can end up with a project focus that is both inspiring and practical.

17.2 Techniques for generating ideas

In the early stages of your project, you may find it quite difficult to clearly identify your topic, let alone come up with an excellent idea for taking the subject area forward. In this section we outline a few methods for getting your brain working in a creative mode.

17.2.1 Mind Mapping

For many people the best way of capturing ideas is with a Mind Map, either on paper or using software. The basis of this technique is covered in Chapter 8 - *Mind Mapping*.

The main reason that this is becoming increasingly popular is that it's essentially a method for recording ideas and associations that your brain generates, without restricting the *order* in which you have ideas.

To use mind-mapping to generate some project ideas, start in the middle of the page with something that represents the topic of your project. It could be a picture that portrays the concept, or the name of the topic, or if you're really stuck – just the word 'Project'. Now each time you have an idea, draw a line radiating out from the centre, and write on top of the line a brief summary of the idea. You may find that this sparks off a related idea, which you can attach to the previous idea (like a branch off a tree-trunk). Or you may find you have completely new idea (this is very common) so start a new line in a different direction, radiating from the centre. You can add diagrams where appropriate, and build this up in whatever way you like. Many mind-mappers find that using pens of different colours helps the ideas to flow.

Sometimes (especially when thinking about the particular focus of your project) you may find that there are several *clusters* of ideas. This is sometimes referred to as a Topic Web, and shows your discovery of the relationships between the different aspects of your subject area.

A mind-map is often quite a good way of explaining a complex idea to someone else, as they can see the structure of your thoughts, and the relationships between them. This is why they are very useful tools for supervisions. Some people use mind-maps in their reports to summarise complex ideas. Still others find that it forms a good visual record of your thought processes about the project. As your ideas develop, you can add them to the map, or change things to reflect your new way of thinking. Also, if you get stuck or distracted, one look at the mind map gives your brain a holistic reminder of where your thinking got up to last time.

17.2.2 Brainstorming

Mind-mapping is a technique for writing down ideas as they occur to you. The more general process of coming up with ideas has often been referred to as Brainstorming. This is simply a state of mind where you give yourself permission to have ideas *without judging* them. What people have found is that if you generate *lots* of ideas, then *some* of them will be good. However, if you start off by restrictively looking for 'good ideas' then there are not many to be found. Brainstorming can be a solo activity, or something you can do in a group. When there is more than one person present, you can take turns in asking questions and jotting them down, or have competitions for the most ideas, or anything to get you thinking.

17.2.3 Focus Groups

A wonderful way of developing ideas is to team up with people who are also studying in your subject area, or at least a topic that has something in common with yours. In Chapter 4 (section 4.3) and Chapter 9 we looked at setting up a support group of like-minded individuals, the Special Interest Group, or SIG.

It is particularly helpful if these are fellow students who understand exactly what you're going through because they are at the same stage in their project. So, when you are all needing to generate ideas about your project, get together to talk about it, either formally in an arranged group meeting or supervision, or individually for example over a cup of coffee.

Check that the other person/people are ok with asking *critical questions* of each other, for example:

- "What exactly *is* your topic then?"
- "Surely that's been done before? What's different about what *you're* doing?"
- "How does that relate to the topic?"

Managing Your Project

- "Why would you want to do that?"
- "Ok, I see what you're saying, but how would you explain this to someone who's *not* done our course?"

Read each other's reports, plans and jottings. Make sure that you understand what each other is saying, and what you have each written. Pretend to be examiners for each other. This can be fun, and a bit scary, but you will begin to respond to critical questions, and to prepare for explaining and justifying your project (more on this in Chapter 34 - *The Viva*).

17.2.4 Radio Interview Technique

A particularly useful technique for formulating your project topic is to put yourself under imaginary pressure to explain it well. The following is a transcript of the sort of conversation I have often had with my new students.

Me: Ok, let's talk about your project. What do you think the focus is?

Student: Well <*sigh*> I don't really know. I've been thinking about it, but it's all rather complicated. . . .

Me: <*holding an imaginary microphone under the student's chin*> Hi, I'm from the local radio station. We're doing a feature on the university, and what students are studying these days. Tell me in 30 seconds what you are looking into and why. Ok? Go . . .

Student: Er, well, Ok, I'm doing a project on computer interfaces. Typically these are not very good for real-time tasks, and I'm trying to find ways to improve this situation, particularly for people with limited movement.

Very often students are impressed with the eloquence of their spontaneous replies, and they reply with "Hold on a minute, I need to write that down". It seems as if a bit of artificial pressure can bring ideas from the subconscious out into the open. Students are often surprised that deep down they knew all along what they were doing. We often use this as a starting-point for writing down the topic of study, and from there we will come up with the title, and the aims and objectives.

I then ask the students to pair up and to interview each other. After an initial look which says "Does he *really* want us to do *that*?" they get interviewing and after several such pairings find that their confidence in summarising their project focus has improved enormously. I encourage the interviewer to ask for clarification if they don't understand something, and this very engagement with the main project focus turns out to be very rewarding and useful.

17.3 Developing your Title, Aims & Objectives

These three attributes of your project are perhaps the most important things to establish early on. The *Title* announces to the world (and to yourself!) what you are studying and what you are doing. The *Aims* define what you are trying to achieve. The *Objectives* describe the main steps you plan to take to achieve the aims. You can always come back and define these later, but an early statement of them gives you the direction and focus you need to begin with.

17.3.1 Working on your Title

It is good practice to spend some time coming up with a working title for your project, as this will provide a sense of focus and direction to your work. The time you spend on this task is an investment, because it forces you to think about the work you plan to do. A good title should define the topic area you are working in and a hint of what you are going to do about it.

Here are some example titles which do both of these:

- A prototype user-interface for helping people with disabilities to make music.
- An investigation into the causes of the common cold.
- Repetitive structures: a critical study of minimalism in the operas of Philip Glass.

The above titles also share another helpful feature – they should, *where possible*, make sense to the person in the street. Titles such as *"Categorisation of multiple spin techniques in the diomorphine substructure using electrolaryngographically derived surface textures"* may appear impressive, but to the average person it is almost as if they are nonsense. (I'll leave it to you to work out if this title is a real one or not!) Many doctoral titles seem to just state the subject area (e.g. Complex Real-time User Interfaces) as they are meant to be an in-depth study on a particular area. But doctoral theses also should be reporting novel work done and so it is a good idea to reflect this in the title whenever possible.

Your title can evolve with the project. Think of it as a *working statement* of your chosen area of focus and activity. The title should lead directly on to your Aims.

17.3.2 Establishing the Aims

People are often confused by the labels 'aims' and 'objectives'. Very simply, the Aims are statements of the things you want to *achieve* by the end of the project. Objectives describe *how to get to each aim* by listing the main stages you will need to undertake. In other words aims are 'targets', objectives are 'strategies'.

Let's assume that you have a single focussed aim. Imagine you are being interviewed for a radio news bulletin, and someone asks you to complete the sentence:

"The main aim of my project is . . ."

or

"The thing that I want to have done by the end of the project is . . ."

You should then come up with phrases like this (taking some of the examples mentioned in the 'Title' section above);

- To design and build a prototype user-interface for people with physical disabilities to make music in non-real-time using computers.

- To investigate the causes of the common cold, considering specifically the airborne transmission of viruses from one human to another.

- To critically examine the operas of Philip Glass in comparison to other twentieth century 'minimalist' composers; focussing on the precise methods for developing repetitive musical structures.

Don't worry if your aim looks very much like your Title; this probably shows that your title is good. However, the aim is typically longer than the title, and gives a little more detail of what you want to deliver at the end of the project. If your aim is very long, with many clauses such as "To do . . . . .and to do . . . and also . . ." then you probably have a *list* of aims. Try listing them separately and see what they look like.

Once you have defined your Aim(s) the next process is to bring your project to life with a list of Objectives.

17.3.3 Crafting your Objectives

Objectives are the steps that you need to carry out in order to reach your aim. There are normally many objectives, which exist as an ordered sequence of action phrases. In other words, 'objectives' often form a numbered list of sentence fragments with verbs (action words), such as *"Analyse the existing work in this topic"* or *"Write a computer program to graph the data"*.

There are different ways of setting objectives, but a good way to start is to look at each of your stated Aims and ask yourself "If I'm going to achieve this aim, what will I have to *do*?"

If you are struggling with how to develop objectives from your aims, then you need a conversation with someone (such as your supervisor, or someone from your Special Interest Group) who will just keep asking you questions. Let's eavesdrop on a typical conversation, using one of the project examples mentioned above, to see how this works.

You: <*sounding worried*> I just don't know how I'm going to achieve my aim.

Other Person: What *is* your stated aim?

You: <*reads*> "To design and build a prototype user-interface for people with physical disabilities to make music in non-real-time using computers".

Other : Ok, good, so what worries you about this?

You: I don't want to reinvent the wheel.

Other : Fine, so what do you need to *do* to *make sure* you don't re-invent the wheel?

You: Do something original!

Other : Yes, ok, but *how* exactly will you ensure that it's original?

You: I'd better find out what already exists?

Other : Good – write that down as Objective no.1

You: <*writes*> 1. Find out what already exists.

Other : Now if you read that objective out of context, would it make sense to someone?

You: <*reads*> "1. Find out what already exists". Mmm – sounds like I'm trying to survey the whole of creation. Ok, so how about "1. Survey literature and web to establish existing methods of making music on computers for people with limited movement"?

Other: Sounds good. So what would you do after that?

You: I'd have to design my own original system.

Other: What would you need *to do* to get started on that right now?

You: Well, I'd have to work out what was *missing* from the existing work. Oh, well, I suppose I could ask people working in this area what they would like to see invented.

Other: Ok, sounds good. Could you write that down as number 2?

You: "2. Contact people working in this area with a questionnaire"?

Other: and . . .?

You: then analyse the questionnaire and decide on an original feature.

Other: Right. Then what? Is the project finished yet?

You: No, nothing's actually built yet. And that's what *really* worries me; my programming skills are not very good.

Other: So what could you put as an objective?

You: What do you mean?

Other: Rather than stating something as a 'worry' (which just makes you *feel* bad) why not rephrase it as a *positive action* which will take you forward?

You: How about 'Get better programming skills'?

Other: Mmmm – yes, but how would you actually *do* that?

You: Ok – I see what you mean. How about: "3. Revise computer programming course; highlighting particular coding problems needed for the novel interface"

etc. etc.

This conversation could continue for some time, but hopefully you get the general idea. By having someone just ask you question after question, you begin to build up a *set of activities that need to be done*, acknowledging your worries and weaknesses along the way and converting them into positive actions. You should revise your objectives and talk them through with your Supervisor and Special Interest Group.

17.6 Bringing together Title, Aims & Objectives

The above example, when completed, looked like this:

Title

A prototype user-interface for helping people with disabilities to make music.

Aim

To design and build a prototype user-interface for people with physical disabilities to make music in non-real-time using computers.

Objectives

1. Survey literature and web to establish existing methods of making music on computers for people with limited movement.

2. Produce and analyse a questionnaire aimed at practitioners in the fields of music, computers and disability to find out what new equipment is needed.

3. Draw up a design specification for the novel interface.

4. Identify most suitable programming language: revise main features of the language.

5. Plan necessary hardware; order components and book workshop time.

6. Build the hardware and write the software.

7. Test completed prototype system in the lab, then with a local special school.

If you are still stuck with your objectives, or they don't yet seem quite right, you may wish to think about whether they make sense from the point of view of *time flow*. Does the first objective lead naturally into the second? Is there something missing? Can the two tasks be run concurrently? Or does one need to be completed before the next one begins?

When you are happy with the above process, you will have a succinct form of words that you can discuss with your Supervisor, Special Interest Group, or anyone else to whom you need to present your project ideas. This trio of Title, Aims & Objectives also forms a valuable part of any initial report that you have to do (see Chapter 18 – *The Project Proposal*) as well as being essential for the final report.

Managing Your Project

The Objectives will also help you to form a more detailed Project Plan, and we will look at that in more detail in Chapter 20 - *Successful Project Planning*.

17.7 Summary

In this chapter we have considered how to select a project, and to make it your own. By the process of managing your ideas, and gradually refining them, you will arrive at a statement of your understanding of the project. This should describe both the topic area and the actions you hope to achieve within that area.

The ***Title*** summarises the whole project very briefly. Ideally it states the topic area and hints at your contribution to that area.

The ***Aim*** states clearly what you hope to achieve. Many people believe that a single Aim is better than multiple ones because it defines a clear focus, but there are no universal rules about this.

The ***Objectives*** provide an ordered list of activities you intend to carry out to achieve the aim.

A series of *Tasks* can be derived from the objectives by gradually breaking them down into more manageable chunks.

We've looked at several techniques for generating ideas, such as discussion in your focus group, a radio interview technique, brainstorming and mind-mapping. The process of moving from the unknown to a working plan is daunting, but ultimately very rewarding. The resulting Title, Aims, Objectives and Tasks will help to keep you focussed along the way, and to communicate with others at an appropriate level for them.

18. THE PROJECT PROPOSAL

In this chapter we look at the first written statement of your project's focus. Sometimes this can be called a 'Project Proposal' because the project focus has yet been fixed up to this point in time. In other places, where your project focus has already been chosen, the term 'Initial Report' is more appropriate.

The major differences between the two is that a Project Proposal is typically very short, and is sometimes just a one or two page overview of the project's area of study. An Initial Report is generally longer, and includes everything that a Proposal would, coupled with a summary of any work done up to the point of writing. It often includes a Literature Survey, because much of the focus of the early stage of the project work is on reading up about what others have done.

In this chapter we look at the Project Proposal, and the Literature Survey is covered in Chapter 19.

18.1 Your first report

Some projects require you to write an initial report in the early stages. Even if this is not a requirement at your place of study, it is strongly recommended that you write one. This report becomes the first statement of what the project really means to *you*. It shows to your tutor not only that you understand the topic, but that you have a plan and some idea of how to bring it to life.

For doctoral studies (and some Masters-by-Research courses) this proposal needs to be presented up-front, i.e. *before* you are accepted onto the course, because you are expected to be responsible for running your own research.

Whichever level you are working at, you should aim to write a report (a few pages long) which states your agreed Title, Aims and Objectives (as developed in the previous chapter. Sometimes this is enough, as it says what focus area you have agreed on, and what you plan to do about it. However, you may also want to add some background or introductory material if you feel that some explanation is needed before the aim makes proper sense.

For some initial reports you are first given several weeks to get started on your project, and you may wish (or may be expected) to also include a Literature Survey (see Chapter 19 for more details), and a time-plan (see chapters 20 & 21).

Whichever format you choose, you should aim at writing a short report which clearly explains what your project is, and what you are going to do about it. Ask for feedback from your supervisor, because the earlier you can establish a mutually acceptable writing style the easier it will be to write your final report.

18.2 Structuring your report

The structure of an initial report is usually a lot simpler than that of the final report. However, it is *always* worth thinking about the structure of any report you have to write, even if it is only a short one.

Things you should consider:

- What is the main purpose of this report?
- Who is going to be reading it?
- What specifications are you given for it?

Let's look at each of these things in turn.

18.2.1 What is the main purpose of this report?

Be clear about what this report is for.

a) If it's written as a *pre-course* proposal, then this is basically an advert about you and what you are hoping to study. The people reading it are going to be deciding whether you are the right student for them, and whether they are the right department or supervisor to take on your field of study. In this case, please make sure that you have first read Chapter 2: Choosing a Project.

b) If it's an initial report required by your department, then you have already been 'accepted' onto a project, and this becomes more of a statement of focus. It is a condensation of the thoughts you have been having about the topic and the aims of your project.

c) It may be a required report following several weeks of work on the project, in which case it more of a showcase summary of what you have been getting up to following your initial meeting(s) with your Supervisor. This is very likely to involve a Literature Survey following the introduction and overview.

18.2.2 Who is going to be reading it?

In case a) above, the intended readership is determined by your type of application. If you are applying generally to a University for higher-level study, such as a PhD, initially your proposal will be viewed by somebody in the graduate schools office. This is very likely to be a non-subject specialist, and so your writing must be accessible and free from jargon. Based on this initial reading, it is likely to be passed to the appropriate department, and eventually to prospective supervisors. If you have already established contact with a supervisor, then target the report to that person, in which case you can be more specific about the details of your project.

For cases b) and c) above, it is likely that the initial reader will be your Supervisor. Please make sure you have already read Chapter 5 on the Supervision Process. Your report - in this case - is a statement of your ideas which becomes the starting-point for a series of discussions about your project's focus and direction.

18.2.3 What specifications are you given for it?

It's important to find out whether the University or Department has a given specification for this report. It might do one of the following:

- simply specify a page-limit;

- give some general high-level expectations (e.g., "submit a short report describing your project focus so far and outlining the key literature discovered");

- give you some headings which you are required to cover;

- give you a template file which you are expected to edit with your information.

It is possible that there is no specification at all, in which case you might like to use something based on the following:

For a short proposal (or early-stage initial report):

1. Introduction - here you introduce the Topic of study for a general audience, and gradually focus towards your project idea

2. Project Aim(s) - the main thing you hope to achieve - see Ch. 17

3. Objectives - the main steps needed to achieve the aim - see Ch. 17

4. Initial Plan - it's important to conclude with a brief summary of what you plan to do over the coming weeks and months. This shows that you are action-oriented and have an idea of what work needs to be done.

For a longer proposal or Initial Report / Literature Survey you will probably need more sections, along the following lines:

1. Introduction

2. Aim(s) & Objectives

3. Topic web - a graphical portrayal of the topics covered by the project; maybe not needed if your project area is very well established

4. Literature Survey - usually a relatively big piece of work, as described in the next chapter

5. Initial Work-Plan

6. Proposed Timetable of activities.

If you have any doubt as to what is expected, please check with the person or office who will be reading it.

Independent of who else this is intended for, this report gives *you* an excellent chance to gain some early experience of writing, and to learn from any response you get back. It gives you:

- practice at writing in the required style,
- feedback and training from the people who know the marking system,

- a written form of your initial ideas and focus, firming up your commitment and focus.

18.3 Summary

A Project Proposal is usually the first statement of your project's main focus. If this is written some weeks after the start of the project, it is more likely to be called an Initial Report, and would be expected to cover your Aims and Objectives, a survey of the literature you have found so far, and maybe a detailed time-plan for the project.

Make sure you know *who* you are writing for, what is the main *purpose* of the report, and whether there is a *specification* that you should follow. This chapter has given a few suggestions for the structure of such a report, if there is no other guidance available.

The act of writing an initial report should give you some experience of structuring and wording your communications ahead the much larger final report. You should also receive some valuable feedback from your supervisor on the topic content and your writing style. More than anything else it becomes your first substantial statement of what your project is about and how you intend to run it, and so will act as a useful reference for quite some time – up until it is replaced by the final report.

19. THE LITERATURE SURVEY

This chapter discusses the purpose of a Literature Survey, and then takes you through the task of planning it, doing it, and writing it up. Whilst this is not a feature of every project, it is certainly an important milestone in many higher degrees, and is a key feature of all research. It would be helpful if you have already read Chapter 18 - *The Project Proposal* because a Literature Survey is often specified as being a key part of any early-stage report.

19.1 The importance of setting your work in context

Before embarking upon any big task in life, it is sensible to ask the following questions:

- Has anyone else *already done* this?
- Has anyone done something *similar* that I can learn from?
- Is anyone *currently working on* this, or something similar?
- What am I therefore doing that is *unique*?

These questions are particularly relevant to a research project, and the higher up the education system you go, the more important it becomes:

> Typically for **school projects**, you simply need to demonstrate that you can *do* what you've been asked to do, although it shows initiative to comment on what other things have been done.
>
> For **lower-level undergraduate** project work, you need to show competence in the *techniques* being studied, and that you can *manage* a project. However, a survey of existing techniques and applications can set a better context for your work and allow you to evaluate your

contribution in the light of other work.

For **higher-level undergraduate** projects and **Masters** work you need to confirm that you know *where your work fits in* with other similar work around the world and in the literature, and demonstrate that your work is *informed* by this research.

For **doctoral level work**, your research needs to be so thorough that you can prove the *novelty* of your work by being critically aware of all major existing literature and progress in the topic area.

So let's now look at how you can answer those important questions (above) that will set the context for your work.

19.2 What has been done?

To answer the question "Has anyone else already done this?" we can really only do two things:

1) Find out what has been *written* about the topic. In the next section, we compare some of the common ways of getting hold of this sort of information.

2) *Ask* someone knowledgeable about this topic.

However, before you do either of the above two things, you need to have a good idea of what your 'topic' is, or you won't know where to look or what to ask. If you have worked through the book up to this point, then you should have developed a Title, an overall Aim and some supporting Objectives, which define in some detail what you think you would like to do.

You can take these as a starting point for defining your project topics and thus knowing what to look out for in the existing literature. Usually your Title will contain a few important keywords. You may wish to revisit Chapter 17, especially section 17.1 - *Setting the overall focus*, to refresh your perspective on your topic.

You might be asked for your Literature Survey *before* you have had a chance to develop your project plan in detail. There is a lot of sense to this approach, because it forces you to examine "what is out there" before you commit large amounts of time working out the details of what you are going to do. It also helps you to operate more in Managerial mode, by examining existing work before embarking upon your own work. A further advantage is that a written survey of literature will usually form an important part of your final project report, and this will give you a good head start on the report at an early stage of the project.

Managing Your Project

So, you have established that you need to discover what has been previously written in your topic area. Let's now examine and compare the different potential sources of the information you are looking for.

19.3 Different types of information source

This section considers the variety of forms that information comes in, and is intended to be a sort of 'travel guide' to these different media, with things to do and areas to beware of. We'll look at the various types of media, and discuss the advantages and disadvantages of each. Remember that a good Literature Survey is not just a list of references (or a concatenation of quotes). Instead it should consist of a carefully reasoned argument which references other people's work, analyses it, comments on it, introduces your own ideas, and leads up to your main project work.

Figure 19.1 shows a list of publication types and compares their principal features of timeliness and reliability.

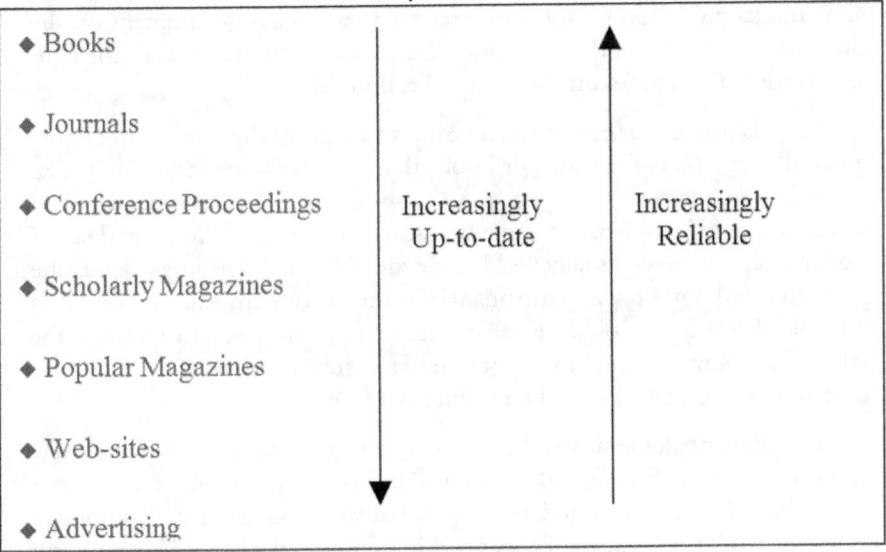

Figure 19.1 Different media types and the timeliness-reliability trade-off

Books are traditionally considered to be reliable because of the editing process, but they typically take a long time to produce and so do not contain the latest information in a rapidly changing field. Advertising is *meant* to be up-to-date, but cannot be considered reliable as an independent opinion. Of course, this list is a gross generalisation (for instance some books may well be **un**reliable, others may be up-to-date, and there is much that can be learned from advertising), but you need to be aware from the start that just because something is *written* does not mean that it is *correct*. In a Literature Survey, the reader will want to know what you *think* of each piece of work that you reference.

In the following sections, we consider each of these media types in turn, and what we can learn from each one.

19.3.1 Books

For hundreds of years books have been an important medium of written communication of specialist knowledge. Conventionally books have taken a long time to complete, and go through many processes of review. This affects the content, and gives time for the material to be considered, revised and checked. Books are often more accessible to the reader than journals and magazines (which tend to use a lot of terminology which requires specialist knowledge). But be aware that because of the long preparation time, books published in the traditional way cannot easily comment on the latest developments, and so are often best used to 'set the scene' for your later reading from more up-to-date publications.

There is usually a strict editorial process to control the quality of a book, especially textbooks for study, or books that summarise research. However, there is one danger that you must consider. Whereas journals and magazines tend to sell via a reasonably steady subscription (to a fixed set of readers), books are usually sold individually via bookshops, and the publisher and author will gain financially for every copy sold. Thus it is possible that a book could be sensationalised in some way to enhance the sales. This is more likely to happen in some subjects than with others, so be careful when considering the reliability of a book.

As a student doing a literature review, you may wish to start with any appropriate book lists found in your syllabus, or given to you by your supervisor. Next, you should get acquainted with your library. Computers are wonderful tools, but the danger is that they can trawl up a huge amount of information of unknown quality, often dependent on the keywords you type into a search engine. In a library, you can locate the section for your subject, and just browse through a whole variety of books that are classified as being relevant to that subject. Physically flicking through books, at a speed your brain is comfortable with, yields completely different insights about what information is relevant, compared with staring at a computer screen for hours. There are also subject librarians who can help you locate suitable books and journals, but you will first need to consider your research topic clearly before making an appointment.

19.3.2 e-Books

The world is changing, and the publishing world is currently being overturned by the technology and marketing of e-Books. These can be in the form of PDF files readable on any computer device, or as a more targeted file format which works only on one type of gadget, or in one 'reader' app. For some books, the electronic version is just a more handy and portable way of reading and distributing material. Such books are published and reviewed in the traditional way and are printed on paper, as well as being distributed electronically.

However, there is another phenomenon occurring, that of mass-market self-publishing. There have always been self-published books, but these have tended to be limited by the budget of the author who took responsibility for writing, editing, printing, and selling their book. But with e-Books, and with the market opening up with worldwide media distribution companies such as Apple (iBooks) and Amazon (Kindle), almost anyone with access to a computer can write a book.

You might be reading this on an e-Device, or at least in electronic form, because as an author this offered me the best way of getting this work 'out there' to a wider and more diverse audience than traditional publishing. Or you might be reading the print version, which is printed to order, rather than pre-printing thousands as was tradition. As a reader, there are pros and cons to this process. As a positive, readers now have ready access to people whose written work may not have been available before; the range of subjects is increasing; and books can be kept up to date and actually become very timely. As a negative, the editorial review process is down to the author, and so there is more chance that you will read something that has been checked less than with traditional publishing methods.

What this does, though, is place the emphasis on *you* being a critical reviewer, rather than having some automatic 'reverence' for anything that has been published in book form. This is a good thing from the point of view of writing a Literature Survey.

19.3.3 Journals

Journals are subject-specific periodicals that are usually available in academic libraries and by subscription. There are around ten thousand journals published in the UK alone. Academics often consider them a good compromise between reliability and speed of publication. Usually a journal has a strong emphasis on *peer reviewing*. This means that before a paper is published, it has to go through a rigorous process of being read, analysed and commented on by (usually) more than one expert in the field of study. This ensures that the papers are acceptable to the current practitioners in the topic, but can make it quite hard to get radically new ideas published.

As such, journals are rather specialist publications, and can often feel relatively inaccessible to someone outside the area. They rely heavily on common knowledge in the area, without the need to continuously revisit the same explanatory material. This means that they are not usually the best way of beginning or 'getting into' a subject, but are excellent for detailed analysis. Journals are generally well respected as sources of specialist information for research, primarily because of the reviewing process. They also encourage extensive cross-referencing, so rather than repeating other people's work, authors *quote* and *refer* to others' work. This makes them an excellent introduction to other references that you may not have come across yet.

You can browse through journals in a library, or ask specialists in your subject area (e.g., your supervisor) if they particularly recommend certain papers to study.

Nowadays, much information about journals can be found online. Most journals have a 'homepage', which contains lists of contents for each issue, often abstracts of every paper, and sometimes full papers. Some journals (known as e-journals) only exist in electronic form, and so do not have a printed-paper copy. You still need to pay a subscription for many of these, so the information may not be 'free'. However it is worth checking out your university or college Library because many of them pay for bulk subscriptions, which can allow you to download certain papers without further charge.

A useful method to get hold of a particular journal paper is to find out if it is available on-line. It could be that an individual author has made the paper available on his or her website. Simply type some keywords of the title (and possibly the first author's surname) into an internet search engine, and patiently review the results - looking for the paper in question. This has the advantage that you may well discover other web-pages or papers in this topic which share the same keywords, or indeed which quote the paper you are looking for.

19.3.4 Conferences

Conferences are gatherings of people (often academics or practitioners in a certain subject) where the main goals are to share ideas, hear presentations, and meet people working in the same area. Speakers at a conference typically have more freedom than those writing for an academic journal. Often, presenters are expected to submit a paper, which is later published in a set of conference *proceedings*.

Sometimes conference proceedings are heavily refereed, in a similar way to journal papers. However, many conferences are considered to be reviewed a bit more 'freely' and a little less rigorously than journals. Some journals can take between one and two years to produce, whereas conferences are usually reporting work or ideas from the previous 6 months or so. Therefore, the latest conference proceedings in a particular subject are a reasonably good overview of "what is going on now" in that subject, but the papers do not carry quite as much 'weight' as a journal. Often you will see work presented at a conference that is later expanded into a journal paper.

Again, most conferences have their own web-page, and it is becoming more common to see the full papers freely available on the conference website.

19.3.5 Scholarly Magazines

There are different sorts of magazine. Some are more like journals, in that there is quite a strong reviewing process. The main differences between journals and scholarly magazines is that journals are really intended for a specific audience and are rarely to be found in a shop, whereas magazines are written for a broader audience and sell most of their copies through newsagents.

The turnaround time for magazines is also much faster. This means that they can report in a more up-to-date manner in fast-changing subject areas, or produce very fast reports from conferences. However, this means that the depth of reviewing is usually less, and thus you have to read them with more caution. The very fact that they are written in a popular style (to make them accessible) means that they are rather restricted in their depth of technical or analytical detail.

19.3.6 Popular Magazines

Popular magazines are designed to sell in bulk, and so are mainly found in newsagents. Often they are produced weekly, so the turnaround times for writing are very short. In many instances there is a very limited review process. This encourages people to write articles that will sell more magazines and which therefore have to be extremely accessible (and thus not technically deep). Quite often, such magazines contain many tutorials, and news pages. The emphasis is more on training, entertainment, and advertising rather than scholarly research. Some articles may even be adverts in disguise. So, while you may find some interesting ideas in magazines, beware of quoting them without following up the information further to discover its true source.

19.3.7 Web Sites

As we have seen above, the internet allows access to journals, conferences, and library catalogues, and so is nowadays regarded as an essential tool for research. But with the freedom and accessibility of the internet comes a warning. Anyone can write anything and put it online. Just because it's on the web, does not mean that it is correct.

The internet is unregulated by default, and so it is vitally important that you evaluate the quality of review.

Positive things you should look out for include:

- Home pages of well-respected authors;
  These are often the source of many ideas and papers;
- A 'virtual community' which monitors or regulates the content of the site, and encourages discussion and sharing of ideas;
- Sites related to journals and conferences where a strong review process is known to take place;
- Sites which primarily give links to other information (portals). Again, weigh up who is providing the information and what their motives are for doing so.

For all other sites beware that you may be reading:

- Advertising material (see next section)
- Spoof material (the internet is rife with jokes and made-up stuff)
- Interesting material that has simply not been tested by the community
- Assignments, which may or may not be technically correct, posted by proud schoolchildren and students.

The guiding rule is to ask the following questions of any piece of information you get from the web:

Managing Your Project

- *who* said that?
- *why* did they say it?
- *where* did they get *their* information from?
- Is this likely to be a *trustworthy* source?

If even one of the above is in doubt, then you are advised not to use this in your Literature Survey.

19.3.8 Advertising

Adverts are intended to make you buy something, or to promote a particular ideology. They are not there to provide you with a carefully considered independent point of view. Be *very* wary of quoting advertising. It is often written in a certain style (intended to manipulate) and this sits extremely uncomfortably in a report which is meant to be objectively surveying the area.

Imagine you have written the following extract from your report on the topic of computer software used in graphics, specifically drawing.

There are many programs available for artists, but the one to be used for this project is the Graph-o-Pad 3 by SuperDuperDraw Systems:

"Graph-o-pad 3 is the only drawing package you will ever need. Years ahead of its competition, this amazing package will allow your creativity to flow, enabling you to produce stunning artwork admired by all your friends" [SuperDuperDraw website, 2013]

Clearly this is the best program to use. The project will allow artists to . . .

As a reader of such a report, surely you will not be convinced by such an argument, which appears to amount to "I chose this system because I was brainwashed by an advert"?

19.4 Learning from other people

In the section above, we considered some of the many sources of *written* information for your literature survey. However, never underestimate what knowledge and advice might be lurking in the heads of people around you.

19.4.1 Talking about your project

At the risk of becoming a project bore, do try to talk to as many people as possible about your project and really *listen* to what they have to say. These could be fellow students on your course, your housemates (maybe at the same educational institution, but studying different subjects), non-student friends, or relatives. If other people do not seem to understand what you're trying to do, then work harder at finding an explanation; this will help you when it comes to refining your aims, and writing the report. However, quite often you will receive some very interesting ideas, some of them that would never have come from an expert in your area!

19.4.2 Your Supervisor

We've discussed the role of your supervisor in detail in Chapter 5. Be aware that talking to this single person will generally guide you to the relevant texts faster than any other method. However, do not be surprised if he or she does not just give you a reading list; they may want you to exercise your research skills by letting you look for yourself first. When you are happy with what you have found, your supervisor is an excellent person to ask "do you think I've missed anything?".

19.4.3 Your Special Interest Group

Your project focus group (or SIG, see Chapter 9) should be an integral part of your literature review process. These are fellow students who are working in a similar area to you. The members of a focus group can work together to:

- *Compare* lists of literature found,
- *Discuss* the contents and relevance of the literature,
- Ask each other questions to see if you *understand* what you have read.

If you haven't already done so, it would be worth setting up such a group just to get some support during the literature review phase of the project.

19.4.4 Librarians

People who work with academic literature every day are great sources of advice on how to use a library and on what written material exists. Many libraries also employ subject specialists. These people know about the structure of the literature in a certain topic area, and may know much of its content too. This does not mean they will automatically understand the aims or details of your project, but they are certainly worth talking to in order to get some guidance about where you should look.

19.4.5 Other Experts

You may wish to contact some of the specialists around the world in your particular subject area. Please read Chapter 22 – *Structuring your Communication* carefully before doing this. There are many people doing research, and far fewer experts, so they do not want to be inundated with requests for information. You should perhaps discuss with your supervisor which people, if any, might be most approachable.

19.4.6 Questionnaires

Another source of information is the feedback that you receive from a carefully designed and distributed questionnaire. This can be particularly useful if you are trying to canvas opinion on a certain topic. The internet has certainly made this sort of information gathering easier, as questionnaires can be sent and received by email. However, you get more of a personal touch if you use physical sheets of paper that you give to people. Again, refer to Chapter 22 for guidance about how best to communicate with busy people.

19.5 Writing the Literature Survey

This section contains some advice about the different ways that a literature survey can be structured, and the most important things that it should contain.

19.5.1 Main Aim

Let us be clear what you are trying to do when writing a Literature Survey. You are demonstrating that:

- You know what other work exists in your topic area
- You have gathered and read some subject-specific material

- You can analyse and comment on existing work
- You know how your proposed work relates to the existing work
- You understand to what extent your proposed work is unique.

19.5.2 Different approaches

There are many ways to write a literature survey:

- An **essay-based** approach is usually text-based, and *tells a story*, referring to other work along the way.
- A **bibliography-based** approach *lists the literature* found, and says something about each one.
- A **topic-based** approach divides the literature you have found into certain *subject areas* related to your project.

A good literature survey (whatever the style) will have a good *flow of argument* and will reference other work in the area. The flow of argument is important because it shows that you understand what your project is about, and how the other work relates to it. The referencing is important because it shows what other work exists.

19.5.3 Arguing your case

The most important thing to remember when you are writing a literature survey is that *your opinions matter* to the person reading it. Therefore, it is important that you apply a personal 'filter' to the material you discover. The literature survey is your selection of what is 'out there'. You are not trying to represent *all* the literature that might be vaguely related to your topic, but instead you are constructing a story that leads up to your specific project focus.

A literature survey should take the reader from a 'general knowledge' of the area, to a specific, focussed description of your project. You should comment on the work of others, feeling free to criticise it if you disagree. Most importantly, you should try to *balance* your ideas with the ideas of others.

19.5.4 Referencing

It's really important that you reference someone else's work when:

Managing Your Project

- You **refer** to it (e.g. This is covered in the book by Hunt)
- You **quote** directly from it (e.g. Hunt says "It's really important that you reference someone else's work").
- You **paraphrase** (re-word) it: e.g. referencing someone else's work is very important.

There are several possible styles of referencing, and you should talk to your supervisor about which one is preferred. Some universities and colleges specify the format precisely, while others leave it more open.

One method is to use footnotes like this[2] but this can clutter up the bottom of a page, and does not automatically provide a complete ordered list of references for the reader.

Another method is to provide a simple number in square brackets for each reference like this [1]. This must be supported by a numbered list of references at the back of the report. This is very popular in short papers where many references can be included in a limited space e.g., [2], [3], [4]-[9]. However, as you can see, this doesn't give any information to the reader, who must then look up the reference. That's fine if the reference is at the bottom of the page or clearly visible at the end of a very short report. However, for longer report, it can be really frustrating for the reader to keep having to turn a Reference section somewhere near the back of the report, just to find out what sort of paper is being referred to.

A very popular method is to include the first author's surname and the publication date in brackets straight after the reference occurs, like this (Hunt, 2015). Towards the back of the report is a full list of references arranged alphabetically by first author, as shown below:

Appendix A: References

...

Hunt, A, Managing Your Project: Achieving Success with Minimal Stress, ISBN-13: 978-1537212203, 2016

...

Extract from alphabetic reference list at the end of the report

---

[2] This is an example of a footnote. Some people put their references down here.

This has a dual advantage:

1) It provides some in-line information about the reference (e.g., if you know about Hunt's 2015 work, then you need look no further and your reading is not interrupted).

2) The alphabetic list of references at the back of the report forms a useful summary of all the material you have found in an easily accessible form.

Using this method, here are some examples of Referring, Quoting and Paraphrasing used together in a single (highly contrived) paragraph.

Three books in particular cover the details of referencing research projects (Berry, 2000), (Hunt, 2005), and (Hunt, 2016). When writing a report *'It's really important that you reference someone else's work"* (Hunt, 2016), because it shows that you understand what other people have written. Where possible integrate the quote into your own text, and make it part of your argument, either for or against.

Establishing the correct format for submission is important too.

"There are several possible styles of referencing, and you should talk to your supervisor about which one is preferred. Some universities and colleges specify the format precisely, while others leave it more open." (Hunt, 2016)

Hunt later describes the dangers of plagiarism, because it is the opposite of good referencing.

In reality if you were talking about 'Hunt, 2016' a lot, you would not need to reference it *every* time – but you *must* show which material has come from other people.

19.5.5 Concluding the survey

Make sure that you finish the survey with a positive statement of what you will be doing for the rest of your project, or at least what the focus of your study is. Try to summarise the literature you have found, and what you thought of it, then describe what you are going to be focussing on and why.

19.6 Plagiarism

Plagiarism is the use of other people's material *without* properly referencing it. It is, in effect, cheating by pretending that the words and ideas on the page are yours, whereas in reality they have come from somewhere else. Most places of higher education treat this as a very serious offence.

The sheer volume of information available on the internet makes it very easy to cut and paste material into your report. If you mark it clearly, list where it comes from, and comment on it appropriately, then this is acceptable. However, many people try to construct their work by finding pieces of it elsewhere and bolting it together, hoping that it will form an essay.

Plagiarism is wrong for the following reasons:

- It shows a lack of thinking and processing
- It is simply unfair to those whose words you have stolen
- It will *not* show you in a good light when questioned further about the work
- It does not show off your research skills.

This last point is important. If you find something relevant and quote it and comment on it – you have demonstrated your ability to find elusive information and analyse its content. If, on the other hand, you pass it off as your own words you simply show your proficiency at cheating. The effort required to disguise someone else's work as your own is much better applied towards proper referencing.

19.7 Summary

This chapter has looked at the important topic of finding out what else has been done in your topic area. Your stage (or level) in the education system determines how important it is to be aware of existing work, and to what depth.

We have considered the different sources of information available to you, and compared their reliability and timeliness. Books typically take a long time to produce and scientific books have a strong editorial process. E-Books are becoming much more common and can be produced faster, making them possibly more up-to-date but less rigorously reviewed. Journal papers are highly specialised subject-specific publications with a very strong peer review process. Conference proceedings report faster-moving updates and findings but are still mostly peer-reviewed. Magazines usually have to sell many copies and are typically lightly reviewed, if at all, so be more careful about quoting information from them. If you're looking on the Web for information, make sure that you evaluate the quality of what you find (determining who wrote it and why, and based on what information?). Advertising should be sparingly used, and rarely quoted.

Don't limit your information gathering to written sources. Instead make sure you talk about your topic and project to as many people as will listen, including friends and family, course mates, your Supervisor, your Special Interest Group, library staff, and maybe some outside experts in the field. You may also gain some new insights by constructing a questionnaire and carrying out a survey.

You can structure your Literature Survey as an essay (telling a story), or as a bibliography (explaining each piece of literature), or split into the topics that make up your subject area. Ensure that you critically analyse each of your references, and show how this relates to your project.

Referencing your work (in the format agreed with your supervisor) is the most important thing of all. It acts as a catalogue of all your information sources, and is a key component in helping you avoid academic misconduct such as plagiarism.

We have thought about how to write the literature survey, and have stressed the importance of properly referencing other people's work. With your literature survey complete, you should know how your particular project fits into the bigger scheme of things, and this should help you to focus on your own individual work with renewed enthusiasm.

20. SUCCESSFUL PROJECT PLANNING

In Chapter 17, we looked at the importance of setting your Title, Aims and Objectives. These were then used to help write your Initial Report (Chapter 18) and to guide your Literature Survey (Chapter 19), which may or may not have been part of the same document. In this chapter we look at how to develop the Aims and Objectives into a fully thought-out project plan, which will help you to carry it out successfully, and will aid enormously in communicating your ideas to other people, and in documenting your thought processes for the final report.

20.1 Turning Objectives into Tasks

The plan you have written down, in the form of your Title, Aims and Objectives, can change. You have the right to change it; it is your project. But for now, at least you have a *plan*. Section 17.3 described the sequential questioning process that gets you from your vague topic idea, to a firm Title with a supporting Aim (or Aims), and in turn helps you to identify a series of Objectives. Something magical begins happening now in your brain. You will find that you begin applying the same sort of questioning process to each of your Objectives – except that the focus is no longer on the whole project, but instead just on one of the key components.

Allow yourself to focus on each of your Objectives, one at a time, forgetting temporarily about all the rest. Take yourself through the process of asking, "Exactly what do you mean by that?" If you do not know the answer – write down at least how you *propose to find out* (e.g., ask your supervisor, email an expert, phone up a local contact, brainstorm the idea with your fellow students, do a web-search etc.).

The human brain has been shown to work well with lists of 7 items or fewer (Miller, 1994). So, try to limit the number of objectives to no more than 7, at least for now, and also limit the number of sub-objectives. We seem to be able to focus on a sub-list of items, as long as they are sensibly grouped together. So, keep on working on your objectives, and sub-objectives, until you have quite a detailed plan of what to do.

To see how this might work in practice, let's take our example from Section 17.6, and break down Objective no. 1 as follows:

1. Survey literature and web to establish existing methods of making music on computers for people with limited movement.

    1.1 Brainstorm main subject areas to establish keywords.

    1.2 Visit library to identify main journals and books on the subject.

    1.3 Web-search on the topics identified in the brainstorm.

    1.4 Build up a database of contacts (inc. web-based newsgroups).

    1.5 Write up literature survey.

Already the original objective is turning into a more definite, ordered plan. We've gone from a single action phrase "Survey literature and web" to five, more specific ones ("Brainstorm", "Visit library", "Web-search", "Build database", "Write survey"). However, none of these are what we might call 'Unit Actions'. A Unit Action is a task you can just get on with, one that doesn't really need any further explanation.

So, let's take the above list and *repeat* the process for each of the sub-objectives.

1. Survey literature and web to establish existing methods of making music on computers for people with limited movement.

    1.1 Brainstorm main subject areas to establish keywords:

        1.1.1 Jot down initial ideas

        1.1.2 Schedule a focus group session to discuss this

        1.1.3 Organise a supervision to discuss ideas

        1.1.4 Run ideas past my contact at the local special school.

    1.2 Visit library to identify main journals and books on the subject:

        1.2.1 Log on to library computer and perform search

        1.2.2 Book appointment with subject librarian

Managing Your Project

    1.2.3 Note down relevant journals

    1.2.4 Skimp-read all relevant journals and books from 1990.

    1.2.5 Photocopy relevant articles

    1.2.6 Borrow appropriate books

    1.2.6 Schedule time to read copied articles and books.

1.3 Web-search on the topics identified in the brainstorm:

    1.3.1 Fix amount of time willing to spend on this task

    1.3.2 Follow-up web links from photocopied journals.

1.4 Build up a database of contacts (inc. web-based newsgroups):

    1.4.1 List all author contacts from journals and books

    1.4.2 Ask supervisor for contacts and recommendations

    1.4.3 Expand this list – with further brainstorming.

1.5 Write up literature survey:

    1.5.1 Check suggested length & level of detail with supervisor

    1.5.2 Read previously submitted surveys (even in unrelated topics)

    1.5.3 Decide on main structure. Check with focus group

    1.5.4 Create reference list from journals, books, web etc.

    1.5.5 Schedule writing of the entire chapter.

2. Produce and analyse a questionnaire aimed at practitioners in the fields of music, computers and disability to find out what new equipment is needed.

Etc. etc.

You may notice that new ideas have started to emerge as part of this process. Many of those individual tasks are simple activities, which you can schedule in your planner to do at a certain time, or put on your Action Lists to do at the appropriate time and place.

Hopefully you can see from this that the art of creating a detailed project plan involves thinking about things in gradually greater detail. If you can find a way to help your brain focus on one particular sub-topic, it will usually reward you by coming up with questions, breakdowns, ideas and solutions *at that level*. However, if you try to address the whole picture, it is simply too complicated and you may get confused and daunted.

To summarise:

- Write down what you *know*,
- List what you *don't* know yet but need to,
- Work on one sub-section at a time and break it down into further sub-topics.

20.2 Project storyboarding

The concept of storyboarding comes from the film industry. Writers and directors need to have a very detailed outline of the story before they allocate resources to filming, locations, actors and crew. A typical film storyboard consists of a series of sketched drawings that show the key points of the action in a film or animation. This is not a frame-by-frame plan of every detail, just the important events that mark out the story of the film. Usually each drawing is on a small card, and these are pinned to a board for all to see, hence the term *storyboard*.

A similar concept can be used to help you to plan your project, by sketching out the main points of action that you anticipate in the project. There is one key difference between its use in the film industry and in project planning. A director knows that the film must eventually bring to life *all* the cards on the board (i.e., the story must conclude by the end of the film). In your project, however, you do not yet know how long it will take to do each section, so you cannot assume that you will complete all the sections *and* do everything well! The project storyboard instead allows you to think about all the things that *could* be done in your project, and to place them in a sensible order. This concept acknowledges that at some point you *will* run out of time. If you are working to a well-organised storyboard, you will have done your best to tackle items in a sensible order, and what is left incomplete becomes 'further work'.

So, the act of putting together a storyboard can help you to build a coherent project plan. You may be worried about using such an idea because you are not yet confident about what the major components of the project are, and more importantly in what order they should be carried out. Yet, if you ask some simple questions, you will realise that you already possess a common-sense approach to the ordering of a project. Can you carry out testing before you've built a prototype product? No, so this tells you that 'testing' needs to come after 'building'. Does design happen

Managing Your Project

before building? Yes – so put it in its place.

Already with just those two 'obvious' questions, we can make a start at producing a storyboard (see Figure 20.1).

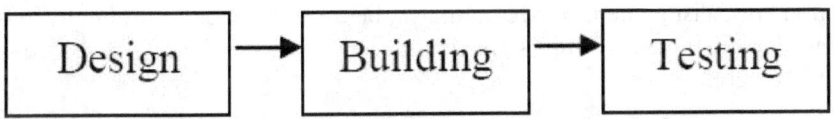

Figure 20.1 First stages of a storyboard

Now, this is so simple that it offers you nothing that you did not know before, but it *does* give you a written, graphical framework to explore, change and expand. After some more thought you might decide that rather than designing it all, *then* building it all, *then* testing it all, you may wish to split up the task into smaller chunks. You may also note that you need to do various things before you start designing. So you might come up with something like Figure 20.2.

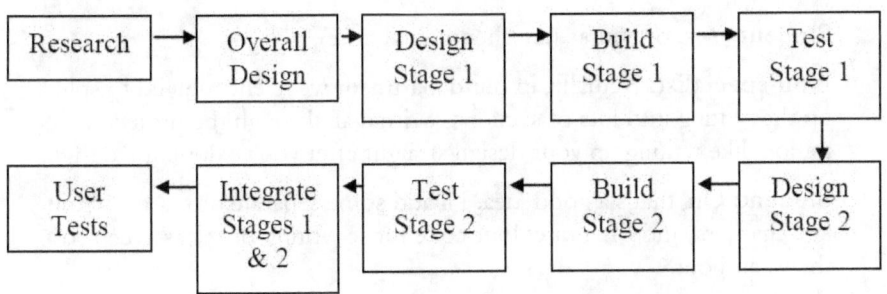

Figure 20.2 Evolution of the storyboard

Your particular project will probably look completely different to this, but all projects have stages and components – they are not a monolithic mass of work. The idea is to gradually flesh out the major components of the project, and place them in time order. Put as much information as you want into each box. Put sketches or pictures in the box if it helps you to visualise that stage. If a box becomes too complex, this probably indicates that you need to convert it into several small boxes, each of which contains a simpler task. Eventually your storyboard may occupy several pages. Keep going until you are happy that the major project components are in the correct order.

Andy Hunt

One of the great benefits of the storyboard is that allows you to discuss your detailed project flow with others. Because it puts onto paper your intended direction, you can get input from your Special Interest Group, your Supervisor, or anyone who will listen to you! In fact, sometimes a non-specialist is the best person to ask, because they point out the obvious, as demonstrated by this semi-fictitious discussion of the storyboard in Figure 20.2:

Non-specialist: So does your project *finish* with the User Tests then?

Student: Yes.

Non-specialist: Really? – don't you need to *analyse* the results?

Student: Oh yes, I'd have to do *that* (makes a mental note to enlarge the storyboard)

Non-specialist: What about writing it up? Do you have to do a write-up?

Student: Of course.

Non-specialist: Won't that take time? Could it go in here? (pointing to end of storyboard)

Student: Yes, of course (another mental note).

Non-specialist: Actually, in our department we're encouraged to split up the writing into lots of sections, written all through the project period, like writing up your design straight after you've done the design.

Student: Oh, that's a good idea. I'll add some separate boxes for writing key chapters, and I might colour code those writing boxes as green so they stand out.

Non-specialist: Why do you have *two* separate phases?

Student: Er- well, I just *have*. (maybe some more thinking needs to be done)

etc.

Every so often, pretend that you are someone who knows nothing about the project. Work through the storyboard from the beginning and jot down anything you think is wrong or missing. You may find that you add completely new sections that were simply forgotten in an earlier version.

Your final storyboard may end up being very detailed with lots of individual steps. Equally, it may represent the project with a few items that outline the main phases. See what develops as the best choice for you and your project. Many people like to add images, or "artists' impressions" of

Managing Your Project

what the project will look like at each stage, or a flowchart of how the interim project stage will work, or what it will contain.

Actually constructing the storyboard can be done in many ways:

- **Single-sheet of paper**: Sketch out the whole flow on one page. This is simple and direct, but messy and time-wasting as soon as you need to make changes.

- **Cards**: Put each item on a postcard. These can be laid out on a table, or pinned to a board like the traditional film storyboards. This provides a direct physical way of moving ideas around, but if you drop the set of cards you have lost your order!

- **Word-processor**: Simply type each item on a new line. You can use bullet-points or indentation to indicate a series of activities that make up an item. This is very quick, and easy to edit, but lacks some of the visual and spatial appeal of storyboards.

- **Computer Slide-show**: One of the best tools for storyboarding is a standard presentation package, such as Microsoft PowerPoint or Apple Keynote, which allows you to prepare text and images in a slideshow for presentations. Each item on your storyboard goes on one slide. It is straightforward to type in text, and add graphics to illustrate a point. Using the 'slide overview' feature you can easily drag slides around to change the ordering. You can then print out the slide overview to give you a paper version of the storyboard with several slides (items) on each page. An added bonus is that you can put it into 'slide presentation' mode and make a simple presentation of your project idea to your focus group or supervisor, for example.

At the end of the storyboarding process, whichever method you have chosen, you should have a list of the most important phases and sub-phases of the project – in the right order. You have not *promised* to get them all done, and you have not said *how long* each phase will take, but you now have an overall plan which is visible to other people. Now we need to think about how to formalise and refine this plan, and a good way to start this process is by deciding what makes a successful project.

20.3 Criteria for success

It is important to think about how your progress can be monitored for several reasons:

- For your own peace of mind, you need to know how the project is progressing towards your desired aim. If time is slipping, you can take corrective action, such as renegotiating the objectives with your supervisor.

- Other people (such as your supervisor or an external funding body) have a concern about how your work is progressing, so you need a way of reporting progress to them.

- It is the essence of any Manager's role to be aware of the current state of progress. Each time you review your project, you need to know *where you are*, so that you can chart *what needs to be done* to get you to *where you want to be*. (Try reading that sentence again, as it's the essence of good regular management!).

Therefore, it is advisable for a project to have a series of targets to meet. In Chapter 21 – Detailed Time & Project Planning, we consider in more detail the use of time-planning tools to set schedules, and to place targets on a measurable time-line. But first, let's concentrate more on the factors you will use to judge your own progress. These factors are often referred to as criteria for success. In other words:

- How will you know that a chunk of your project has been achieved?

- What exactly would need to happen for you to 'tick off' an objective as *done*?

- What makes a successful objective?

The distinction between an objective and a *successful* objective is subtle, so here is an example to clarify it. You may have written down an objective which says "hand-in initial report". So surely if you hand in your initial report, you have achieved your objective? Well, not if it was handed in *late*. Not if it gets a *fail* mark. Not if it's rushed and insubstantial so that it doesn't actually *help* you to push the project forward. So, maybe the criteria for success (the things that will make it an excellent report) are more complex. Here is an example list of criteria drawn up to define what a successful outcome of 'handing in the initial report' might look like:

- It is handed in **on time** (so, specify the deadline here).

- It meets the **specification** in your departmental handbook (specify the details here – e.g., number of pages, topics covered, referencing style).

- It is **understandable** in detail by a member of your focus group (specify how and when you will get a statement to that effect from a member of your group).

- The main aims are understandable by a **non-expert person** (specify how and when you will get such a statement from, for example, a member of your family).

- It gets a **good mark** (detail the criteria the marker - usually your supervisor - wants to see in an initial report, and schedule when you are going to proofread it prior to hand-in).

- It forms a **'springboard'** for the work that is to follow (imagine yourself sitting down with your report, ready to work on the project. What sorts of things will be written down in order for the report to help you start work on the project details?).

Note how each of the above criteria will cause you to do *extra work* (read a handbook, note down specifications, proofread the document according to those specifications, schedule in time before the deadline to get feedback from focus group and external people, etc.), and that is precisely the point!

If you think about each of your objectives in detail, considering what would make them excellent, you will end up with more work to do. However, this extra work improves the quality and value of what you produce. As a by-product, the whole thinking process supporting the project will become more rigorous. The characteristics which make a successful project will take place, simply because you have thought about them and have taken action to ensure they get done.

Compare the detailed criteria we just listed above with the original specification ("hand in initial report") and you get a good idea of the extra depth of thinking required to produce a smoothly running project. Most people don't bother with this extra work. Most people don't get top marks and a feeling of great satisfaction of a job well done.

Each of your main objectives should be analysed in this way; to establish what a 'successful outcome' would be like. Make sure that you schedule time in your Calendar to ensure that the required actions are carried out.

20.4 Establishing Key Deliverables

Now that you have established what would constitute the successful completion of each objective, it is useful to list the *deliverables* that will occur as part of the work towards that objective. A deliverable is simply something concrete that you produce. Typical deliverables are:

- **Reports** e.g., initial report, final report, literature survey, questionnaire summary, project web-page
- **Products** e.g., computer code, or a piece of hardware
- **Presentations** e.g., concert performance, or talk to an audience.

In other words, a deliverable is typically something you show or 'deliver' to other people. It is important to identify your deliverables, and build them into your schedule. Sometimes other people will give you fixed deadlines for certain deliverables, and for others you will need to set your own time-limits. We discuss this in more detail in following sections.

20.5 From Objectives to Work Packages

If you are dealing with a complex project, or a funding application, you may wish to formalise everything we have said so far by converting your objectives and your Project Storyboard into a series of Work Packages. What is presented here is simply a suggestion of how you might do this. You should customise the procedure to your own situation, but this is a reasonable model to start with.

We will assume that by now you have the following:

- A Title
- A main Aim
- An ordered list of Objectives to reach that aim
- Several levels of Tasks which constitute each objective
- Criteria for Success for each objective
- A list of key Deliverables associated with each objective
- Some idea of the overall flow of the project (e.g., a Storyboard).

Let's now produce a set of Work Packages – one for each Objective – which will encapsulate the project work to be done in well-defined chunks. Each package will take the form outlined in Figure 20.3, but you are encouraged to edit this into something appropriate for your type of project.

Managing Your Project

Work Package <number> : <name>

Objective:

Overview:

Main tasks:

Key Deliverables:

Criteria for success:

Figure 20.3 Template for a Work Package

Each work package has a *number*, and it is useful to give it a *name* (such as 'research work', or 'implementation') to tag briefly its main function.

The *Objective* is listed next, and this is taken directly from the major objective you have already written (see Chapter 17 - *Title, Aims & Objectives*).

This is followed by a descriptive *overview*, which outlines in plain language the focus of the work that needs to be done to carry out the objective.

Next are listed the *main tasks*, which come from the breakdown of the objective into smaller, more precisely defined, work elements (as we saw above in Section 20.1). You may list as many levels of your task hierarchy as you think are appropriate here.

Finally you list the *key deliverables* and the *criteria for success* associated with this objective.

Taking up again the example we worked with in Chapter 17, we can now build up an example work package based on the first objective (see Figure 20.4).

Note how in the *main tasks* section, not all the levels of task breakdown have been entered. How much detail you put in here is a matter of judgement, but your main concern should be that the work package looks clear and coherent.

> **Work Package 1:** *Research*
>
> **Objective:** Survey literature and web to establish existing methods of making music on computers for people with limited movement.
>
> **Overview:** This work-package launches the project by investigating available literature, both in written form and on the web, and establishing a list of the main contacts that can be followed up later.
>
> **Main tasks:**
>
> 1.1 Brainstorm main subject areas to establish keywords.
>
> 1.2 Visit library to identify main journals and books in the subject.
>
> 1.3 Web-search on the topics identified in the brainstorm.
>
> 1.4 Build up a database of contacts (incl. web-based newsgroups).
>
> 1.5 Write up literature survey.
>
> **Key Deliverables:**
>
> - Database of contacts
> - Literature Survey
>
> **Criteria for success:**
>
> ☐ Supervisor has approved draft report by October 20th
>
> ☐ Tick-sheets filled in, approving final draft in all main categories (readability, coherent plan, grammar & style) by two proof-readers: a subject specialist & a non-specialist.
>
> ☐ Literature Survey handed in by November 11th.

Figure 20.4 An example Work Package

Consider the lower-level subtasks of the type we developed in in Section 20.1:

> 1.2.1 Log on to library computer and perform search
>
> 1.2.2 Book appointment with subject librarian
>
> 1.2.3 Note down relevant journals

1.2.4 Skimp-read all relevant journals and books from 1990.

1.2.5 Photocopy relevant articles

1.2.6 Borrow appropriate books

1.2.7 Schedule time to read copied articles and books.

Maybe, if these were included, the impact of the work-package would actually be *reduced*. Note the irony here - that **putting in more information does not always aid clarity**. The human brain can only deal with a limited number of items in one 'sitting'. The phrase "You can't see the wood (forest) for the trees" speaks of too much detail actually preventing you from perceiving the higher-level structure. Use this knowledge, and some common sense, to make sure that your work packages appear *readable*, and coherent. The full detail can appear in your own personal Managerial plan, which is intended to help you get the job done and not necessarily to be shown to other people.

20.6 Relationship between Work Packages and Timing

Finally all the work packages can be pulled together into a larger section, sometimes known as a Work Plan. This would typically contain a general introduction to the work to be done, followed by the main Aim, the list of Objectives (top-level only), and then the Work Packages. Work plans nearly always go on to indicate the *timing* structure of the project, and that is what we will now consider in some detail in Chapter 21 - *Detailed Time & Project Planning*.

20.7 Summary

Once you have come up with a Title, Aim and Objectives, you can use these to help you come up with a more comprehensive project plan. Focus your attention on one Objective at a time, and break it down into a number of sub-tasks. Keep repeating this process until you reach a set of Unit Tasks – things which you can carry out in one 'sitting' and which require no further breakdown. Number your tasks and sub-tasks hierarchically, and now you should have a list of things to do. The list will be much longer than your list of Objectives, but each line should be easier to conceptualise and carry out. In the example in the chapter, you may find:

- Task 1.2.2 Book appointment with subject librarian,

easier to schedule and complete than:

- Task 1.2 Visit library to identify main journals and books on the subject,

which in turn is easier than:

- **Objective 1 Survey literature and web to establish existing methods of making music on computers for people with limited movement.**

Storyboards are a very good way to help you develop (and explain to others) the overall flow of your project. These can be created simply on paper, on postcards, or by using computer tools such as presentation packages. Each stage of the project goes on one card or slide, and the overall picture becomes the workflow of the project. They are useful because they allow you to construct and modify the order of the project's work, without having to worry about how long each stage will take.

For each main stage of your project it is helpful to establish the Criteria for Success. These are the things which will need to be true, in order for you to be able to 'tick off' this section as complete. It takes more work to think through in detail what is *really* meant by succeeding at an objective, but that extra thought and work will make it *much* more likely to happen. For each stage, it's essential that you identify the key 'Deliverables'. These are things you show or give to other people. Sometimes it is the outcome of a project stage that is needed by a subsequent stage.

You can then produce a professional project plan by constructing Work Packages. Each work package is focussed on one of your key Objectives. It brings together a statement of the Objective, and Overview of what's involved, a list of detailed Tasks needed to carry it out, a list of Deliverables and Criteria for Success.

20.8 External References

Miller GA (April 1994). "The magical number seven, plus or minus two: some limits on our capacity for processing information". Psychological Review 101 (2): 343–52. doi:10.1037/0033-295X.101.2.343

The original 1956 publication is available online here: http://psychclassics.yorku.ca/Miller/

21. DETAILED TIME & PROJECT PLANNING

In Chapters 10 through 15 we considered the issue of personal time management. Here we are considering *project* time management. It is important to note the difference. In personal time management, you are trying to organise *yourself*, and to manage all the activities which exist on several levels within your life. With *project* time management, you are focussing purely on completing your project, by charting the way that time is allocated to different phases. This section will help you through this process.

21.1 Establishing all external deadlines

Before we calculate timings for the project, it is vital to note down what external deadlines already exist. Here are some questions you might want to ask:

- When is your final report due in?
- What is the last date for submitting a particular proposal?
- Are there certain periods of the year when certain activities have to take place (e.g., weather-dependent field-trips, or the availability of collaborators)?
- Do you have regular meetings with your supervisor that can be scheduled now?
- Are there specific dates when you are to do presentations?

Build up a list of all the fixed timings for the lifetime of your project. Put these in your diary immediately if you haven't already done so. These are the major events that you need to work towards, and you cannot afford to forget. However, really good projects are driven from *within* and do not rely on external prompting.

21.2 Working backwards from fixed deadlines

This process is similar to that discussed in Section 14.10 - *Thinking backwards from an event*.

You should 'work backwards' from your fixed deadlines, to ensure that everything is ready ahead of schedule. You can do this by deciding on times that you will have completed specific things to make certain that the final deadline is met.

As an example, if your final report is due in 4 months' time, you can work out a specific schedule guaranteed to get it completed on time or ahead of time. There is probably something you can do about the report *right now* (see Chapter 24 - *Organising the Final Report* for some ideas). Make a list of all the sections of the report that need to be written. Try allocating deadlines to each section.

21.3 Working forward to allocate time

However, you should also work forward - allocating time sensibly for all the tasks in the Work Packages that you created in Chapter 20.

Inevitably you will have to compromise. There are various ways of handling the fact that you simply do not know how long each stage of the project will take. One of these is project Storyboarding, which is why Chapter 20 began by producing an ordered outline of tasks, without worrying too much about exactly how long each task was going to take.

In a typical project there are more tasks to do than you really have time for. So a good project plan will:

- contain a list of all major activities in the *order* in which they need to be carried out
- allocate these sensibly to the time available
- be flexible enough to change as the project develops.

Managing Your Project

21.4 Storyboard or time-chart

In a research project, it is often the Storyboard that turns out to be the most useful tool, because it helps you to concentrate on the logical *flow* of events that your project could address, rather than trying to predict accurately *how long* each section will take to complete. It is often better for a supervisor to receive a well-thought-out ordered list of tasks to be done, rather than a badly thought out time-based chart.

Imagine for a moment you are a supervisor and you receive Figure 21.1 from one student and Figure 21.2 from another.

- Literature Survey (4 weeks)

- End-user questionnaire (1 week)

- Analysis of results (1 day ?)

- First stage design process (1-2 weeks)

- Show to end-users: more feedback (A few weeks? not sure yet)

- Top-level software design (2 weeks ?)

- Software analysis: which package? (By end of term 1)

- Coding phase 1: Core algorithms (no idea; help please)

- Test phase for core algorithms (2 days maximum)

- Coding phase 2: Interface device handling (again, help)

- Test phase for interface algorithms (1 day ?)

Etc. etc.

Figure 21.1 Student project plan example A

Week no.	1	2	3	4	5	6	7	8	9	10	11	12	13	14	15	16	17	18	19
First stage	■	■	■	■															
Supervisons		■				■		■		■			■			■	■		
Coding					■	■	■	■	■	■	■	■	■	■	■				
Testing															■	■			
Report Writing																	■	■	■
Final Presentation																			■

Figure 21.2 Student project plan example B

Would you agree that there is something quite convincing about Plan B (Figure 21.2)?

"He's done a time-chart, so it must be ok!"

Maybe Plan A (Figure 21.1) looks a bit too undecided?

On closer inspection it becomes clear that there is more substance to the planning that has gone into Plan A compared with Plan B.

Plan A shows an ordered series of tasks, which demonstrates that the student has been thinking not only about the product, but how it is perceived by the end user. It has an honest list of durations, with question marks to show what is not yet decided, and direct calls for help to the supervisor (who might be able to offer some guidance as to how long these things tend to take). In summary this is a good start for a project plan, which looks as though it would be a good basis for a detailed discussion.

Plan B, by contrast, is accurate to the week number, and each phase seamlessly passes on to the next. Real-life tends to be neither time-accurate nor smooth. The student has also made the classic mistake of planning to write the report at the end of the project (see Chapter 24 - *Organising the Final Report*). There is also little indication that much thought has gone into *what* the project will actually do. Yet Plan B is the sort of plan most often submitted. It is a triumph of form over function. "We need a time-chart, so here is a time-chart", yet it would be of little actual use in the project.

However, there are many situations when you *have* identified all the phases and they simply *must* be done within a particular time-slot. This is where a time-chart becomes particularly useful, as it forces you to think about the relative proportion of time that each section of work should take. Remember though that if it turns out that things take longer, you will have a decision to make; do you reduce the number of phases you plan to get complete? Or do you still aim to get all the planned phases complete but cut down on your expectations, doing less within each phase, or doing it to a lower quality?

21.5 Creating a time-chart

Many software packages exist to help you manage your project, and these include a wealth of sophisticated features including time-charting. However, they cannot actually do the project *thinking* for you. There is no substitute for sorting out your Aims and Objectives, finding out what has already been done, placing the work into a logical order, and carrying this out effectively by managing your own time.

The most common form of time-chart is the Gantt chart (named after its inventor Henry Gantt). A Gantt chart is a table of information that uses word descriptions of tasks (arranged vertically in time-order), and graphical representations of the time which each task is meant to occupy (on a horizontal scale). The ideal Gantt chart takes up a single sheet of paper, and shows the entire project timeline in a single view. However, for bigger projects they can be made extremely complex.

The act of constructing a Gantt chart forces you to ask certain questions about each and every major task:

- Roughly when in the project time should this task occur?
- Are there other tasks that need to be done *before* it can be started?
- Does this completion of this task naturally lead on to other tasks?
- How long should it take to complete?

If you have put a good deal of thought into a project storyboard, you will probably already have a good idea about the answers to the first three of these questions. The last is always the hardest to answer, and is the precise reason why any form of time-charting is only ever going to be a good guess. However, it is a very useful tool for managing your project because you can always use it to compare what is *actually* going on with what you *thought* should have been going on.

Figure 21.3 shows a typical Gantt chart, produced using Microsoft Project software, following through the ideas presented in Plan A.

Notice the following features:

- The tasks are listed in a column, working downwards in time order.
- The horizontal blocks represent the time allocated for each task.
- Relationships have been added, where one task 'feeds into' the next.
- Some tasks take place independently of the others.

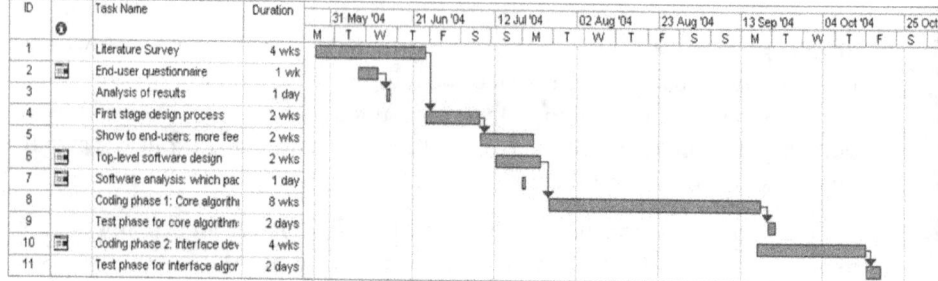

Figure 21.3 Gantt chart taken from Plan A

It would be possible to expand on this Gantt chart by adding the following features:

- **Deadlines** (e.g., initial report, final report, presentations)
- **Milestones** (things you really want to have happened by a certain time)
- **Work Packages** (If you have developed these, you can have tasks grouped together, but linked to an appropriate Work Package).

21.6 Being realistic about what time you have

When you write '3 weeks' on your chart, make sure that you know what that really means for you in terms of working hours. Is this a full-time project where you are sure you will be working 40-hour weeks? Even if it is, how many of those 40 hours are *really* productive? Or, maybe you have other commitments in your studies or your home-life which mean that each week has only 10 hours in which to work. Being honest about the number of hours you actually have available will help you estimate how long things should take. This is easier, of course, if you have done this sort of task before, because you can infer from your previous experience how long the new task should take. Otherwise you might want to ask other people for advice.

Alternatively, you can take the approach of simply setting the time, and doing what you *can* within that time. This is particularly useful for more open-ended tasks such as 'testing' or 'editing', where you might never finish to a perfect standard. In these situations why not set a time-limit, and then stop work when the time runs out? Ask for outside help if you are unsure, but make sure you have first had a go yourself before asking someone else for advice.

21.7 Summary

It is important to have an overall plan of the timings for your project. Firstly, make a complete list of all external deadlines for your project (dates when reports are due in, times when collaborators are available etc.). Then work backwards from those deadlines to produce your own set of 'internal' deadlines, making sure these times are clearly visible to you in a project planner or Calendar. Then plan 'forwards', allocating time for tasks that you have identified in your Work Packages (see Chapter 20).

Time-charts (such as Gantt charts) are classically associated with Project Management, yet sometimes a more flexible Storyboard is a more appropriate planning tool.

Gantt charts specifically help you to focus on the passing of time and the major fixed deadlines in a project. They also help you to think about the time relationships between your tasks (such as Task 8 needs to be completed before Task 9 can start, whereas Tasks 6 and 7 can be carried out simultaneously.) Make an estimate about how long each item in the time-chart will take to complete. Estimates get better with practice, so you may choose to seek some advice from people who have seen or done these sorts of tasks before.

At this stage of the project, you should have a storyboard (or at least a list) of key events in your project, in the *order* in which they need to occur. You may have worked these into a Work Plan which includes packages of related tasks, or you may be content with a single task list. At each stage you should know what would make a successful outcome. You should also have some idea of how you are going to spend your time on the project, and what is to be produced at each stage. You may have this all summarised on a time-chart, which you can use to monitor and manage the project as it progresses.

SECTION 5
COMMUNICATION – WRITING AND SPEAKING ABOUT YOUR WORK

Your project, however brilliant, is no good to anyone else if it just remains in your head. You have to find ways of communicating your ideas, plans and results to other people. This section helps you to communicate with others more clearly, and with the reader/listener in mind. It breaks down the process into the following sections.

- **Ch. 22 Structuring Your Communication** – *because most project students find it quite difficult to write an effective report and speak about their project*. This is usually because not enough thought has been given to the point of view of the reader or listener. This chapter explains the importance of logical flow, setting the context, and focussing on a specific audience. It also considers your everyday communications and how to get the most out of them.

- **Ch. 23 Giving Presentations** - *describing your project effectively by talking about it to other people*. Though many say that Public Speaking is their worst fear, it's an important part of communicating your project plans and results, and is often a key part of the project process. This chapter guides you through the process of planning and presenting a talk to an audience, and explains why it's a superb way of organising your thoughts.

- **Ch. 24 Organising the Final Report** - *the most important part of your project*. This chapter gives some good and bad examples of planning and writing your final report. It's a major undertaking, and needs to be given high priority in your planning. Guidance is offered here about how to start, how to write regularly, and how to cope if you are running short of time.

- **Ch. 25 Writing Style and Format** - *how the report should be actually written*. Although each subject and department will have its own guidelines, this chapter takes you through some common considerations that all project authors should think about when writing their final report.

22. STRUCTURING YOUR COMMUNICATION

Most of the things we've discussed so far in this book relate to an internal dialogue that takes place in your head and as you plan. This chapter concerns the external communications that will occur during the project, as you interact with other people. Chapter 5 - *The Supervision Process* has already considered the key communication path in any project - that between student and supervisor. So, in this chapter we discuss a range of insights into the communication process in general, to ensure that you are aware of how others might view what you write and say. This leads to some specific hints about how to structure your phone calls, emails, presentations and documents.

22.1 Other people's mind-sets

There is a time in most children's development when it suddenly dawns on them that not everyone sees the world through their eyes. In other words, at some point we gradually realise that we're not the centre of the entire universe, though it feels to us as if we are. Even in adulthood we often see a particular situation only from our own perspective. Actually, everyone else is seeing a different view and thinking unique thoughts. Every person's brain has built up its own way of viewing, listening to and interpreting the world. Two people may look at the same space yet see completely different things. This may seem a very philosophical discussion to be having at this point, but it is at the very core of the art of communication. Successful communication bridges the gap between one person's view of the world and another's.

22.2 Revealing information logically

Imagine that someone said to you:

> "The banana is brighter in colour, and therefore it should score higher than the fish. However the burger is hidden within its packaging, so you have only your knowledge of the advertising to tell you what is actually inside. The can doesn't feature as I have implied that you are hungry."

Would you have any idea what that person was talking about? It sounds rather like the ramblings of someone whose mind is altered by various chemicals. Imagine now that you heard the following preamble, leading up to the same words:

> "Welcome. This is the third session in our series of lectures looking at the health issues surrounding food in the western world. Today we study the effect of food packaging and advertising on the choices that people make when confronted with several, visually different, alternative foods. Let's start with a rather artificial exercise. On the desk in front of me, I have laid out some examples of different food types that clearly look distinctive. We have a banana, a can of fish, a burger in a cardboard container, and a can of fizzy drink. Imagine that you come into the room and are hungry. I'm going to ask you to choose just one item, but you only have 2 seconds to do this. Choose now, 1, 2, STOP. Hands up if you chose the burger? The banana? The fish? Interesting – most of you went for the burger. Do you know that if you were *reading* this most of you would go for the banana? Somehow, your visual system is influencing the choice. So, how did your visual system and brain handle this? Well, suppose your eyes and brain have a 'points' system to rank the items. **The banana is brighter in colour, and therefore it should score higher than the fish. The burger is hidden within its packaging, so you have only your knowledge of the advertising to tell you what is actually inside. The can doesn't feature as I have implied that you are hungry** not thirsty. ..."

Whatever you thought of the fictitious lecture, did you find that the second extract flowed better? Notice that the exact same text at the end (the words in bold, which initially seemed rather bizarre when seen out of context) made reasonable sense when your brain had been given the correct 'cues'.

If we analyse what your brain was saying when it first read the original paragraph, it would probably look something like this:

Paragraph: The banana ...

Your brain: What banana? Who *are* you and *what* are you talking about?

Managing Your Project

Paragraph: ...is brighter in colour..

Your brain: brighter than *what*? I still don't know *which* banana you're talking about, and now you're comparing it with some *other* object I don't even know about. And I *still* don't know why I'm listening to you anyway.

Paragraph: ...and therefore it should score higher than the fish.

Your brain: Now come on – you're just having a laugh! Even if I knew *which* banana you meant, are you now saying that because it is *brighter* than some other, as yet undescribed object, it scores more *points* (in some, as yet unspecified competition) than a *fish* which has just popped out of your mind? And who *are* you anyway? This is too hard. All this talk of food is making me hungry. Now, what shall I have for tea? Now I *should* have some fruit but I *have* got that half-eaten burger from yesterday . . .

And thus another student switches off in a lecture before the first sentence is complete!

Actually, keeping people awake when teaching is another issue altogether. But at least a lecturer who follows the second paragraph would have a chance of engaging with the audience. Let us consider how this was achieved:

- It reminded the listeners of where they were (third in a lecture series)
- It stated the overall topic (health issues relating to western food)
- It stated the purpose of this particular communication (choices and adverts)
- It then used a visual example (bananas etc. on a table)
- It used audience interaction (making a real choice)

etc. etc.

In other words, because everyone comes to a lecture with a different mind-set, it makes sense to reveal the context in a logical order. This gives every listener's brain a chance to catch up with and process what the lecturer is trying to say.

Peter Thomson (1994) describes how the brain is like a computer filing system, which needs prompting to open each file. A good piece of communication will provide prompts for the listener to 'open the appropriate file' in their heads.

So, for example, if you have been struggling with a piece of computer code, and you decide to see the lecturer or teacher concerned, it would be best ***not*** to jump straight in like this:

Student: <*knocks on lecturer's door without an appointment*>

Lecturer: <*Sighing, as the grant application is put aside yet again*> Come in!

Student: Hi – I've got a problem with this bit of code <*pointing to it*>. It won't do what I want. What's wrong with it?

Lecturer: Wait a moment, remind me; which course are you on . . . ?

This understandable 'diving in' on the part of the student happens often, and occurs because the student's brain is highly focussed on the problem. The lecturer, in contrast, is still thinking about her own work, and (as you can tell from the above dialogue) is not even sure who this student is.

22.3 Your starting-point is not theirs

So, people get confused if you just 'dive in'. This applies to students talking to lecturers, just as much as it applies to lecturers delivering material to students. But it is also true for everyday conversations. Have you ever stopped someone in mid-conversational flow and said, "I'm sorry, but I have absolutely *no* idea what you're talking about"?

People typically do not think about the point of view of the person they are talking to. So, when you start talking to someone, make a point of helping their brain to catch up with yours, by setting the context.

Let's return to our student with the coding problem. Maybe this next encounter would be more productive?

Student: <*knocks on lecturer's door*>

Lecturer: <*Sighing, as the grant application is put aside yet again*> Come in.

Student: Hi – my name's Michael, and I emailed you earlier?

Lecturer: Ah yes, I remember. I asked you to call round.

Student: Yes, thanks. I'm on the second year computing course unit, and we've got the flight control assignment to do. It's due in at the end of the week but I've got stuck with one section and don't know how to move forward.

Lecturer: Ok, do you have a print-out of your code with you?

Student: Yes, here it is. Ok, so there are three main sections: <*pointing to the code*> the stored data, the incoming flight data, and the processing algorithm. My problem is in the processing stage. It's around here <*pointing to the general area*>. This particular section should combine the stored data with the incoming data, but I don't think it's working.

Lecturer: Which bit in particular do you think isn't working? . . .

etc.

In this second example, the student implicitly acknowledges that the lecturer has been concentrating on something else, by reminding him of the context ("my name's Michael, and I emailed you earlier?"). The rising pitch indicated by the question mark is subtle, but important. It's a polite way of saying 'remember'? And of course as soon as the lecturer remembers, half the battle is won. The lecturer temporarily puts aside the grant application and now needs to know what the problem is. The student now sets the context brilliantly by declaring which course he is on and which assignment the problem concerns. This 'opens' these topics in the lecturer's mind, and Michael now explains his situation ("due in at the end of the week but I've got stuck with one section"). The process continues, and the encounter is focussed and creative.

How could you plan to improve your next communication so that the listener/reader is more prepared and therefore follows what you are saying?

22.4 Different forms of direct communication

Having considered how to reveal information to the person you are communicating with, we now take a brief look at the ways in which you might actually perform the act of communication. In the next sections, we compare the use of email with phone calls and visits (both unplanned and pre-arranged).

22.4.1 Email

Most people in a college or university use email extensively. Members of staff will use it every day as part of their jobs, and so will be carefully monitoring it (although you will discover that different people have varying rates of response when sent a message!). The best thing about email is that you do not actually disturb anyone's thought process by sending it[3].

---

[3] Actually, if they *are* disturbed by your incoming message going "ding" and they stop work to answer it, this is at least their *choice*. I turn off all email sounds, and respond to incoming messages only when I am ready. This means that emails

People tend to read their email when they are ready to do so, or when they just need a break. The main point is that they are actively *expecting* new messages and new information. This is a good state for your recipient to be in when you wish to initiate a communication. You might be able to carry out the entire process by email (e.g., a request for information, a summary report, or a question about an assignment etc.). However, you can also use an email to arrange a phone conversation if needed, or to meet in person.

Therefore, if in doubt – *start the communication process with an email.*

If you get no reply, don't be afraid to send a copy a few days later. Sometimes emails get accidentally deleted, or removed by filters, so politely point out that you sent an email a while ago and that you have taken the liberty of sending it again. You might want to check that you are providing sensible message 'subjects'.

Consider the following emails arriving in your Inbox. Imagine you were a lecturer (receiving over 100 messages per day) and you were trying to prioritise your Inbox. Which ones would you delete without opening?

From	Subject	Size
Druggy005@aol.com	Cheap drugs BUY IT NOW	15KB
DittyBoy	help me	2.4MB
Henry James		3KB
Michael Connor	2nd Year Flight Control assignment enquiry	7KB
Helen T. Robbetts	Sell your endowment policies today	16KB

Most people would *only* open Michael Connor's message because it had a clearly relevant subject line. Poor Henry James is a first year student (whom the lecturer isn't familiar with yet) who has put no subject message

---

do not interrupt me, and they are therefore less disturbing.

in his desperate email about exam problems, so it is promptly deleted as if it were SPAM. And what about Jim Fisher, the 3rd year who needs to talk to you about his urgent financial problems? You never received his email? Or does he unfortunately use the 'fun' alias-name DittyBoy, and the emotional but completely unhelpful 'help me' in the subject line, and a suspiciously large attachment which makes it look like a typical SPAM appeal?

We will return to the content of the email in the next major section 'Asking people for help'.

22.4.2 Telephone

For some communication tasks telephoning is a much better way of getting in touch. People in certain types of job (such as receptionists, secretaries, personal assistants, journalists etc.) treat incoming phone calls with top priority. Others are best contacted by phone, as they carry it with them everywhere but rarely check email. You also have the satisfaction of having spoken to 'a real person' and thus have some feeling of how successful the communication has been.

However, there are many downsides, including the following (fictitious) responses:

- "I'm sorry but he is in a meeting at the moment. He might be free in about twenty minutes, if you wanted to wait, but the meeting may run on"

- "Welcome to the automated menu service. I will now automatically take up an unspecified amount of your time, and give you a list of services which do not cover the reason for your call. If this is ok, please press 1 now..."

- "Er – hello – I can't talk right now as I'm in a meeting. <*whispering*> Sorry Jean, it's a student of mine. Er, can I call you back? Better still, call my PA and he will take a message"

In other words you cannot guarantee that the person will be available to talk, and you need to be prepared to wait, leave messages, call back later, or use another form of communication. You are also disturbing that person's current work-flow, and it is advisable to minimise this disruption where possible. This is the reason for the suggestion to email *first* where possible (which also gives you a written record of the communication), *then* arrange to speak on the phone at a given time if you need to discuss things more interactively.

For the person who 'lives in their phone' a text (SMS) message can be a good way of getting a non-interactive message to them. Remember though that if you need to track or remember the response, they are likely to send a text message back, and you need to make sure that you are set up to receive and respond to this.

22.4.3 'Dropping in'

Please think twice (or more) before making a random call to someone's office door. You will either find them:

- Not there
- Busy in a meeting (which you have just interrupted)
- On the telephone (which is awkward to leave to answer the door)
- Working on something else.

In other words you are almost *guaranteed* to be interrupting the person you want help from, and almost certain to find them in a mental state *not* conducive to answering your problem. When you are on the receiving end of such a visit it is rather frustrating when the visitor looks around the room and (even if it's full of people) says "sorry – are you busy?", or "is this a good time to see you?" The true answers to these questions are "Yes, I *am* busy" or "No, by definition, this is *not* a good time to visit"[4].

Use email instead to *arrange* a visit, which you are both then expecting, and which will be much more constructive as a consequence.

22.5 Social Media

A huge change has occurred in the world of computer communications over the last few years. There has been a blossoming of short conversations occurring through various social media sites, such as Twitter and Facebook, and 'chat' or 'messaging' apps.

It's been interesting to notice a bit of a gap opening up between the first generation of computer users (such as myself) - who have let computers slowly into our lives - and the new generation (today's students) who have

---

[4] The exception to this rule is if the person is known to operate an 'open-door' policy, where dropping in is actively encouraged, maybe in a particular time-slot. In such a situation there is still no disadvantage with making the first contact by email, saying "Is it ok for me to drop round at 3.30, to talk about . . . ?"

Managing Your Project

been born into a computer-savvy world.

The main difference seems to be that the older generation still use traditional methods of communication (such as writing letters) but in computer form. So, we use email to send long communications full of information, and large attachments laid out like a magazine, business brief, or a structured assignment. In contrast, the younger generation appears to be more concerned with short, interactive messaging between large numbers of people.

It's not an insurmountable barrier, but it's worth considering how to bridge the gap, and what are the advantages and disadvantages of both modes of working.

22.5.1 Facebook

Many people have adopted Facebook as their main method of communication. What seems to have encouraged this was the integration with smartphones in the late 2000s. The seamless blending of text messaging (SMS) and Facebook chat, for instance, meant that people could text on their phones and the messages might get an instant response, or might be stored for later retrieval either on a phone or on a computer when they logged into Facebook. And that's when a lot of people *stopped* regularly checking email. People who work in an email culture find it hard when some people they need to contact are NOT checking their email, but are always checking their Facebook account.

The following advice has been collected and from the personal experiences of many students who have shared their communication woes. I'm aware this sounds like advice from an old fashioned 'internet dinosaur' who remembers the web being *invented*, but social media has caused quite a few problems for students, as well as being part of the fabric of their lives:

- think carefully about what you really *mean* by 'friends'; don't just collect friends as trophies in their hundreds and thousands.

- be careful about what you share - I know many people who are haunted by what they posted when drunk, and have lost jobs because their boss read it all. You *do* know that interviewers look you up on Facebook to see what you're actually like, don't you?

- restrict your use - social media can be a huge time-waster when you have other things to do. At times it can even become a burden, as people expect you to instantly respond[5]. You don't need to be "on" all the time.

- minimise its use for work, apart from the suggestion below about Groups.

- retain a regular (daily as a minimum) check of your email - because at least for the next few years the people supervising, assessing and marking your work will come from an email culture. Email is direct, storable, scalable (you can send to one or many) and forms part of the organisational fabric of higher-education institutions. Ignore it at your peril. You have been warned.

22.5.2 Social Media Groups for Discussions

Many of my students have found - for the sort of discussion and sharing that happens naturally as part of their Special Interest Groups - that a Facebook *Group* page is well suited. It allows people to chat on various sub-topics and the membership can be set to 'closed' so that you are not broadcasting to the world. It has built-in features for arranging events and meetings, and can easily synchronise with people's calendars.

To keep things completely clear, as a supervisor I never join these groups. This allows students to chat away without somehow fearing that I am 'watching over' or 'grading' these discussions.

What I *do* set up and join is a Google Group. Chapter 9 (and specifically section 9.9) describes the different options for managing Special Interest Group discussions over email, web-sites or social media groups. A Google Group allows everyone to set their own mode of interaction (e.g., access to discussions from a web-page only; getting a daily 'digest' of discussions by email, or receiving every email as soon as it is posted).

As mentioned before, it is best that anything to do with *organising* or *managing* (arranging meetings, specific questions to your supervisor, deadlines & assignments etc.) is handled by email. Leave the Groups as a

---

[5] One of my students was totally distracted in an important group supervision – constantly checking her phone and tapping away on it. I asked if she needed to leave to sort out something important. For some reason, she actually showed me the screen with a message from one of her 750 friends who had messaged "I'm bored. Entertain me. Now". The student felt she had to engage with this (at the expense of her degree) because this 'friend' had the power to make people socially 'in' or 'out' depending on how well she felt entertained. That was the start of an important conversation, and an eye-opening insight for me.

place for more open, ongoing discussions and sharing of specific information and thoughts.

22.5.3 Twitter

Twitter has become so popular that it is integrated into tens of thousands of apps and now, even operating systems. This is remarkable for a short-text-based service that was set up in 2006. It's referred to as 'microblogging' and users are limited to 140 characters per message. What you 'tweet' about is potentially visible to the world, and stays on record as people 'retweet' (RT) your message to their network of contacts. Many people have landed in big trouble for tweeting dangerous or slanderous remarks that possibly were just a quick vent of frustration to their friends.

My strong recommendation is that for work / research / project purpose, you simply use this as a *read-only* research tool. Companies and researchers will tweet about their inventions or products, so it's a good way of 'following' those you are interested in. Or you can *search* for keywords of interest.

Many students use it successfully as a newsfeed for topics of interest, and to sift the world of information by keyword, to get an idea of the latest announcements. Slightly worrying are those students who have grown up with Twitter and Facebook and use these as their main source of information and communication; abandoning email, web-searching and "dinosaur" information repositories such as libraries. To those students, I say that the latest, trendiest, most controversial and most popular topics do not always give the best information about research and ideas.

22.5.4 Other Social Media

This whole section will go out of date very quickly, as the whole phenomenon of social media is relatively recent and in great flux. At the time of writing, this link to an article by Dave Chaffey gives a well-written summary and analysis of how the world is using social media:

   http://www.smartinsights.com/social-media-marketing/social-media-strategy/new-global-social-media-research/

It explains what sort of activities people tend to do on each social medium, and ranks them in terms of usage and take-up around the world. Various discussions are had regarding how the figures are gathered, and which medium is the most 'up and coming'. Much of the activity appears to be summarised as:

- uploading photos and videos for sharing
- small details of everyday life ("my coffee's not nice this morning")
- responding to broadcast tv or news
- advertising.

In other words, it seems that for all the huge media and personal interest in which social media you are using, it is being used for localised and worldwide everyday communication and sharing.

This does not necessarily make it the best environment for coordinating a project.

22.5.5 Mobile Phones as Communications Centres

The rise of the multi-touch smartphone in the late 2000s has given rise to a great opportunity - that of an individual mobile, multi-media communications centre. If you'll forgive a personal anecdote that will clearly mark me out as prehistoric, for years I only kept a cheap, pay-as-you-go mobile phone for emergency breakdowns etc. I didn't give everyone my number, and the phone was powered off until *I* needed it, as I didn't want to be disturbed wherever I was at any time day or night. It still amazes me that so many people *do*[6]. However, I know that I'm in the minority in wanting some peace and to be able to concentrate uninterrupted on what I'm doing, so I shall return to eating my Jurassic Ferns.

In the last few years though I have re-joined the 21st century and got a whizzy smartphone. The main reason for this is that in one small (and thus portable) device, I now can see at a glance if there have been any:

- incoming phone calls
- text messages
- emails from work
- emails from home/friends
- Facebook updates, etc.

---

[6] Folks - do you realise how *rude* it is to answer a call or a text while you're talking to someone else! Really. It's like saying "Yeah yeah, whatever you were saying, but shut up now while I get this message because any old text or call is going to be more important than talking to you." Nice!

Managing Your Project

I have to say that it's still not the easiest of devices on which to *reply* to any of these things, but I am not blessed with 'young person's thumbs' and so will often tap out a brief reply, and respond more fully (if needed) when I'm next on a computer.

I *still* don't give everyone my number, and it never actually *rings*[7] - it just quietly buzzes for a limited set of my contacts - but I can look at it whenever I want an update of all my communication channels.

You probably know all this anyway, but it's worth just giving yourself a 'communications audit' - checking and reviewing all the communication channels in your life and that they are actually working *positively* for you rather than a negative drain on your mental resources.

22.6 Asking people for help

Even though your supervisor will be your main contact for help throughout your project, there will be times when you need to ask others for help. You might, for example, be asking another academic for some information on their research, or asking a company if they can give you some technical guidance on their product. In this section we consider some of the good (and bad) ways to ask people for help.

22.6.1 How *not* to do it

Imagine for a moment that you are an academic in a university. You are just wondering how to proceed with the day's jobs when the following email arrives. Read it now and note your reaction.

Dear Professr,

You are an expert in computers. My supervisor is ill at the moment, and I need some recumendations how I can do my project which is in your area. Please cud u send me the most important references in this area, and tell me the most imprtant things I shud be doing. Please get back to me promptyl as I have only a few weeks left on my projectg.

Awaiting your prompt reply,

<student at another university!>

How does it make you feel? Does it make you want to help the person?

---

[7] (always guaranteed to disrupt a meeting, conversation, tv show, dinner, lecture, concert, visit to the toilet, etc!!)

Maybe you reacted with some of the following thoughts:

1) The whole thing is shoddily put together as if the sender doesn't really care about this communication at all.

2) This is a student from *another* university, of which you have no contact with or commitment to in any way at all.

3) Why *should* you do somebody else's work for them?

4) Surely the student should urgently contact people in his own department to get something done about their supervision process?

5) The student is asking you to spend time (that you are desperately short of) in reading his mail, putting together a list of references (which is not well defined at all), and giving project guidance about a completely undefined project!

6) He has the cheek to request a prompt reply, without any reference to the fact that you might have something else to do, and have nothing to do with them anyway! etc etc.

So, you see, just a few hurried words, written from the student's own perspective, can create a very bad reaction in the reader. You, the reader, felt imposed upon, and the student ended up with nothing as the academic deleted his email.

Yet this is the sort of message it is easy to write if you are fully immersed in your project and simply think of other people as "ready sources of information" rather than individual people with their own commitments and mind-sets.

22.6.2 Decide when communication is necessary

A golden rule of communication is to do it sparingly, and after much thought.

Maybe some of you have been plagued by SPAM emails or junk post? The people sending this stuff do not care about you or your overloaded email Inbox, or whether you are offended by its contents. They just fire their message to as many people as possible in the hope that one or two will answer and buy their product.

So, an uninvited message that has little relevance to you, and is sent out to many people, is SPAM. The above message from the student was practically SPAM. If you are going to communicate with someone, you need to make sure it is not perceived as such. In the following section, there are some hints about how to do this.

22.6.3 Ensuring your communication creates a good reaction

- Make it *personal* (i.e., a single message written and sent to one person).

- Explain why you are contacting *them* (and not somebody else).

- Make it *interesting* for them (the person reading it is a person with their own priorities. Why should they spend any time on this at all?).

- Be as *specific* as possible. Ask a simple question that seems appropriate for that particular person to answer.

- Be aware that the recipient will have little time available, so make sure that what you are asking them could be done *quickly*, if not immediately, and that you do not appear to be demanding it.

- Consider what you are *offering* the person. Re-read the above email, and consider how *you* would react to it. There is nothing to be gained by replying. A good communication should acknowledge that the recipient needs to get something from this.

All of this takes time and effort. And this, once again, is the heart of it. Rushed, sloppily worded communications are not usually effective, yet the email and text culture has made speedy messages possible. Carefully worded, interesting communications that offer something to the recipient are more likely to get a positive reply.

Imagine that the same student had sent the following letter. This example includes one of my own research fields as an example of how such a letter needs to be customised and relevant to the person you are writing to.

Dear Professor Hunt,

I am a student from <*another University*> working on new electronic musical instruments. I have been reading about your work on Sonification, but I am unsure how the two fields relate. I know this is a busy exam time, but I wonder if you would be able to help me with a short answer to a particular problem in your field?

In your paper for the Multimedia Data Workshop you described an ideal interactive sonification system as requiring "control intimacy similar to an acoustic musical instrument". Would you be willing to explain this comment further, as I would like to refer to it in my thesis?

Alternatively do you know of any other information sources which deal with this problem? I would be very happy to send you the completed thesis at the end of the project if you are interested.

Many thanks in anticipation,

<Student's name>

This is a completely different entity from that earlier email, and if I received it, I would probably give it a positive reply, maybe almost immediately. The person has clearly been reading my work, and has a question to answer, which explains their motivation in specifically contacting me. They are interested in what I have to say, yet acknowledge that I probably will be busy. They offer something in return (a copy of their thesis in an area of interest to me) as an extra incentive to reply (although this is not always necessary). So to summarise, address your communication in an unassuming way, explain clearly why you are contacting a particular person, and ask specific questions that can probably be answered.

22.7 Summary

This chapter has looked at how to communicate your work with other people.

The most important thing to realise is that everybody's brain has its own context, memories, concerns, skills, energy levels, and preferred way of working. Therefore, the first rule of any effective communication is to set out the *context* of what you are talking about. In other words, because the content of your brain is *not* the same as that of the listener, you are doomed if you communicate while expecting the listener to magically know the contents of your head. So, you should take time to prepare what you say so that it briefs the listener, step by step, to what is on your mind.

In the main chapter, we gave some imaginary examples to show how the same piece of text (or spoken request) can be either helpful or incomprehensible, depending on how it is introduced. Remember that when you start talking or writing about your project – what is currently in your head is probably not yet in the head of the listener / reader. You have to place it there in the correct order.

Be careful how and when you approach other people for help. Be aware that they carry with them a huge list of unseen problems and priorities, and you need to ensure that your communication is received well. Choose the appropriate medium, starting where possible with email, and following up if needed with a phone call or visit. There are times when social media can be

Managing Your Project

a useful coordination tool for projects, but it can become an all-consuming habit that detracts from your work.

People's brains do not start out containing the information that you wish to communicate to them. The essence of communication is to find a way to get your message across. This is true whether you are in a supervision meeting, writing an email to a person who does not know you, or presenting your work in front of a group of other people.

22.8 External Links

Thomson, 1994 - Conversation the Power of Persuasion by Peter Thomson, Nightingale Conant Audio CD set, ISBN-13: 978-1905453627

23. GIVING PRESENTATIONS

This chapter gives a brief introduction to presentations, how to think about them, and how to plan, prepare and deliver them effectively. It would be helpful if you have already read Chapter 22 - *Structuring your Communication* as you need to know something about what it's like to be in the audience before you can start to prepare to talk to them.

If giving a presentation is part of your assessment process, then there is some advice coming up on how to practice with your Special Interest Group in a safe environment. But even if not - giving a presentation is one of the best ways of sorting out what you are really doing and focussing on. Preparing to describe your work to others has a very special effect on your focus and clarity, and students have often reported that it was only after doing their presentation that they really knew what they were doing. Plus it gives you the opportunity for some useful feedback and questions.

23.1 Presenting your ideas to others

At some point in your project you may be required to do a stand-up presentation to explain your work. This may take the form of a research seminar where an unknown number of interested people come along to hear about your project. Or it might be a formal part of the assessment where everyone doing a research project is expected to present the outcomes (or the progress) of their work. You might also be asked to present your work at a conference (see Chapter 35 - *Publishing your Work* for more on this). Some postgraduates get involved in teaching and may be given the chance to deliver a lecture or seminar to students.

Whatever the setting, it is natural to worry about public speaking, but in this section we look at a few practical techniques to help you to prepare better for the talk, and – who knows – maybe even *enjoy* the process!

23.2 Establishing the audience

By far the most important thing you can do is to work out *who* you are talking to, and determine their *reason* for being there. It matters enormously whether people have specifically *chosen* to come to your talk. If so, it means that they are already an interested audience. On the other hand if people *have* to be there (for example as a requirement for a course or assessment) then you will need to work a bit harder to interest them in what you are saying.

A really good hint is to work out "what they know already". As an illustration, imagine that the audience consists primarily of your fellow students. In this case you can assume your common knowledge of the entire course so far, but you *cannot* assume knowledge of your particular project area. Your job in this case is to take the audience from the knowledge you had *before* you started your project (which should be similar to their current mind-set) up to the point you are at now.

It is also useful to gauge (in advance if possible) the predicted numbers of people in the audience. This will affect how you choose to deliver your talk. For a small number of familiar people you can be chatty and informal, but a larger audience will require more energy from you, and more of a performance.

23.3 Methods of presentation

Your next choice should be to choose which method you will use to deliver the talk, as this will determine the way you gather materials for the presentation. Here we consider some of the options available to you, and consider the pros and cons of each.

1) Talking without notes is quite a scary way of proceeding, but may be appropriate for a small audience (or any other environment which is more forgiving). You need to be confident about what you are saying, and have either memorised your talk, or be willing to improvise it. The advantages of this method are that you will be looking at your audience the whole time, and are more likely to interact with them. When done well this can come across as a natural, engaging and effective form of talk, because it sounds like it's coming straight from the heart. It's also easy to use a blackboard or whiteboard to illustrate your talk as you go. When done well, it can make for a compelling and confident talk, but it takes *lots* of practice.

2) Talking with notes is a 'safer' (and more common way) to proceed with a talk. This allows you to think through the structure of the talk in advance, and to give yourself cues (for example *"play sound example no. 1 from the CD"*) at certain points.

The detail that you put on the notes will determine the style of the delivery. At one extreme you could have a **pre-prepared speech**. Here, everything is written down in full, and you simply read out your own words. Whilst this reduces the potential error (because all your words have been formed in advance) it also drastically reduces the potential for change and opportunities for eye-contact with the audience which would help you to respond to their reactions. Also, unless you are well-practised at speech-giving, it can sound very stilted. A final problem is that the words we *write* are usually different to those that we *speak*. Phrases that work formally on paper can sound very 'stiff' when delivered to an audience.

So instead you could use **'bullet-pointed notes'**, such as:

- Welcome
- Why I am talking about TV advertising
- VIDEO example

These are intended to act as reminders to you. You will need to turn these into sentences *as you are delivering them*. If this sounds daunting, just remember that this is what you do every time you have a conversation with someone. So, the above bullet-points might become:

"**Welcome** to the afternoon session. I hope lunch wasn't so big that you all fall asleep! Today I'll be talking about the effect of **TV advertising** on the dietary habits of the general population. Let's start by taking a look at the following **video example** . . ."

The advantage is that you can change the style and mood of your delivery according to the specific audience. This is something that gets easier with practice.

Some people have their notes on A4 paper on a **Lectern**, whereas some write them on **Postcards**. The lectern is more formal, whereas the postcards allow you to move around more easily. Nowadays many people are also using **electronic notes** - handheld smartphones or tablet computers to display their notes.

3) Talking using a Slideshow is a very common way of delivering a presentation nowadays. Your talk is marked out by a series of slides

Managing Your Project

(containing text and graphics) which are displayed to the audience. This is typically done by using either **pre-printed acetates**[8] or (most common nowadays) **computer presentation software**. The audience can also be a given a printout of the slides, often many slides to one page, with space to take notes.

Nowadays most people are likely to associate presentations with using **computer-based slide projection**, via software such as Microsoft Powerpoint, Apple Keynote, or and independent package such as Prezi.

Triggering the slides takes just a press of a button, but it's also worth looking into a remote control or 'presenter' device if you are going to be doing many presentations[9]. There are the advantages of being able to trigger sound and video material from within the presentation. However, many presentations are done with a standard (usually the default) layout and text font, and what should be dramatically different talks can ironically end up 'all looking the same'. It is also harder for you to see what is coming up next[10], which makes it vital for you to have a set of notes, showing the slide order, and any extra comments you wish to make. Alternatively you can rehearse the presentation so that you *know* what is coming up next. It always looks a bit odd when the person presenting appears to be constantly surprised about what appears on the screen, even though they have prepared it.

---

[8] **Pre-printed slides** (which can be handwritten using acetate pens, or can be printed out from a computer) allow you to physically manipulate the current slide. This has become less common as computer presentations have taken over. But, if this is done well, it can be a highly effective way of working. Some advantages are that you can re-order your slides (or miss some out if running short of time), and that you can reveal sections of the slide to your audience by placing a sheet of paper on the projector. You will be able to see what is coming up next, but the audience cannot. This helps your flow. However, some disadvantages are that if the slides are dropped, the talk becomes hopelessly out of order, and if handled wrongly you can point with a shaking hand to a slide which is slanting on the screen and this is very disconcerting for the audience. Another problem is that many audiences now simply *expect* the use of computer slideshows and are not prepared for anything else.

[9] This will allow you to move around freely rather than being stuck in front of the computer. They often come with laser-pointers so you can highlight key information on the screen.

[10] This is not impossible as most software also allows you to configure a 'presenter's view' on your computer which shows several slides in context - and your notes - whilst the projector just shows the current screen.

Here are some guidelines to help you with the layout of the slides if you are preparing your first presentation:

- Keep the text on each slide short. The audience will then listen to what *you* have to say, rather than just reading the slide (which gives the unfortunate impression that the slide is somehow in charge and you are just following it).

- If you want your slides to contain lots of detail, make a 'full details' version for yourself. Print this out as your 'notes', then make an abbreviated version for the audience to see on the screen. Sometimes students find these 'extended' slides useful as printed material to take away or to be posted online.

- Try not to read out the text that is on the slide (unless you specifically want the audience to remember a particular statement by rote). This doesn't help the audience as everyone is reading at different speeds and it's guaranteed to be different to the speed at which you are talking.

- Supplement the text with graphics. It can make your presentation look more individual, as pure-text slides tend to get boring. Also lots of people in your audience will respond better to graphical ideas (such as cartoons, photographs, block diagrams etc.) than to text.

- Be careful with the use of animated effects (such as each bullet-point whizzing in from the left, accompanied by a 'wheeeeeeee' sound). This causes great amusement when you are setting it up, and you may get one laugh in the presentation. But after that it becomes annoying to everyone, and to some people it is visually disconcerting and can make them a bit 'seasick'[11].

23.4 Planning the presentation

The planning phase is vital. It is here that you consider what the audience currently knows, and what you want them to know by the end of your presentation. Don't start making slides or notes until you know *why* you are giving the talk, and *who* will be listening.

---

[11] I really like using animated text (and changes between slides) because it draws the audience's attention to what is changing on screen, rather than expecting them to constantly 'spot the difference'. However, a few people do find it visually disturbing, so I try not to use it all the time.

The order in which you reveal information to the audience affects how it is received. A lot can be learned by watching TV documentaries, and studying the ways in which they attract and keep a varied audience. A typical documentary will begin with something to catch your attention – maybe even before the main titles! Then it will give you some background to the story. Note carefully the mix of styles: a formal, plainly spoken narrator tells you the 'facts', which are often supplemented by interviews with the people involved, telling their stories in lively first-person language, often supported by pictures, photos, dramatic reconstructions or computer-generated images. Now imagine if this programme had presented you with 30 identical-looking slides of bullet-pointed facts.

You may find it helpful to draw up a mind-map (see Chapter 8 - *Mind Mapping*) of ideas for your own presentation, which you can then annotate in numerical order. This allows a good compromise between free-thinking (mind-mapping) and ordering information into a sensible flow (numbering).

Finally, you must rehearse the talk. This is especially important if (as is often the case) you are speaking to a time-limit. You can rehearse it 'in your head', but it is much better to speak it through out loud, and even better with a friendly audience (made up of your family, friends or focus group).

23.5 Giving the talk

On the day of your presentation it is strongly advisable to get to the room as early as possible. This will allow you to ensure that your slides can be shown properly. This is particularly important if you are hoping to connect up your own laptop to some existing audio-visual equipment. It also gives you time to 'get the feel' of the room – working out where you are going to stand, and what it feels like standing in the position you will be doing your presentation.

If someone is 'chairing' your session it is good to meet with them and to make sure that they have enough information about you to be able to introduce you appropriately to the audience. You should double-check how much time you have been allocated. Ideally agree a signal with the session chair to inform you, say, when you have five minutes left. Work out in your own mind how you will react when you receive this signal, depending on where you are in your presentation.

Another advantage of arriving at your presentation room early is that your setting up is done privately, instead of frantically in front of a waiting audience. You also get to see the audience arriving one by one. This can help to calm the nerves by seeing your audience as individuals who have come along to your talk.

As you are being introduced, take some deep breaths, then begin your presentation with a confident smile and a welcome (no matter how you are feeling). Most presenters learn to appreciate the nerves beforehand, knowing that it gives them the edge of concentration that they need for their talk.

It seems to be a natural law of presentations that they take longer than when you rehearsed them! So be prepared how to handle running over time. If you receive a signal that you are nearing the end of your time, then by far the best thing to do is to calmly say "Thank you. Ok, I'm running a bit over time, so I'll move straight to the conclusions", then do exactly that and finish on time. No audience will thank you for rushing through all your slides at high-speed and still finishing late. Once a time warning has been given – accept it, and gracefully bring your talk to a conclusion.

If you get a chance, encourage some people you trust to give you some feedback on the talk. Did they understand what you were saying? Was it too fast or slow? Were the slides readable? Do they have any other suggestions for improvement? Write down their suggestions and refer to them next time you plan a talk.

23.6 Summary

There are several points in a degree or project work that you might be required to do a spoken presentation - either individually or as part of a group. The most important piece of preparation is to think about the audience - who they are; why they are attending your talk; and what you can assume that they already know. Your task then becomes to take the audience from what *they* know to what *you* know in logical flowing steps.

The size of the audience affects how formal your talk needs to be. In a small group you can chat, whereas a large audience requires more of a performance. Determine whether or not you will use notes in the talk, and if so - how detailed they will be. At one extreme you could deliver the whole talk without looking at any notes. At the other extreme, you might read out your pre-prepared speech. Both of these methods can work, but are likely to have problems for first-time talk givers.

The most common way of giving a talk is to have a series of visual slides to accompany what you say. Nowadays this is mostly done with presentation software, such as PowerPoint or Keynote. Each slide contains a combination of text and images, but you can also trigger soundfiles and display videos. As a general rule keep your text points short, don't read them out verbatim, and supplement the text with images. Consider using a remote-control presentation device so that you are free to move around the

Managing Your Project

presentation area (and perhaps the room) and thus gain freedom from the computer on the lectern.

Plan your talk carefully, thinking about the audience all the time. On the presentation day, get to the room early and do as much setting up as you can. Seeing the audience arrive as individual people is more comforting that walking in to a full room. Because presentations tend to take longer when you give them for real, you should plan what to do if you run out of time. Prepare a calm response (such as moving to your conclusions) in case you receive a time warning. If possible, ask some trusted people for feedback on your talk.

23.7 References

Links to Presentation software:

- Microsoft Powerpoint:

  https://products.office.com/en-us/powerpoint

- Apple Keynote: https://www.apple.com/uk/mac/keynote/

- Prezi: https://prezi.com/

PC Magazine article on Free Presentation Software: http://uk.pcmag.com/office-suites-products/8076/feature/top-free-software-picks-presentation-software

Links to Presenter devices (remote control):

A review of the top-ten presentation devices:
http://wireless-presenters-review.toptenreviews.com/

Books about giving presentations:

The Presentation Lab: Learn the Formula Behind Powerful Presentations, By Simon Morton [Kindle Edition or Wiley Paperback, ISBN-13: 978-1118687000].

24. ORGANISING THE FINAL REPORT

24.1 Introduction

The final report for a research project may well be the biggest piece of creative writing you have ever done (and possibly ever will do). There are other books and resources that explain in more detail about the art and craft of composing a research paper. By contrast this chapter concerns making sure you *manage* the whole process effectively.

The final report is certainly highly important, and yet many people start work on it far too late, and fail to manage the process effectively because it is such a large task. This chapter guides you through the process of writing a large report. It encourages you to begin this process early, and advises on how to structure your sections and your writing time. There are some warnings from real-life experiences, accompanied by some principles which will maximise the effectiveness of your report, and ensure that your work has the best chance of being understood by those who are reading it or examining it.

24.2 Report-writing as an ongoing process

One of the biggest mistakes (and unfortunately one of the most common) is leaving the report write-up until the end of the project. This stems from the natural thought that you "must finish your project, before you can write it". However, the truth is that every project naturally falls into *phases*.

These generally (but not always) include something similar to Figure 24.1.

Managing Your Project

- research
- specification of aims & objectives
- creative thoughts about how to tackle the project
- detailed design and planning
- practical execution of the project work
- testing, evaluation and refinement
- analysis and conclusion

Figure 24.1 Typical phases of a project

Since each phase tends to conclude at a certain time (rather than continuing throughout the project) it is rather like having an ordered series of mini-projects. These are likely to be closely related to any Work Packages you drew up in Chapter 20 (see section 20.5). It makes sense to take notes about each phase *while* it is in progress, then to write it up in its final form *as soon as the phase is complete*. There are several reasons that this is a good idea:

- Your brain can only actively hold so much information. You will forget crucial details if you don't write them down.

- The best time for writing notes on a subject is *while* you are thinking about it, or *immediately after* thinking about it and deciding on something. If you leave it too long you won't be able to recall the details.

- At the very end of the project your mind is nearly always focussed on 'fine-tuning' – e.g., serious computer code to get the program to work, auditions of your composition with feedback from others, analysing your test results etc. You may not easily remember, for example, the ten alternative design possibilities for your product which were so clear in your mind in the design phase.

- Writing an ongoing report is a good discipline because it ensures that you think deeply about each project phase, rather than just rushing on with the next one.

- Other people (such as your supervisor and focus group) can read what you have written and give you feedback which may guide your project direction.

- Your supervisor, or another person, can also give you feedback on your writing style and report layout.

- You will get the satisfaction of seeing your report 'grow' as the project progresses. This also gives the reassurance that your most important deliverable is taking shape.

Therefore your report-writing should be scheduled into your management system as an ongoing process throughout the project. You should still allocate a special block of time for the report at the end of the project. This can be used for:

- Reviewing the report with the experience and perspective that can only be gained at the end of a project process;

- Proofreading (by yourself, and ideally by at least one other person);

- Writing the Conclusions and Abstract (typically the last things to be written);

- Printing (and binding if appropriate).

Some people find that scheduling a regular time (or times) each week throughout the project encourages them to get into the habit of writing up their work. Others build blocks of time into the larger scale project plan, so that after completing a phase, there are several days put aside for writing it up. They often find this gives a useful sense of 'closure' on that phase, effectively shifting detailed information out of their brains onto paper, and leaving thinking space for the next phase. One thing is clear - it is never advisable simply to wait until you *feel* like writing. Experience seems to show that it never feels right and this can be fatal to a project.

24.3 Writing as a daily activity

Many professional writers schedule daily writing time. They find that if they write regularly their books and articles actually get written. In contrast, those who 'wait for inspiration' often never find it and the book never gets completed (or in the case of a student project, there is an almighty rush at the end, and quality suffers greatly as a result).

The Artist's Way, by Julia Cameron, gathers together wisdom and advice on creativity from authors and artists. One of the things that comes through strongly is the need to have regular creative time - and for writing this means setting aside a time every day when you will write. It almost doesn't matter what you write, but it does matter that you do it. Out of the discipline the creativity will emerge. A similar thing could be said about your project writing. Nobody wakes up suddenly *wanting* to write up their project, so you either plan it, or wait for panic.

Some people rebel against such an idea, viewing writing as a creative task and, as such, not subject to management or organisation. However, creativity often needs a structure within which to operate.

Artists and writers often report that their greatest moments of creativity come about precisely *because* they carry out the discipline of scheduling regular times for writing (often at the same time each day) so that their brain and body can slot with ease into writing mode. The greatest musical performers can only play and perform and improvise with apparent effortlessness because they have practised for hours every day.

The website *750 Words* is partly responsible for the existence of this book. It takes some of the concepts of The Artist's Way and gives a web-based environment aimed at encouraging people to write every day. The discipline of daily writing 750 words (about 3 pages of longhand or 2 pages of computer typing) causes big projects to come into being, step-by-step. You might want to try committing yourself to daily writing for your project. Write what you can each day, inspired by what you are currently thinking about in your project. You can always edit it later. Or you can more carefully structure your writing plan, as outlined in the following sections.

24.4 Scoping your writing time

Whenever you choose to schedule your writing time, you will need to carefully manage the process.

Your time will be used completely differently depending on what your mind is focussed on. Imagine that you have scheduled a two-hour writing session and you sit down with one of the following mind-sets:

1) This is my hallowed writing time and therefore *this* is the time to be *creative*. I must produce *excellent* work, starting *now* . . . .

2) In this two-hour slot I know that I need to make significant progress on chapter two. In particular I must review its structure, and then complete the writing of sections 2.1 and 2.2. Given that I have a total of two hours, I should spend:

- 15 minutes on the structure,
- 45 minutes on section 2.1,
- take 15 minutes to relax,

- 45 minutes on section 2.2, and then
- 15 minutes to review what I've written.

Option 1 is what is really in many people's minds when they sit down to write. However they find it far too threatening when it actually comes to it. They sit looking at the page (or the computer screen) feeling distinctly guilty and uncreative. *Writer's block* usually happens when you're waiting for the inspiration to get you writing. Many writers say that they have to *just start writing* to overcome such a block, even writing rubbish if necessary just to get in the flow.

Maybe option 2 appears a bit too organised for some, but it demonstrates the awareness of a grander plan. It implies that the author (acting as a Manager) has creatively organised the report, is aware of the contents and the sub-sections, has worked out the total amount of writing time available, and has allocated certain sections to be written at certain times.

There are two benefits that spring directly from such an approach:

- During each of the 45 minute writing slots there is no need to worry about *anything else* other than writing the current section. As a worker you are reassured that the management has everything in control, and so you can concentrate on the job at hand.
- You know you have 45 minutes to write a particular section, and you can aim to get it finished within that time.

This concept of 'writing to a fixed time' is very useful. Some people insist they take as long as is necessary to write a particular section. These are usually the same people who run late and miss their deadlines. If you know you have a fixed time, you can take a range of approaches to ensure that the section gets finished on time. Here are two examples:

1) If the section is quite open-ended and you just need to 'discuss the topic', you can simply start writing, and (rather like an exam) just stop writing when the time is up.

2) If there are a number of definite points that need to be addressed within a section, then you should take a more structured approach. Start off by typing in the main points in brief, maybe even as bullet-points. Then, go back and write a 'killer sentence' for each point; one that perfectly sums up the concept. If there is time, then go back again from the top and expand on each killer sentence – making it the start of a paragraph. Keep going, refining your work and adding more material until the time runs out.

Approach no. 2 has a number of advantages. At every stage of the writing process your section covers its main points. At first, these are just titles or outlines, but by the second and third stages you have short paragraphs covering what you need to say. You can carry on adding layer of detail, but maybe you already have enough? Don't *over*-write, describing things in more and more detail, unless you're actually adding valuable content by doing so.

Whichever method you use, just stop writing when the time is up. Briefly look over your work, noting down anything you wish to change later. Then schedule time for *later* (ideally on another day), to read it through and make corrections.

24.5 Contents as a springboard for writing

Most students nowadays are used to working with a word processor. If you are not yet familiar with the use of a computer for writing, then this is the time to learn. Even though there are several very good reasons for working with pen on paper[12], the advantages of word-processing are numerous:

Your final report needs to be printed, so save time and work in that medium by typing things up from the beginning.

- Copies can be made easily (actually safer than a single piece of hand-written work).

- Work can be emailed to people for information and review.

- It is much easier to experiment with your structure by moving around blocks of text, as opposed to re-writing various sections or physically cutting and pasting pieces of paper.

- Certain useful functions are built-in, such as spelling checks and word counts.

A particularly good way of structuring a report is to type in the Contents page at the earliest opportunity. Discuss this with your supervisor and focus group, and refine the structure. Then make a copy of the file. This copy then becomes your working report. The contents file (for this book) might have contained this:

---

[12] The physicality of pen or pencil and paper can cause you to think in different ways to using a computer. This is particularly good at the ideas stage, where you can utilise the free-space on a page of paper to jot down ideas, concepts, diagrams, and topic links (see the section on mind-mapping in Chapter 8).

Chapter 24: Organising the Final Report

24.1 Introduction

24.2 Report-writing as an ongoing process

24.3 Writing as a daily activity

24.4 Scoping your writing time

This becomes the template for chapter 24, where the writing for each section is allocated a particular time-slot. In this way the report is gradually built up, following the model of the Contents page. As you write, inevitably your ideas will develop and the structure may change, in which case you should adjust the original contents file accordingly.

Some writers use a method where every section has its writing slot marked in the file, like this:

Chapter 24: Organising the Final Report (week 4)

24.1 Introduction (Monday: 9.00-9.30)

24.2 Report-writing as an ongoing process (Monday: 9.30-10.30)

24.3 Writing as a daily activity (Tuesday: 9.00-9.30)

24.4 Scoping your writing time (Tuesday: 9.30-10.30)

Just like the storyboard concept, and your overall project plans, you are not to be *ruled* by these time-slots. It is just that experience shows that for most people a disciplined, carefully planned schedule is more likely to yield success than total freedom.

The other advantage for using your Contents section as a planning tool is that you can see it growing and can track your progress. Many students like to see their report physically becoming real, so every time a chapter is completed it is printed out and placed into a ring-binder. At the front of the ring-binder is the latest version of the Contents page showing what has been completed and what is still to be done. It is a great motivation to see the report taking physical shape like this.

24.6 Backing up your work

As well as building up a physical print-out of your report, it's also vital to keep electronic records of what you are typing. As mentioned earlier in the book, PLEASE keep more than one back-up and in different locations. This - for many people - is one of the biggest and most time-intensive writing activities that they will ever do in their lives. It is more than scary to see how many people type this all up on a laptop, and keep it only there, unaware of how fragile a thing is a laptop hard-drive and how easily it can break or the machine get stolen. Equally, some people invest all their storage in a tiny memory card or USB drive which can easily be lost or accidentally put in the washing or dropped down a drain.

So make sure you do the following things:

1. Save your work regularly *as you are typing*. A good guide is to save whenever you catch yourself thinking "ah, that was a good paragraph", or if you have any sense of achievement in your writing. But remember this may only get saved to your local disk.

2. After each writing session (e.g., of about an hour or so) make a copy of your work onto *another* medium, e.g., a USB drive.

3. Every so often - at least every week - get your data for that week to *somewhere else*. If you had a fire and your laptop AND backup perished you have still lost everything. So either make a physical backup to another medium which is stored elsewhere, or use an online backup (cloud-based) service to store a copy of your data.

24.7 Summary

If you leave your report writing until near the end of the project, you will probably get a poor result. This is because you will have forgotten the details of the work you did earlier, there will be so much pressure towards the end to 'be creative' and write a good report, and you will miss out on the opportunity of feedback from other people. Instead you should plan to gradually build up your report by writing up sections while they are still fresh in your mind.

Plan carefully when you are going to do your writing. Don't just wait for creative inspiration, because that can lead to a mad rush at the end of the project. Many authors recommend writing each day, without worrying about the quality. Other students have found that they can use the Work Packages in their project plan to schedule whole sections of writing on completion of certain activities in the project. Here, the writing is not only done when the work is fresh in your mind, but it acts as a way of getting 'closure' on that topic.

During your writing time it pays to use a structured approach. If you prepare in advance to write a particular section within a specific length of time, then you can simply write as much as you can on that sub-topic in the time available. Students have found that this approach does take a lot of planning, but somehow reassures your inner panicker that there is a grand plan and that the writing will get completed. A very good way of doing this is to use your Contents page as a planning tool, breaking down the report's structure into multiple sub-sections, and possibly allocating the time-slot when that section is planned to be written, and copying that into your diary/planner.

Remember to back up your writing in multiple places. This is one of the most important pieces of work you have ever produced, and represents a large investment in time. Most universities will not accept loss of data as an excuse.

24.8 Further Reading

Other resources on writing a final report:

Check out your own department's or University's resources for writing the final report. For example look at this one from York's Computer Science Department: https://www.cs.york.ac.uk/projects/howtowrt.html

Writing Your Dissertation, The Bestselling Guide to Planning, Preparing and Presenting First-Class Work (The How to Series) by Derek & Ruth Swetnam, ISBN-10: 185703662X, ISBN-13: 978-1857036626

Academic Writing: A Handbook for International Students (Routledge Study Guides) by Stephen Bailey, 2014, ISBN-10: 1138778508, ISBN-13: 978-1138778504

Julia Cameron, The Artist's Way: A Course in Discovering and Recovering Your Creative Self, Pan, 1995, ISBN-10: 0330343580, ISBN-13: 978-0330343589 (see also http://juliacameronlive.com/).

750 Words - http://750words.com/ - a website to help you establish a daily writing habit.

Overcoming Writer's Block, by David Tuffley, 2011 (Kindle edition) (see also http://goinswriter.com/how-to-overcome-writers-block/).

25. WRITING STYLE AND FORMAT

In the previous chapter we looked at some of the issues surrounding writing and managing your final report. In this chapter we continue the process by thinking more about *what* you need to write along with some advice on *how* you should do this.

25.1 Establishing the readership

The main message of Chapter 22 - *Structuring your Communication* - was to think carefully about the person (or people) you are trying to communicate with, and then to reveal your information, starting from what they *already* know to what you *want* them to know. The same is true for a final report. So it is vital that you develop an understanding of for *whom* the report is written. Too often students assume it is written for their supervisor who might well be an expert in the subject area. Accordingly such writing often misses out explanations which would make the report more understandable and useful to a wider audience.

Instead of writing personally for your supervisor, ask him or her to explain to you who your target audience is. I often recommend imagining a fellow student who has done most of your course, but knows nothing about your specific project. Therefore you need not waste valuable space and time covering details which are clearly outlined in textbooks or course notes, but instead can concentrate on revealing the information that you have discovered during your particular project. This has two added benefits:

1. Your supervisor (or any other examiner) will be able to judge what you have learnt *beyond* the taught course.
2. Your report will be readily usable for future students because you have written it for that particular knowledge set.

It is good to have a *specific* person in mind as you are writing, so you can ask questions such as "would Jim know what I'm talking about here?" Imagine you are at the beginning of one of the 45-minute writing sessions mentioned in Section 24.4, and you know that you need to cover a topic called "The future of transistors". If you are stuck as to what to write, just try visualising 'Jim' sitting in front of you. Your job is to explain to him the future of transistors, and you haven't got long to do it in. Try imagining the conversation in your head, and type up what you say to Jim. This will naturally be at the right level because he is your typical 'target audience' and you know roughly what he already understands. You can probably start with an overview of the topics that will need to be covered (and these will become your bullet-points). You can then explain each point in turn, and write down the key sentences; these are the single concepts that Jim needs to hear in order to understand what you are saying. Then you can go back and explain in more detail.

Don't worry too much about the writing style being too conversational; this can be corrected later. Often when you re-read something (especially the following day) you realise that certain phrases should be expressed differently. However, it is better to succeed at explaining your concept in a relaxed style, rather than having beautifully structured prose that your readers cannot understand.

25.2 House-styles

Check with your academic institution or department whether there are particular writing or formatting rules that you need to follow. They may allow you to choose the style, but you should check to see if there are restrictions on line-spacing, text-size, use of headings, use of numbering, formatting of figures, and referencing styles[13]. There may be rules to follow about writing style, e.g., whether to write in first person, ("I carried out the following experiment)", or third person ("The following experiment was carried out").

The earlier you discover these guidelines, the better. If you are using a word-processor you can then produce a writing *template*, which contains the appropriate paper layout and font styles etc. If there are no specific guidelines, it is still wise to discuss the format with your supervisor. Look at various books and journal papers, and previous reports from your institution, to find out what is permissible and to see what you prefer.

---

[13] For more information on referencing see Chapter 19 - *The Literature Survey*.

25.3 Tenses and 3rd vs 1st Person

Whilst the section above urges you to look closely at the localised 'house styles' for your report there are a few general guidelines about reports that it would be good to make clear.

Students are often strangely attracted to writing in the *future* tense when they are reporting work that is already done.

"The experiment must be designed so that it is statistically valid. Therefore a detailed specification needs to be drawn up. This will be covered in detail in the next section".

Let's be clear; you're writing about work that has been *done*, so this should be in the past tense, and your report is being read in the present tense, not the future.

So the above section would be better written as follows:

"The experiment was designed so that it was statistically valid. This process began by drawing up a detailed specification. This is covered in detail in the next section".

For many reports the reader does not need to be reminded about who wrote the report and did the work - after all your name is on the front cover.

There are times when you might want to refer to yourself as "I", but - particularly in science writing - this is rather frowned upon. Instead think of yourself as being a reporter, telling the reader about work which has been done.

Imagine tuning in to the News at Ten and hearing this:

"Good evening. Here is the news. I will be reading you the news and will enjoy telling you about what happened today. A new conference took place in Madrid today. I'm so happy to hear this because I've visited the place a few times and it's lovely. The conference . . . "

It would be shocking, because although the newsreader *is* a person (an "I") their job is to portray information to you without personally getting in the way. The same is true for a report.

Students often try to commentate in a personal tone and this rarely works.

"In the first section I will cover the first world war, and then I shall proceed to analyse the second world war".

'I' does not need to appear at all. We know that you wrote it, so it serves no further purpose. Instead, use third-person passive writing such as:

"The first section covers the first world war, and this is followed by an analysis of the second world war".

Some students try to avoid "I" by substituting a phrase such as "the author". This actually gets even more confusing and a bit annoying. This sort of writing is very common:

"In the first section the author will cover the first world war, and following on from that the author shall then proceed to analyse and write up the second world war".

There is a notable exception, which is when you really are talking about yourself. Then it is ok to use "I". Students who are writing up their experiences (for example of a placement in the company) get confused about the use of "I".

When you are describing personal experience and contribution then first person is actually better.

But when you are documenting a system or a product or a development process, that's when 3rd person works much better.

So, for contrast:

(personal writing)

> *AWKWARD*: When the author joined the company placement scheme he was made extremely welcome and his mentor met him daily.
>
> *GOOD*: When I joined the company placement scheme I was made extremely welcome and my mentor met me daily.
>
> *3rd PERSON ALTERNATIVE:* The company has an excellent mentoring scheme which ensures that students are made to feel welcome, via daily supportive meetings.

(technical writing)

> *AWKWARD*: I decided to choose the iPad for my development environment. I wrote code daily in my journal and showed it to my mentor each week, who gave me constructive feedback.[14]

---

[14] If your goal was to write a journal or a diary, then this is fine. But if it's to document processes and decisions, then the sheer amount of first-person words just gets in the way, as if you were *writing "me me me, technical bit, now more about me".*

GOOD: The code was developed for the iPad. Weekly meetings with the company mentor ensured that specific feedback was built into the design.

A final way of thinking about it is this . . .

If you really are referring to *yourself as a person*, then you can't beat phrases such as "I joined the company" etc.

BUT if you are really describing a technical product or a process, it's no longer about you - it's about the *'thing' being built or designed*, so "I" gets in the way and sounds like a diary "I did this then I did that and I chose this then debugged that". Because your report has your name on it - we *know* it's you who built the thing, so there's no need to use 'I'.

But whatever is suggested here, do make sure that you check it through with your supervisor and ideally anyone else who will be reading/marking your report, to see what they are expecting and what matters to them.

25.4 Revealing information to the reader

Those of you familiar with, and maybe good at, novel writing or poetry know that language can be used to maintain suspense. The reader can be kept waiting, basking in a flow of words that sets the scene and builds the tension[15]. When writing for information, however, it is better to use plainer language that carries your reader logically through your argument, and unveils the information you wish to portray in a sensible order[16].

In Chapter 23 - *Giving Presentations* we discussed the art of giving a talk, and how to reveal information to your audience in a logical way. In Section 23.4 - *Planning the presentation* we saw how much can be learnt from the way a TV documentary captures the audience's interest, maintains their imagination, and leads them through a series of logical steps supported by sound and vision.

---

[15] For example, consider the following. *"Entering the room via the creaking door, unaware of her location because of the pitch black surroundings, but smelling a damp, musky aroma, and creeping slowly down the rickety stairs, Eva held onto the wooden handrail, and - sinking one stair at a time - plunged into the doom, when suddenly - a hand grabbed hers!"* Ok, it's rubbish and that's why I'm not a fiction writer, but it breaks many rules of academic writing.

[16] In academic style the previous story would read more like this. *"Eva descended the old stairs into a dark room that smelled damp. She was frightened. She was grabbed by another hand."* More factual. Perhaps more boring? Less evocative description? But plainer and more direct language in shorter sentences.

You may wish to revisit Chapter 22 - *Structuring your Communication* in the context of writing your final report, in order to think again about how other people's minds work. What is in your head at the very moment you start writing should be as close as possible as to what will be in your readers' heads when they start reading.

25.5 Writing flow

The most important thing for you to do is to regularly read your own writing to check that it actually makes sense for the reader. Remember that your primary task is to feed information into the reader's brain in a sensible order.

It is useful to check that *at every level* there is a logical flow of information. If you were to read your chapter titles in order, there should be some sense of progression. It might sound like this:

1. Introduction
2. Overview of Previous Work
3. Focus of this project
4. Design
5. Construction
6. Testing
7. Evaluation
8. Conclusions
9. Further Work

Now, here's a useful test. Do your first level subsections also flow well?

If the above list represents chapters 1, 2, 3, 4 etc., then what would the flow be like looking at 1.1, 1.2, 1.3, 2.1, 2.2, 2.3, 2.4, 2.5, 3.1 etc? Try it on your own writing. If the topics appear unrelated or jumbled, this might give you a clue that it's going to be hard for the reader to follow.

If you're feeling ambitious you could try the same exercise with the next level subsections (1.1.1, 1.1.2 etc.).

Finally you will get down to the level of the individual paragraphs. A well-crafted report will have a sensible flow between paragraphs. Each one should have its own focus and should try to cover one small topic. There should also be a logical flow between sentences within each paragraph.

Even within a sentence there is much that can be done to make it succeed or fail. Try to keep a good balance with your writing style - not too stylised nor too informal.

Contrast the following summaries of the same event:

1) I wanted to test this stuff to make sure it all worked ok. I asked a few of my friends over and most of them thought it was great. One guy said it was rubbish but what does he know? He doesn't even play an instrument.

2) This project needed to facilitate a multi-person experimentation protocol, to be preceded by an informal evaluation exercise. Several non-expert participants were recruited and took part in an extensive trial of the pre-release prototype. 80% of the test subjects subsequently reported positive experiences, whereas 20% had issues and reported negatively. It should be noted that due to the lack of subject experience of the 20% it is perfectly possible to dismiss this data. Alternatively this data may henceforth be useful in determining the participatory make-up of the upcoming evaluation exercise.

3) It was important to test the prototype on an informal group of people, before testing the project on the general public. Five colleagues were asked to try out the instrument and to give an honest appraisal. Four were impressed with the system and were pleased with the sounds that they made. One person, who does not play a musical instrument, did not like using the prototype. His experiences should be useful in deciding which sorts of people we recruit for the larger test.

25.6 Use of Diagrams

A good report should include a good balance between text and diagrams[17]. Some readers find it hard to wade through large blocks of text. Diagrams are one way of helping to break up the text (along with subtitles, tables, bullet-points, and sensible use of paragraphing).

Many readers will respond better to diagrams because they are visual learners. As you do not know all your future readers it is good to provide for a variety of learning styles.

Some information is inherently better shown as a diagram. If you find yourself saying things like *"at first the data goes up, but after 30 minutes it starts to*

---

[17] In reports, diagrams are often called Figures. In other publications they might be referred to as illustrations or pictures.

go down again, but not quite as low as when it first started, and way below what it eventually gets to at the end" you probably require a graph instead.

Please make sure that every Figure is 'anchored' in the text like this (see Figure 25.1). Don't let them just float about unannounced. There should be a specific place where readers are directed to jump away from the text and look at a figure.

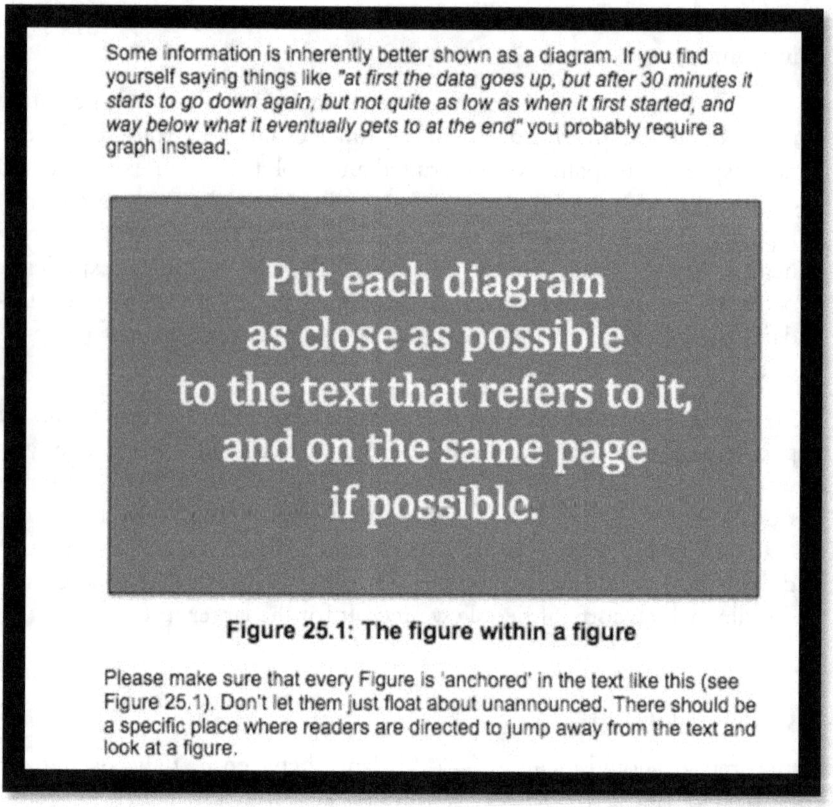

> Some information is inherently better shown as a diagram. If you find yourself saying things like *"at first the data goes up, but after 30 minutes it starts to go down again, but not quite as low as when it first started, and way below what it eventually gets to at the end"* you probably require a graph instead.
>
> ### Put each diagram as close as possible to the text that refers to it, and on the same page if possible.
>
> **Figure 25.1: The figure within a figure**
>
> Please make sure that every Figure is 'anchored' in the text like this (see Figure 25.1). Don't let them just float about unannounced. There should be a specific place where readers are directed to jump away from the text and look at a figure.

Figure 25.1: The placement of figures

25.7 Appendices

You can place material in an appendix if you want your reader to be *aware* of it, but not *required* to read it as part of the main body of the report. In other words, if you have things which you and your supervisor agree should be included in the report, but that seems to interrupt the 'flow' of the report, then consider putting them in an appendix. Label your appendices alphabetically.

Managing Your Project

Many authors use Appendix A to be their list of References.

Likewise Appendix B is often the Bibliography (i.e., a list of books and papers that have influenced your work and writing, but are not necessarily referenced nor quoted from.

Other uses of appendices include:

- Questionnaire forms (the summary goes in the main body, but the detailed responses from your survey can be kept in an appendix).

- Relevant correspondence (e.g., from an expert in your topic area).

- Information (such as printouts of web-pages or adverts) which has influenced your work, but would look wrong inserted in the main body of the report.

- Computer code listings (although these are increasingly being submitted electronically, see next section).

Ensure that details of your Appendices are listed in your Contents page.

25.8 Submitting Electronic information

Nowadays many final reports are submitted with a disk (such as a CD-ROM, a DVD or a USB flash drive) which provides information in electronic form. Here are the sorts of information that typically go on such a disk:

- An electronic copy of the report (i.e., the computer files from your word processor that made up the report)

- Computer code (source files, libraries and executables)

- Web-pages (text & images) from your literature survey

- Sound files of musical compositions or other sound examples

- Video demonstrations of the product in action.

The electronic copy of your report is especially useful as it can be sent via email, edited into a publication (see Chapter 35 - *Publishing your work*), and stored in a much smaller space than the paper version. Computer code takes up a lot of printed space, and is inherently more useful to future students if available and ready-to-use on a disk. If you have found useful information on web-pages (particularly that which is not stored in published, printed form) it is good to store those pages in electronic form on your disk. This is because the web is a precarious place for storing information – web addresses can change and sites can disappear completely, and it would be a shame to lose relevant information. Any media, which are not text or static graphics, can be included. Video demonstrations[18] of your product in action show the examiners that it works, and allow you to control the filming conditions. You can also include sound or music examples to illustrate points throughout your report.

A good electronic appendix should be fully indexed, both on its cover and within the printed report. If, for example, you are referring to sound examples from within your text you might be advised to include the reference as follows:

Beethoven used the oboe as a bridge in the 5th symphony [CD track 4].

Or if you are referring to a file on the CD (e.g., a web-page) use something like this:

This information is available on the accompanying CD [/research/sound/index.htm].

This implies that you have structured the CD in a sensible way, using carefully named folders and sub-folders to hold the information in a logical place.

As with standard printed Appendices, ensure that details of the contents of your disk are listed in your Contents page. If it contains too many individual items, then produce a high-level index which outlines the most important folders on the disk.

As a final point, you should always ensure that the report can be read *without* the accompanying disk, should it get lost or damaged. The disk should enhance the report and offer further insights into the project rather than being a mission-critical part of your explanation.

At some point in the future the whole submission process may go electronic to save paper and give an easily accessible record of previous work. Some institutions already do this. At those places where paper copies are still required it's good practice to make an electronic version of your document anyway.

---

[18] Many students are now creating videos and storing them on YouTube, and simply providing the link to that video in the report. This is excellent for an electronic report, as the reader can just click on your link and instantly see the video playing. It is still good practice to provide the video on disk along with the report, in case (for unforeseen reasons) your video is not available online in the future.

25.9 Summary

When you are writing your final report, talk first to your supervisor about who it should be aimed at. A good idea is to imagine writing for a student who has done your particular course, but who knows nothing about your specific project. Focus on one topic at a time and write down what you would say to explain it to your fellow student. Concentrate on revealing information in a logical order, such that a typical reader can pick up your meaning as they read. Go back later and correct any grammatical errors or to correct the phrasing.

Another thing to check with your supervisor is the appropriate 'House style' for the report. Departments and institutions often have their own detailed list of requirements for layout, fonts, writing style and referencing format. It is also good to discuss some details of the writing style, particularly whether you are allowed (or expected) to use first person writing ("I think" etc.), and how tenses are used to report facts and explain report structure.

Check your writing at regular intervals, and pretend that you do not know all about your work (although this is hard to do). Ensure that it flows well at chapter level, but also that the sub-sections make sense when read in order. The topics in each paragraph should also flow easily from one to the next, as should the sentences within each paragraph. In other words you should review your writing at different structural levels, as well as proofreading the flow of text.

Make sure your report uses plentiful diagrams (often called 'figures'). Refer to each one in the text, and place it as close to that text as possible. Each figure should have a number and a title (caption). Use Appendices at the back of the report to hold information that you wish to include, but would otherwise interrupt the flow of the report. The Reference list is often Appendix A, but others can include questionnaires, data sheets, related papers and computer code listings. It is often advisable (or required) to provide an electronic appendix (e.g. on disk or USB stick). Here you can include supporting media, computer code and other technical information better stored on a disk than printed on paper.

25.10 Further reading

Academic writing

Dissertations and Project Reports: A Step by Step Guide (Palgrave Study Skills) Paperback by Stella Cottrell, Palgrave Macmillan (2014), ISBN-10: 1137364262, ISBN-13: 978-1137364265.

Andy Hunt

How to Write Dissertations & Project Reports (Smarter Study Skills) by Kathleen McMillan and Jonathan Weyers, Prentice Hall; 2 edition (2011), ISBN-10: 027374383X, ISBN-13: 978-0273743835 and Kindle edition.

Do an internet search on "academic writing style" to see a large number of guides from different higher education institutions. Remember to check your own institution's guide first.

There's a very good article online at Wikiversity, that covers many aspects of clear writing for technical reports:

https://en.wikiversity.org/wiki/Technical_writing_style

For more detailed information, such as more about tenses, you might like to look at the supporting documents about academic and thesis writing here:

https://www.scribbr.com/category/academic-writing/

SECTION 6
TROUBLESHOOTING - COMMON PROBLEMS

This section contains a series of chapters focussed on particular problems which seem to strike project students at various times. Over the years I've noticed which negative situations are most common, and have spent lots of time helping students through these times, working out solutions, overcoming the problem, and often turning it into a positive strength. For easy reference each chapter deals with a particular problem.

- **Ch. 26 Procrastination** – *when you can't get going.* We can be incredibly creative at finding ways *not* to work. Sometimes this provides a useful break or release, but it can easily become a painful time of stagnation. This chapter looks at *why* we put things off, and gives some advice about how to kick-start yourself into action again.

- **Ch. 27 Perfectionism** – *when you don't know how to stop!* Perfectionism in mild doses can help you to improve your work, which is a good thing. However, it can rapidly get out of control and become a real problem, leading people to get caught up on certain activities at the expense of others, and to never be happy with their work. Here we look at the causes and solutions to strike a good working balance between self-critique and finishing promptly.

- **Ch. 28 Getting Stuck** - *when you can't see a solution.* If you come to a halt, this chapter will help you get moving again. It includes a series of methods that help you to address the problem, think around it, and involve others where necessary; all with the aim of getting you *un*stuck.

- **Ch. 29 Losing Focus** - *when you're not entirely sure that you're working on the right thing.* This can be a tricky situation because you can find yourself slogging away at something, but at the back of your mind you are really not sure that you're making progress on your project. This chapter helps you regain focus by re-launching some of the management techniques covered in other parts of the book.

- **Ch. 30 Losing Motivation** - *when you just don't feel like working*. This is an important issue to address because it can have many causes, each of which is addressed with its own recommended solutions. This chapter helps you to identify the cause and suggests appropriate remedies.

- **Ch. 31 Discovering Similar Work** - *when you find out that somebody else "is doing your project"*. This is a situation which happens more often than you might expect. You spend a lot of effort coming up with what you think is a unique project, then - half-way through - you find that someone else around the world is doing the same thing. This chapter helps you convert the initial disappointment into a series of positive drivers for your project.

26. PROCRASTINATION

Procrastination is the act of putting off (until sometime in the future) what should be done now. This is not to be confused with 'active deferral' – where a proper decision is made that this is not the right time to do a particular thing. The Procrastinator is so daunted by each new task they receive that they attempt to run away from either Managing the task or Working on it. Consequently they fill their time with unrelated stalling activities.

26.1 Stalling Activities

These can take many forms. Procrastinators find themselves actively focussing on something totally unrelated, such as a social activity, or a long series of videos on the internet. Or maybe passively avoiding starting to work, for example sitting hopefully at a desk for long periods hoping for inspiration.

Please don't misunderstand – life should have plenty of opportunities for socialising and daydreaming, but *not* as a masking activity that ultimately prevents you from making progress on your major piece of work. This is the Ostrich effect – the hope that by sticking your head in the sand the problem will somehow just go away.

Sadly, procrastinators tend to go through life oscillating between a state of denial (unconsciously thinking "I won't make any decent progress on my project if I do it now, so, I'll go for a drink instead") and panic ("Oh no, my 3000 word essay really *is* due in tomorrow morning"). Unfortunately a solo project seems like an easy thing to procrastinate about; it's scary, it's big, and there's lots of time for stalling activity. It is amazing how fast time will pass, and the pressures of starting a project late and completing it under panic conditions are strongly not recommended.

26.2 The Psychology of Procrastination

Procrastination is the putting off of things which you know you *should* be doing now.

Why do we do it?

Usually it is *fear* of the feeling that we think we are going to get when we start the job. We fear that we are going to:

- feel inadequate and not know what to do
- feel uncomfortable as we interact with someone we have to talk to
- feel unsure of the outcome of what we are planning
- feel pressure and tired by the amount of work.

In all these things it is usually a worry about how we are going to *feel* when we are doing the job.

This is really strange, because - almost without fail - we feel instantly MUCH better once we have done the job, or even *while* we are doing it. Yet time after time we forget this.

Isn't this true in other parts of life as well?

We fear the discomfort and effort of exercise, which stops us time and again from doing it, yet whenever we DO it we almost invariably feel terrific.

The opposite is true with eating. We try to diet, yet are tempted by the short-term pleasure of eating the food, then regret it later and feel bad about what we ate.

So it seems that we are somehow are programmed to avoid unpleasant situations even if we know that a more pleasurable one lies beyond it. If this is a really big issue in your life you might like to read *"Feel the Fear and Do it Anyway"* by Susan Jeffers. This book has numerous examples of the sorts of situation which make us anxious but that just need to be done, as well as many strategies for overcoming the fear and even using it to your advantage. This is well known by stage performers, who have to deal with stage fright for most of their lives, but who learn how to channel it into a productive mode of optimal concentration and performance. As a performer you ought to worry (rather ironically) if you are *not* worried about an upcoming performance, because that usually indicates you're not putting enough preparation into it.

26.3 When is it NOT Procrastination?

The word Procrastination does not apply to every situation where you put something off until a later date.

There are many instances when the *correct* managerial thing to do is to delay an activity. Some examples of this are:

- when you don't yet feel you have the right information
- when you feel you are being pressured into a quick decision (e.g. by advertisements or sales people)
- when you are too busy with other more important things
- when you have a hunch that the situation might resolve itself if you leave it for a bit.

In all these cases, delaying the action should work in your favour, and this is NOT Procrastination.

However, when you KNOW that you should be getting on with something now, and you don't, that's when you need to start asking yourself "Why am I putting this off?".

If the answer is simply to do with the fear, then you need to *just start* on the activity and stop worrying about it. It will take less psychological energy and you'll feel so much better when it's done.

If, however, when asking "why?", you come up with a really good answer, e.g. "I really need that specific piece of information before I can make this decision", then you are probably right not to do it now.

So, the heart of whether it's procrastination or not can be seen in whether you make any *progress* about the situation or get some *closure* on it.

The true Procrastinator does *nothing* about that situation, and nothing gets done, and the situation does not get resolved. You still feel bad and you've wasted time.

In contrast, the good Manager immediately says "Ok, where can I get that information?" and sets out an action plan to resolve the situation, entering tasks in the working diary (or other time management system) in order to move the situation forward. In this case the problem has been 'managed' and commitments are in place to do the task at a more suitable later time.

So Management can delay a task by planning effectively around it IF it requires further action, whereas Procrastination simply lets your fear win and keeps you feeling bad.

26.3 The Solution

If you have a tendency for procrastination the remedy is quite simple – you must just start. Once you have begun you have crossed the main hurdle, and you may even find the creativity beginning to flow. How many times have you put something off for ages, only to complete it in a few minutes and think "that wasn't so bad; why did I avoid it for so long?" If in doubt, just start with something small on the project. Many of the earlier chapters of this book have discussed how to divide the project or report into manageable sections.

26.3.1 Getting Started

For some people the worst part of any project or task is actually getting started. One of the best methods of 'unsticking' such a project, and making a start, is to allocate a small amount of time in one of your peak energy periods (see Chapter 11 - *Establishing your best times for working*). When you find yourself in that allocated time-slot, you just insist that you write something. Often writing *anything* is better than writing nothing. This is partly because as soon as you have committed something to paper, you have something in front of you to amend, change or criticise. This sets up a creative 'loop' where suddenly you find you are making progress.

If you really have no idea what to write you may want to try one of the following 'tricks':

- List what you **already know** about the project.

- List what you **want to achieve** (this often turns into the final structure of the piece of work).

- Imagine a **radio interviewer** has just shoved a microphone in front of you and has asked "so then, what's this piece of work about ?". Write down your answer, and keep it short. This is often a good starting point.

- Ask yourself "Are there some **unanswered questions** that are preventing me from getting on with this?", then write down the questions. Now apply yourself to each question in turn and come

Managing Your Project

up with some answers, or suggestions on how you might find those answers.

Sometimes, you will reach the end of the time period and wish you had longer to work on it. That's the time for a management decision; can I carry on now while the flow is happening? Or do I have other tasks that I really need to tackle instead?

26.3.2 Are your tasks small enough?

In Chapters 17 and 20 we looked at the idea of breaking down a big task into smaller, more manageable tasks, and ideally into a list of Unit Actions. A Unit Action is something that can be done without further explanation.

Many of us will procrastinate about a task because it's too big or vague, and so what we feel is the fear of not knowing what to do.

There are several things you can do to overcome this. The first is to break down your tasks as far as it goes so that the task is a 'no brainer', then maybe you will feel less resistance and will just get on with it.

Imagine that the task you were avoiding was 'User Tests'. That's actually a really deep and complex statement covered in two words, and it's no wonder you have been avoiding it.

The first thing you need to do is to spend some time working out what you *mean* by that phrase, what's expected of you, and what are the sub-units of work involved.

Maybe you might come up with this:

- Identify the purpose of the user tests
- Decide on the number of test subjects
- Design the test strategy
- Write the computer program to handle the data management
- Invite users to participate in the tests
- Schedule the tests and book the room and equipment
- Run all the tests on all the test subjects
- Analyse the results.

Ok, that's already quite a big list. But are these 'Unit Actions'?

There are a few questions you can ask about each of the above bullet-points, which will help you to recognise whether you've got a Unit Action yet.

- What would I **specifically be doing** when I got this done? Can I explain to someone where and what they would see if they saw me getting on with this?
- Are there any **obvious sub-tasks** that make this up?
- If I break this up into simpler, lower-level tasks, **does the explanation seem clear** or has it suddenly got silly?

Let's try these 3 questions on a couple of the above sub-units.

Firstly let's take: *Identify the purpose of the user tests*

1. What would I be doing (and what would people *see* me doing) when I was in the process of "identifying the purpose of the user tests"?

I might sit at a word processor and type up the reason for the experiment, and come up with a form of words for the experimental hypothesis. I'd then want to check this with my supervisor. That's probably all that's involved.

2. Are there any obvious sub-tasks?

Well, taking the above paragraph the following steps become apparent:

- Type up experimental reason/purpose
- Type up hypothesis
- Email the purpose and hypothesis to supervisor.

3. If we break this down further does it help or get silly?:

- Type up experimental reason/purpose
    - Sketch on paper an image of what I want the experimental outcome to achieve
    - Open up my word processor and type up a description of the purpose.
    - Save the file. *(This feels like it is getting silly now because it's not really adding anything that I didn't know, so I'll stop here).*

. . . and you can continue the process.

So far the list has become:

- Identify the purpose of the user tests
    - Type up experimental reason/purpose
        - Sketch on paper an image of the experimental outcome
    - Type up hypothesis
    - Email purpose and hypothesis to supervisor.
- Decide on the number of test subjects
- Design the test strategy
- Write the computer program to handle the data management
- Invite users to participate in the tests
- Schedule the tests and book the room and equipment
- Run all the tests on all the test subjects
- Analyse the results.

When you have worked your way through the whole list you might well end up with 20 to 30 Unit Actions. It may take you an hour to think this through properly. But the very fact that you needed to take an hour to break down 'User Tests' into over 20 more detailed Unit Actions probably explains why you were procrastinating. Your stated task should not have been 'User Tests', but 'High-level planning for user tests (1 hour @Computer)'.

Most procrastination can be solved by a) just starting, or b) breaking down the task into more manageable Unit Actions.

26.4 Positive and Negative Procrastination

Sometimes you need to be kind to yourself. If you are procrastinating about something which is already very well defined, then why not *positively* procrastinate by doing something else on your list instead? At least this way you are still achieving your tasks, and it might even give you the motivation and energy to get on with the delayed task.

If, however, you decide *not* to do a task that you *know* you need to do - and you do something not positive (e.g., watching trash television, sulking, eating snacks etc.) then almost inevitably you will feel doubly bad - once for not having the strength or courage to get on with what you've identified as being important to you, and secondly for doing something you know is bad for you.

So, if you're tempted to put something off, try to do something else positive instead.

Now there is a subtle, but important, difference in *deciding* that you are tired, and need to stop work, and that an hour's trash TV is just what you need. That is a *management* decision. You can usually tell which one it is by how you feel at the end. If you're thinking "That was indeed a load of rubbish, but now I feel refreshed, and I'm ready to get on with my work" then it was a good decision. If you're feeling guilty and still not inclined to do anything, then maybe that was just good old procrastination, in which case you now need to address it with some of the above techniques.

26.5 Summary

We tend to procrastinate about complex tasks because we fear the feelings that we predict we'll have to endure when faced with the task. Ironically, when we get going with the task and complete what we have to do we generally feel great - yet this doesn't stop the fear time after time (just like trying to exercise regularly).

However, often it is the correct managerial decision to postpone something until a later date. Usually though, in these situations there is a very good reason, and you feel good about your decision and your plans. You know it's procrastination when you can't really say why you've not done it and you feel bad about the whole thing.

The two main remedies for procrastination are 1) to just start (as this is the biggest hurdle and once you've begun you will generate creative energy, and 2) split your tasks into smaller and more manageable units, then work on the simplest.

If you are going to procrastinate on a task, why not do so by doing another task from your list, so at least you are being productive. Or, if you're really just very tired, why not be kind to yourself and make a managerial decision to take some time off. That way you can feel good about not working.

In summary, sometimes we procrastinate:

- for a good reason, in which case this is *good management*, so stop feeling bad about it

Managing Your Project

- because we don't want the feelings of doing the task, so *just start* it!
- because the task is not properly defined, so take some time to specify it more clearly and break it down into more manageable Unit Actions.

26.6 Further Reading[19]

"Feel the Fear and Do it Anyway" by Susan Jeffers, Vermilion, (2007), ISBN-10: 0091907071, ISBN-13: 978-0091907075 & Kindle edition.

Student Procrastination: Seize the Day and Get More Work Done by Michael Tefula, Palgrave Macmillan (2014), ISBN-10: 1137312459, ISBN-13: 978-1137312457 or Kindle edition.

Overcoming Procrastination (Overcoming common problems series) by Dr Windy Dryden, Sheldon Press (2000), ISBN-10: 0859698157, ISBN-13: 978-0859698153

MindTools website on overcoming procrastination:

http://www.mindtools.com/pages/article/newHTE_96.htm

---

[19] Although do make sure that this is not just an excuse to avoid getting on with whatever you know you *should* be getting on with!

27. PERFECTIONISM

Some people experience the opposite problem to Procrastination – they can start easily, but can never finish "because it's not *perfect* yet". Perfectionism is a serious impediment to successful time management, and we will consider this in more detail in this chapter.

27.1 Striving for Quality is good

Many people use the term 'perfectionist' to describe themselves (or someone else) who is constantly striving for things to be as good they can be. Striving for good quality is a positive trait. It stops us with being comfortable with mediocrity. It allows us to be proud of what we have produced. It helps us to feel reassured that we have done our best. More often than not it helps us to enjoy our tasks because we're actively involved in doing things well.

If things are done to a high quality, and within the agreed deadline, without too much strain being put on yourself, on people around you, or on other things you need to do, then this is a good thing. Many people work hard, do as much as they can to make things better, then stop at the right time and feel pleased with what they have done. This is *not* perfectionism.

27.2 What is Perfectionism?

Perfectionism is where the striving for top quality becomes all-consuming, typically such that it affects the following:

- your ability to meet **deadlines**
- your own **satisfaction** with what you hand in
- your own **well-being**
- your **relationships** with others
- your **judgement** about what is acceptable to others.

Let's look at each of these in turn.

27.2.1 Ability to meet Deadlines

The great irony is that many students - in a vain attempt to get something 'perfect' (presumably to get the highest marks possible) - submit their work late and get their marks drastically penalised.

This can become a habit that continues into the working environment. Imagine being late to turn up to a critical company presentation because you were working on getting the slides perfect. Everyone's waiting. Everyone's mad at you. The slides may even be near perfect but you were not there at the time you needed to be, and this has ruined any effectiveness. Long-term job prospects damaged because you weren't there on time. Sound silly? Maybe, but sadly this occurs far too often.

If a deadline is *externally* fixed (such as a report hand-in, or a lecture/presentation to give) then it should be utterly respected. You must have something to hand in / deliver at the right time. If you tend to be late for things because you *started* them late, then that is down to bad time management (and in several chapters of this book, we have seen how to make progress in that area). If, however, it is a deep-seated dissatisfaction with the fact your work is not complete or perfect, then this needs to be dealt with as perfectionism.

27.2.2 Satisfaction with what you hand in

The ideal situation is that when you hand something in, you know that you have done your best, given the time and resources available. If you are a perfectionist, you are unlikely to feel good about what you hand in, because you live in a constant state of being dissatisfied with your work.

Don't get this confused with feeling guilty for handing something in that you *know* is bad because you've not given it proper time or effort. Perfectionism tends to make you feel bad *even if* you have worked on something in good time and with lots of dedication.

This is not a psychological (or even psychiatric) book, but perfectionism can be deeply embedded in people's characteristics, and might have a lot to do with the way they were raised or taught. An overly-critical upbringing or education can cause people to constantly dwell on the negatives, rather than striving for the positives and accepting calmly when they need to stop.

Even if perfectionism runs deep, it *can* be overcome. The moment you realise that it's perfectionism that's making you hand-in late, be dissatisfied etc, then you can apply a little trick. You can actually *use* your perfectionist tendencies to your advantage. Be a perfectionist about the following things:

- be as kind to yourself as possible
- respect the deadlines perfectly
- study and celebrate the good points in your own work
- be as nice as possible to other people you're working with.

27.2.3 Well-being

Perfectionism is often associated with stress and stress-related problems. If you live in a state of worry or negativity, this affects your mind, body and soul. If you see someone working really hard to get something right, but loving every minute of it - then this is probably not perfectionism in action. In contrast, if you find yourself or others saying things like:

"It's just not *good* enough (sigh)"

"I'll *never* get this right"

"Why can't I *ever* do things properly?"

"No, this is *rubbish*. I have to tear it up and start again."

"How long til the deadline? That's *ridiculous*! This is nowhere near done!!"

then you might well be listening to a perfectionist.

All of the above statements are packed with negative feelings of frustration and inadequacy. Bursts of stress which cause us to take action (which is then resolved) can be useful, but if sustained over a long period this can be damaging to health and general well-being.

27.2.4 Relationships with others

Perfectionists can be so wrapped up in their own feelings of frustration that they lose an awareness of how this affects people around them.

Friends and relations have to live with the irritability, bad moods and general angst that can be associated with perfectionism. But it can have a very bad effect on co-workers. If you're the only person in the team who is unhappy with what you're producing, it *could* be that you are surrounded by a bad team of people who don't care, OR it might indicate that you are being a bit precious about some aspects of the team's task.

Having a perfectionist as part of a project team can be really tricky for other people to manage. This is sometimes due to the over-focussing on one aspect (e.g. the appearance of a product) at the expense of another (e.g. costings or deadlines). This can cause tensions in the group, and needs a good manager to channel the perfectionist's tendencies to good use, but not to dominate the group.

The real problem comes when the *boss* is a perfectionist. (And remember that *you* are the boss of your own solo project). The negativity of 'that's not good enough', 'do it again', 'no, that's not what I expect', 'how many times must I say this?!' can have a truly dispiriting effect on the people in the team. A huge part of being a good boss is to provide motivation and encouragement to the members of your team; and perfectionists tend to find it hard to praise and encourage others for what they see is poor quality work. Of course bad work needs addressing, but when *everything* looks like bad work to you, then it's possible that the problem is in your own judgement.

In a solo project, if you keep giving yourself negative messages (as in 27.2.3 above) your ability to keep motivated on the project will be damaged.

27.2.5 Judgement about what is acceptable to others

Perfectionists tend to have the most amazing attention to detail, noticing things that nobody else would have a problem with, or never being satisfied with a good job.

Again, do not confuse this with Quality Control, where a product is rejected because it fails certain standards that a customer/examiner would expect to see. This is where a really well-written specification can help. If you can spell out what is *essential*, and what is *desirable*, then you can manage expectations more realistically.

Perfectionists often know that they have unrealistic expectations. However those that don't know this may find themselves in conflict with those around them who really cannot see what the problem is.

Everybody has room for improvement on *every* task. Sadly the following phrase (or something like it) is often encountered by perfectionists.

"Even after I spent ALL that time on that darn (project / report / product / task) the customer / examiner STILL wasn't happy with it".

It's a horrible irony that the things that the perfectionist obsesses about are often NOT what is being judged in the final assessment by others. Students can feel that they should be given 100% because of all the time and effort spent on a piece of work. Examiners do not mark time and effort but results, accuracy, inventiveness, etc., and it is often the case that the perfectionist was not looking at those all of those things, and so ironically gets a far less than perfect mark.

Examiners will often give good marks to the section that has been done well, but are then forced to give poor marks (or often zero) to the section that was missed out completely as a result of perfectionist obsession.

27.3 Managing Perfectionism

In Chapter 6 - *The 2-stage Work Process* we saw the power of realising that there are two key roles that you have to play, regularly, when you're doing a major project. You are a Manager, who oversees the entire process and allocates time to each major task. But you also have to play the role of the Worker, who just gets on with the allocated work. For an effective project, both roles must alternate.

27.3.1 Manager-Worker conversations

Let's assume that your Manager is doing a good job, and is keeping all things (such as deadlines, progress, all tasks, quality etc.) under scrutiny and in balance. Then Perfectionism is what happens when your inner *Worker* is not satisfied that their current job (the one in focus) is completed to a good enough standard, and demands more time, more effort, more cooperation from others, etc.

If, as a Worker, you over-run your allocated time in a vain attempt to make something perfect, you are now using up time that was allocated to another task. By all means strive for excellent work, but learn to stop at the end of your time-slot, or hop up to management level and have a conversation with yourself that should go something like this:

Managing Your Project

Worker: I need more time to get this right. It's just not good enough.

Manager: But we agreed to finish at 11.00am

Worker: Yes, I know, but this isn't up to standard yet, and I need more time.

Manager: But we have these other 3 tasks which also have to be done this morning.

    etc.

It's probably best that nobody witnesses you having this conversation with yourself! (It is usually just a mental process where you weigh up alternative viewpoints). Actually this is about the only time that you need to acknowledge the needs of the Worker and the Manager at the *same* time. Effectively you are negotiating between the high-level context of the Manager, and the recent practical experience of the Worker. You will either come to the conclusion that the Manager was right, and you need to move on to the other tasks, or you decide that improving the current piece of work really *is* more important than doing the tasks you originally planned. Either way this is a *Management* decision. The Worker makes a request, but the Manager decides.

To overcome any of your perfectionist tendencies you must stop when your Manager said you should stop (because it is *never* going to be perfect), or hold a management-level meeting to decide if the current priorities are correct.

27.3.2 Applying the 80:20 rule

The 80:20 rule was described in Section 10.6. It is a useful antidote to the trap of being stuck in a perfection loop. It strikes at the heart of perfectionism by effectively declaring "Take a *lot* less time to do your work; do it well *enough* - no more- and then stop". This can be a bitter pill for perfectionists to swallow.

However, ask a perfectionist to object to this, and - if they are honest - they are probably going to have to object along these lines:

"I want to spend ALL my time on this small task, converging on - but never actually reaching - perfection, and squander all my other time and all my other tasks and goals. Even when I have wasted all that time I will still not be happy with this one task that I've focussed on".

When you put it like that it seems pretty raw, but take this seriously; if you strive for perfection by taking all your time on a few tasks you may end up achieving very little. As a consequence you are very likely to feel bad both about the tasks you DID **and** all the tasks you DIDN'T achieve.

So, the key is to know *when* it's ok to *stop* working on something.

This can be done by a hard application of time ("we've done 10 hours work on this, so wherever we're at this will have to do!") or sensible and detailed quality criteria.

27.4 Summary

Perfectionism is not the same as a striving for good quality. If you work hard to make things as good as they can be within a given time limit, and other things in your life (and in those you work with) do not suffer as a result, then this is simply good standards at work.

Perfectionism, When taken to extremes, borders on obsession and can actually result in one or more of the following:

- poorer work quality
- bad relationships with others
- general dissatisfaction and depression
- missing essential deadlines
- negative effects on your own health and general quality of life.

There is a great irony here that very poor results can emerge from behaviour which worries about getting things perfect. Watch out for (in yourself and others) overly critical judgemental statements about work quality.

There are tricks you can play in order to bypass this tendency. Aim to be perfect in your respect for deadlines, your own well-being, your attitude to others, and in your planning and time management.

If you really are psychologically stuck in perfectionism and you know that it's harming your productivity, then please seek some help. You could start with your supervisor, but also might want to consider talking to a student counsellor as they may be able to help you with some counter-strategies, or look a little deeper to see where this tendency comes from.

Managing Your Project

27.5 External References

Overcoming Perfectionism (Overcoming Books) by Roz Shafran, Sarah Egan, and Tracey Wade, Robinson (2010), ISBN-10: 1845297423, ISBN-13: 978-1845297428 or Kindle edition.

An interesting blog on perfectionism and solutions:

http://personalexcellence.co/blog/overcome-perfectionism/

Wisdom from people who have overcome it:

http://tinybuddha.com/blog/one-thing-need-know-overcome-perfectionism/

28. GETTING STUCK

One of the most common negative situations that people experience when running a project is 'getting stuck'. It happens to nearly everyone at some point in a major project[20]. You just do not seem to be making progress with part or all of the project. This is usually accompanied by feelings of fear ("I'm going to fail my degree") and inadequacy ("I'm just no good at this"). In this section we encourage you to face the fear, identify the problem, and work through a tried and tested means of 'unsticking' the problem to get you moving again.

28.1 Introduction

One of the worst experiences of working on a big project is when your work grinds to a halt. Sometimes the reason is an obvious *external* failure. For example you may be trying to print out a report and the printer breaks down. This is a problem, but its solution has a clear external focus; in this case how can you mend / replace the printer, or find an alternative way to continue the printing process? But this is not really 'getting stuck' - this is just one example of the many obstacles, challenges and problems which appear in any project.

Most external problems are a nuisance but because you are looking at something outside yourself (such as the broken printer) you tend to get annoyed with *it*, and sooner or later that annoyance turns into a motivation

---

[20] You might be interested to know that this entire chapter came about as a direct result of being stuck for four weeks on another section of this book (I'll leave you to guess which one).

to do something about the problem and to sort it out. Or you realise that you can make better progress by finding an entirely new way to achieve what you are trying to do.

Getting stuck is worse than this. At its root is an *inward* problem. Something happens inside you that brings you to a standstill. Because there is no obvious external problem to point at, it is easy to feel bad about yourself.

Some people think that the psychology of how you feel has nothing to do with project management. In my experience it has much more effect than you can realise. If you're well organised you might not even see that effect. But - keep a note of this chapter so that if you find yourself not working AND feeling bad about it, you can return to it as needed.

The aim of this chapter is to help you become UNstuck, by recognising the debilitating mental states that are commonly encountered when doing a project, and then showing a simple algorithm to follow to get you working again.

28.2 Why are you *really* stuck?

The first thing that you need to do is to face the problem. So often, we discover that being stuck is not the result of an external event, but rather an unsolved *internal* mental block. Because of this you might well be experiencing being stuck as a *mental state of failure*.

- "It's *no* good – I'm just not making *any* progress"
- "Everyone else is really getting on with *their* projects"
- "I just *don't* know what to do"
- "I'm just *not* engaged with this project"

Have you noticed how each of the above statements is an expression of negative emotion? You can imagine each one being said with a big sigh and drooping shoulders.

Notice something important: each statement says *nothing* about how to take action to get out of the situation. It just dwells on the emotion of being unstuck. This is particularly tricky for people who pride themselves on being logical, organised and unemotional. You're a human being - you are bound to experience this at some time or other.

However, the act of noticing that you are feeling like this is exactly what you need to do to get unstuck; **you first need to flick a mental switch** from this position:

- "I'm not feeling very good about my lack of progress"

to this position:

- "I have encountered a problem; now I am going to find a solution to it"

Without this switch being flicked, you would probably remain depressed and continue to blame external events, however relevant or irrelevant.

As an example, imagine a student saying this[21]:

- "I'm completely stuck on my project because my supervisor is ill."

This places the blame somewhere else and gives you an excuse not to do anything! Flick the mental switch and the same situation turns into this:

- "My supervisor is ill, so I either need to identify something else in the project that I can be getting on with, or (if the illness is longer than a week or so) get in touch with the Department to see if there is any other temporary support."

This switch-flicking is a very simple concept, but it works because it reminds us that we really are in charge of our own work, not anybody else, nor any undesirable external event.

28.3 Exactly what is stuck?

Once you have acknowledged that it is *you* that are stuck, and that you are going to do something about it, then you can move on to identifying exactly what is stuck. Some of the negative feelings outlined above are allowed to thrive simply because you have not defined exactly what the problem is.

Taking the above example, if you think that you are stuck *because* your supervisor is ill, you are thinking in a limited way. That is simply a *fact* which relates to your project. What you probably mean (if you think about it for a minute or so) is more like this:

---

[21] This is just one variation of a type of statement I've heard hundreds of times from people. Somehow when we're feeling down we still find the energy to blame the inaction on anywhere/anyone but ourselves. Thus nothing gets done and the cycle continues.

Managing Your Project

- "My supervisor is ill. I was not expecting this, and I was rather hoping to get a decision this week about whether I should take 'path A' or 'path B'. I feel rather unprepared to make that decision, and I wanted some advice."

This is not only much more honest, but it throws the problem back to you:

- "I need to make a decision on whether to do A or B, but I feel unprepared"

Because this problem is back with you, *you* can start to do something about it. So let's spend a little time to remove the negative feelings and start thinking of some positive action. The next section encourages you to focus on possible solutions to, or ways around, the problem.

28.4 What will 'being un-stuck' look and feel like?

To help you think positively, you need to be thinking about *solutions*, rather than wallowing in the negative feelings associated with the problem. So, ask yourself the question "What will being un-stuck look like or feel like?" Imagine for a moment that sometime in the immediate future the problem is solved, or you have found a way round. You may come up with several ideas, so write them down quickly, or produce a mind-map (as in Chapter 8).

Taking our situation above that you need a decision about option A or B, but your supervisor is not around to discuss it, here are a few mental pictures you might paint to visualise the problem already solved or worked around:

a) you imagine yourself working away happily on another part of the project, which you can make progress on without your supervisor's presence *(working around the problem)*

b) you visualise yourself exploring options A and B in more depth, so that you gain confidence in making the decision. When your supervisor returns you are able to recommend one particular option *(taking charge of the problem of your own understanding of the issues)*

c) you see and hear yourself in a meeting with your supervisor, having a discussion about options A and B, and imagining exactly what he or she would say about each option. *(creative thinking to give yourself some extra information)*

The irony is that while picturing mental scene c) (above) you might realise, with a smile, that your supervisor would be quite likely to say "well, what do *you* think?"[22] So the whole notion that you are "stuck because they are ill" is false. You are stuck because there is a decision to be made, and all you needed in this case was the courage to make the decision yourself, once you have gained further information.

28.5 How can I put this into action and get un-stuck?

The final step is vital to becoming un-stuck. You need to turn the creative ideas into definite actions which you schedule into your management system. This might mean entering a slot in your calendar where you will do the work, or it might be an action on your planner, or even an entry in your project list. If you have identified a specific action and you can do it now, then do it.

However, you may have come up with creative ideas that are not immediately actionable. You will need to break these down into Action Steps using the sorts of processes described in Chapters 10, 12, 15 and 20.

Imagine, as an example, that your creative breakthrough is that "you need to know more about options A and B, and then make the decision yourself". In this example you might identify the following tasks that need to be done:

- Do a web-search on options A and B
- Create a mind-map with the pros and cons of each option
- Make a decision (by Friday) concerning which option you should take
- Write a one-page summary of the options, the decision and the reasons for choosing it. (This will be an invaluable memory aid for later discussion with your supervisor, and for putting in your report. It also acts a 'statement of closure' which declares in writing that you have taken charge of the problem, considered the options, made a decision, and have now moved on.)

Each of the above steps would need to be put into your system either as an action or a mini-project. Put deadlines on them, then get them done as soon as you can. You are now free.

---

[22] And they would be *right* to throw the question back to you. We saw in Chapter 5 that the role of the Supervisor is an advisor who helps you to work on your project - not a manager to impose decisions on you.

Managing Your Project

The act of getting going again after being stuck can often be enough to completely turn your feelings around; from complete resignation to successful productivity. So if you are stuck on something, try following the above steps until you have something specific which you can *do* to get you moving again. This process is summarised in the diagram shown in Figure 28.1.

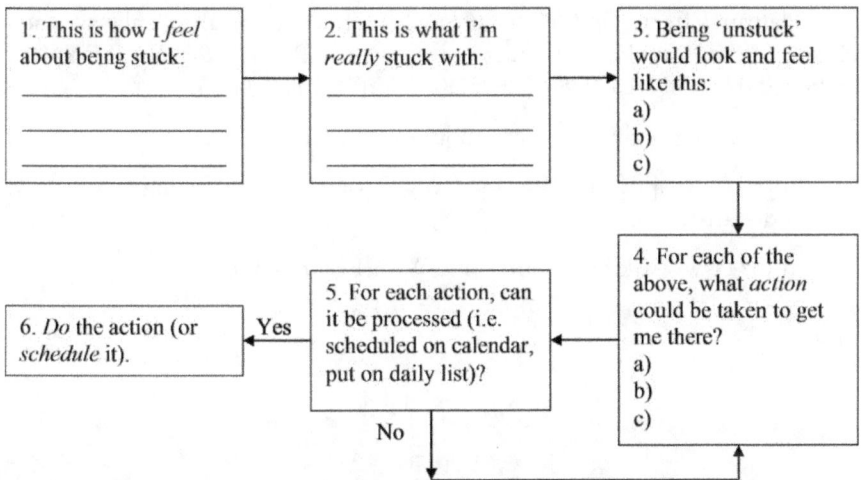

Figure 28.1 Summary of the process of becoming un-stuck

28.6 Summary

Problems occur as a natural part of any project. When these problems have clear *external* causes (such as a broken printer) the solutions are reasonably obvious. However, getting stuck - where your work on the project just comes to a halt - usually indicates an *internal* problem or unsolved dilemma.

This state of being stuck is usually associated with one or many negative emotions. Humans have a tendency to focus on this cycle of emotions, but the way out involves deciding to flick a mental 'switch' and begin to focus on solutions, rather than how bad the problems make you feel.

Take some time to work out what exactly is stuck. Phrase this in such a way that you are back in the centre of the control loop. In other words, stop feeling bad about things and take back the control to get things moving again. A good way of doing this is to visualise "what being UNstuck will look and feel like". While you are doing this jot down ideas, maybe in the form of a mind-map, and allow yourself to look for as many solutions or work-arounds as possible.

Very importantly, enter the best solutions as Actions or Projects into your planning system, and - if possible - do something immediately to get the project moving again. The freedom you gain from becoming unstuck can give rise to a surge of productivity, so make the most of it.

28.7 External links

The Plateau Effect: Getting from Stuck to Success by Bob Sullivan and Hugh Thompson E P Dutton & Co Inc (2 May 2013), ISBN-10: 0525952802, ISBN-13: 978-0525952800, and Kindle edition.

Some interesting online thoughts about overcoming stuck-ness:

> http://www.pickthebrain.com/blog/7-ways-to-stop-feeling-stuck-and-start-feeling-free/

> http://www.wikihow.com/Cope-With-Feeling-Stuck

29. LOSING FOCUS

As you get to the core of your project, where a lot of practical work is done, it is possible to lose your focus and become *too* engrossed in your work. This may not sound like a problem - surely working hard is good? However, as we discussed in Chapter 6 - *The 2-Stage Work Process* it's really important to balance the dual roles of Manager and Worker. Losing focus often happens when you have so much work to do that your inner Worker is so busy that you forget to look at the project from a managerial perspective.

29.1 Identifying your loss of focus

The worst thing about this problem is that you do not notice it happening. At least with Getting Stuck (see Chapter 28) you *know* when you are stuck! With loss of focus you are often busily working away, but possibly on the *wrong* things.

You will eventually discover your loss of focus by noticing one of the following symptoms:

- Someone else asks you what you are doing. You reply in enthusiastic detail. They counter by asking "but how does that meet your main *goal*? I thought you were doing . . .". And then it dawns on you that you are not actually working towards your aim and objectives.

- You develop a gnawing sense of unease that 'something isn't quite right', but you do not let yourself think about it because you are 'just too busy'. One day you realise that the unease was simply your Manager crying out to be listened to[23].

It is easy to lock away the Manager in this way when you are busy, because you have so much to do and so little time. But, if you think about it, this is not the wisest thing to do. It is precisely *when* there is a lot to do, and time is short, that you *need* good management. However urgent the circumstances, you should *always* make some regular time to take stock of the current situation and to create and maintain an up-to-date plan.

29.2 How your focus is lost

This loss of your managerial focus often happens when you are deeply involved in your work (analysing a piece of music, searching for references, writing a piece of computer code etc). In general when you are immersed in Worker mode, you can easily get side-tracked from your plans without even noticing.

This is a natural human state. Have you ever wasted some time browsing on the internet? Maybe you started looking for a reference about Wagner's *Ring Cycle* but somehow ended up browsing the intricacies of Mongolian pig farming. How did this happen? Well, humans are naturally inquisitive, and perhaps an advert caught your eye while searching for 'The Ring' and you decided to look at it "for a moment". This advert led you to a whole set of discoveries that were intriguing. After several hours something in your subconscious made you think "Now the ring through the end of this pig's nose wasn't the sort of ring I started looking for".

The same distractions can happen more subtly when you are working on the main feature of your project. You may be regularly losing time working on something that is not taking you forward towards your goal. For example, a common distraction in computer programming is "making it look nice". When you first see the results of your coding appear on the screen, it is natural for you to want to go back and improve the 'look and feel' of this interface. However, many programmers do this to the detriment of getting the program to *work* properly. As you might imagine, if you let this trend continue, this will not go down well with the examiners:

Examiner: "So then, as far as I can see - your program does not actually *do* what it is *meant* to do"

---

[23] Ok, that's a bit over dramatic! But I'm trying to describe a real problem that happens more often than people give it credit for. Being busy looks good. Surely I'm doing ok?

Managing Your Project

Student: "True, but it really *looks* nice".

We are easily distracted, and we need help to maintain focus.

29.3 The importance of regular Manager meetings

To counteract our natural tendency to get distracted, it is important to find ways of regularly involving your Manager. This can be done by learning to listen to that quiet inner voice which says "remind me – *why* am I doing this?" A simple solution is to schedule[24] a *daily* management meeting, where you review:

- the main aim and objectives,
- the overall time-plan for the project,
- how far you have progressed,
- what is the most important thing you could be doing today?

Regular (but relatively short) meetings like this also help with your general motivation (see Chapter 30), because it forces you to take stock of the results of your work so far.

As an analogy, if you are walking in the countryside, climbing a hill in the rain, you will probably spend a lot of time looking at the ground watching carefully where you are placing your feet on the slippery ground. The irony of this is that even though you are steadily making progress, you do not notice that progress because every step looks the same: 'footstep on muddy soil', 'footstep on muddy soil' . . . . If however, you stop at regular intervals to look round, you will get a chance to take in the view. This not only shows you how far you have come, but is also rewarding in itself. Even a few steps forward can change your perspective. Some might say that looking around is the whole reason for taking the walk in the first place. But the other reason for looking up is that otherwise you might just discover that you have been walking in **completely** the wrong direction for the last hour.

---

[24] and that means putting it in a place you will be reminded every day. This could be in a diary or on a daily planner, or a daily electronic reminder by email or notification.

29.4 Managerial Self-Assessment

It is therefore important to mark regular slots in your diary (e.g., every few weeks) when you plan to take stock of where you are. These will be in addition to your daily management focus meetings. Figure 29.1 shows a series of questions that you could ask yourself. This is a self-assessment form where you ask yourself a series of Manager-level focussing questions. However, you may wish to discuss your answers to the questions with your supervisor or focus group.

Project: Self Assessment Form

Purpose: This form is intended to help you keep a top-level 'managerial' overview of your project, and to encourage you to think about the overall direction and scheduling of the work.

1. State the major points of originality of the project

2. What are the main *aims* of the project?

3. Give a *brief* summary of the work done so far.

4. How far do you feel this has taken you towards your main project goal?

5. Comment on your time management of the project workload.

6. Do you know yet what you would like to present in the final viva/demo?

7. What steps will you have to take to ensure that happens?

8. What 'risk management' plans do you have, to ensure you have *something consistent* to show if your final goals are not reached?

9. What areas of the project are you particularly worried about?

10. What steps are you taking to ensure these are addressed, and that you get support/help/information?

11. Are there any other comments which should be fed back to your supervisor?

Figure 29.1 Self-Assessment Form

Managing Your Project

Initially, it might be good to fill in such a form about a month or so into your project. However, many people find it very useful to ask themselves the same questions regularly - perhaps on the first day of each month[25]. Even though the questions are the same, your own perspective, knowledge and progress will be different each time.

You might also want to develop and fill in your own management progress form (see Figure 29.2).

This can be used to give regular (for example, fortnightly) reports to your supervisor or focus group. Decide with your supervisor if this would be a useful method of reporting your work, and then plan it in your diary as a regular commitment[26].

At the top of the form (under "Progress since last meeting") you write down things you have achieved since your last supervision meeting, and the things you are still working on, specifically concentrating on the Actions you *wrote down* on the previous form. This ensures that nothing is forgotten and that there is a consistent flow from one meeting to the next.

The section "Summary of Progress to Date" is specifically designed to ensure that you consider your *whole* progress so far, since the start of the project. This helps you summarise the context of your work, and helps you reflect on your progress up til now. It also helps you to regain focus on the big picture, and stops you from being side-tracked by other activities that may seem more compelling but are not aligned with your goals.

The 'Actions for next week' (or two weeks, or whatever) is a list of major targets that you plan to achieve before the next meeting. Try to make these specific (e.g. "Get all journal papers and produce a summary", rather than "Make progress on literature review").

If used well, this sort of form can provide an invaluable way of regularly noting your progress and making executive decisions. It is useful for you even if it is a private exercise. However, knowing that *someone else* is expecting the report, and will read and comment on it, really helps to make you do it regularly and to think more deeply about what you are writing.

---

[25] or - towards the end of the project - every week or two.

[26] Some institutions will require you to do something like this on a regular basis. For example, you might be asked to send an email report to your supervisor every two weeks, or a few days in advance of each supervision meeting. If not, it is good practice to do this anyway. Demonstrate to your supervisor that you are proactively managing your project.

Andy Hunt

Regular Progress Form   Date:_____

Progress since last meeting:

Summary of progress to date:

Actions for next week:

Other comments:

Figure 29.2 An example regular management reporting form

29.5 Summary

Losing Focus is a problem that people often do not realise they are suffering from. You may feel uneasy that what you are working on is not the most important thing, or someone may remind you of your main goal and you realise suddenly that your current preoccupation is not going to get you there.

Ironically, at the most busy times, when you feel like you should just be getting on with the work - that is the most important time to take regular 'management' breaks to reappraise your progress and the validity of your current activity.

Humans are easily distracted, and the same applies to our goals. If you don't regularly review your goals, targets, actions, etc., you are likely to drift onto something else. The most useful solution to this is to schedule a short daily management meeting (which you get reminded about in your planner or task list), where you take stock of your project's overall aim, the timescales of the project, your progress so far, and thus identify the most important thing for you to do today.

This chapter includes a Project Self-Assessment Form, which you could use (or adapt) every few weeks, as a way of regaining your focus, and making sure that everything is still moving in the right direction. Also included is a Project Progress Form, which can form the basis of regular reporting to your supervisor. Some institutions will expect you to do this anyway, but even if not it is a useful discipline and demonstrates that you are actively managing and monitoring your project. It also helps you to regain and retain your Focus on your main goals.

30. LOSING MOTIVATION

Everyone loses their will to work every now and again. This is not the same as 'getting stuck' or 'losing focus' as covered in previous chapters.

Getting **stuck** means that you *know* what you want but cannot see *how* to get it.

Losing **focus** means that you are working away busily on the *wrong* things, that will not ultimately take you towards your goal.

Losing **motivation** means that the very *act of working* becomes hard.

30.1 What does losing motivation feel like?

If you find yourself making comments such as:

- I just *wish* this project was over!
- *Why* do I have to get up this morning?
- I just can't be *bothered* to do any work.

then you have probably lost your motivation, and you should take some time out immediately to sort out the problem.

Let's be clear - everyone feels like this every now and then, about any big task that you're working on. Just encountering a negative mood is totally normal. It's what happens *next* that determines whether it's a real problem. If you're just a bit tired, then a nap or a good night's sleep can change your perspective. This indicates that it was just a passing mood.

If you have lost your motivation, then the sort of comments listed above are usually accompanied by feeling 'down' or tired, and they usually persist over several days or longer. If this is a *change of state* for you (i.e., you were not like this a while ago, and this is not your normal personality), then you should take this as a warning signal from your mind and body that something needs to be addressed.

Maintaining motivation is often associated with *balance, tiredness* or *perspective*. Let's take a look at these in the following sections.

30.2 Project – Work - Play balance

Students working on a large-scale project often find that there is a complex balancing act to be accomplished between the following three elements:

- Project Work
- Other Work and Commitments
- Play and Relaxation

Work too *hard* and you will gradually find yourself becoming tired and dispirited.

Work too *little* and you will know deep down that you are not making enough progress. This will affect your overall feeling of wellbeing and sense of self-worth.

Work too intensively on your *project* and you may find that you have other commitments that are not being met.

So the balance is to find the right combination of work and play that keeps life feeling fun, but also reassures you that you are on target and making measurable progress. It's important to plan time for all of these, and to treat this balancing act as a very important part of your personal Managerial process.

30.3 The effect of tiredness

If you are tired, please take a break. You probably know this already, but pushing yourself to work when you are really tired can produce some bad work, and a feeling of resentment towards that work.

So take breaks whenever you can. If you do a web-search on 'taking breaks while studying' you'll find many examples of advice, but the following points come up repeatedly:

- For every hour of work, make sure you take a 10 or 15-minute break.

Managing Your Project

- Don't do sitting work for more than 3 hours at a time.

- Concentrate on one task at a time (don't multitask - especially with TV, social networking or phones)

- Get a good night's sleep, and allow yourself some 'wind-down' time before you try to get to sleep.

However, if you take are taking plenty of breaks and you are *still* feeling very tired, and this feeling of tiredness persists over several days or weeks, then you might wish to talk to someone about this – a friend, your supervisor, a counsellor or a doctor.

All educational institutions have support networks for students, including people to talk to when you are struggling. For example at my university, there is an Open Door network of people who will listen and help you to work through and get over your struggles. In the reference section for this chapter is link to a list of some of the common problems that students have (with links to useful advice).

Many students resist seeking help because they see it as a sign of failure. I often explain how as I was growing up my world became more and more blurry until I could not study in class and I had to see the optician. Once I'd got my glasses, everything was back to normal. It's the same with the common problems listed above. By getting help you are being proactive, and sorting out a problem, just as you would be if you went to see your supervisor about an academic problem.

30.4 The importance of perspective on motivation

If, on the other hand, tiredness is not the problem (for example you find that you have plenty of energy for *other* things) then you have probably just lost (or misplaced) your 'driving force' for working on your project. You need to take some time (at Managerial level) to rediscover that driving force.

If someone said "Get up at 5.00am tomorrow morning, write two pages, and then I'll give you a million pounds" you would probably find the motivation to get up and write! You might even be excited about it. If on the other hand the person told you instead to "Get up at 5.00am tomorrow morning, and write two pages because I *told* you so!", you would probably resent the whole experience. And yet the task (getting up and writing) is the same in both cases. This tells us that it is not usually the task *itself* that is the problem, but the picture you have in your head of *why* you are doing the task.

So, if you are not motivated to work, try looking at the task from different perspectives. Let us take the example that you are trying to write Chapter 3 of your final report, and you just cannot seem to get on with it. Assume that you are not stuck (i.e. you know *what* you should do) and are not particularly tired overall, you just feel as if you want to do anything but write this chapter.

Get your inner Manager to ask your inner Worker *why* the work isn't getting done. Listen carefully to the answer – it might reveal something you can deal with straight away.

Manager: Why don't you want to get on with this?

Worker: I just don't feel like it.

Manager: Why? – what's the matter?

Worker: It's just too complex.

Manager: Would a Managerial meeting help? Maybe we could think about it a bit more and break it down into simpler tasks?

In this case, a short conversation with yourself has revealed the problem; that there's a bit more thinking that needs doing to make the work clearer or more manageable in smaller chunks.

If this does not help, and the Work-plans are clear enough, we need to *change* the perspective to find the driving force. The first way of doing this is to raise the perspective by simply looking back at your overall plans. You might then see that according to your schedule, this chapter *needs* to be finished by the end of this week for you to keep on time. Or you might be reminded of an email to your supervisor where you promised to get this done so that they could look at it before they go away. These little bits of higher-level knowledge might be the push that your inner worker needs to get on with it.

If not, you may want to raise the perspective again – noting, perhaps, that the final report deadline is only three weeks away, and handing this in on time is important. You will know by the adrenaline rush whether you have found the motivating reason to start work on the chapter[27].

---

[27] This is the reason that some people seem to have to wait until the very last day before a deadline before starting on a piece of work. They need the panic of the upcoming deadline to motivate them to begin work. By far a better way is to induce *mild* panic on a regular basis by thinking through the project deliverables, so that you know that the chapter *has* to be written this week in order to achieve the final goal in a calm way.

Managing Your Project

If you are *still* having problems motivating yourself to begin work, then you should raise the perspective yet again, and look at the negative consequences of **not** submitting the project report (failing the project, thus failing the degree, thus damaging a career path and so on). Imagine holding these possibilities in one hand in front of you. At the same time think of the positive consequences of doing the work (feeling of satisfaction, a good chapter, a report that is on time, a good qualification, the subsequent career and financial results). Hold these in the other hand. Weigh them up. Know that the difference between these two future possibilities really *does* come down to whether or not you do the next little bit of work. This should help you to make a start.

If you get all the way up this chain of perspectives and you still have no motivation to work, then you really should seek help urgently from your supervisor and other people to get some advice on what is holding you back.

30.5 Summary

Everyone feels tired at regular intervals, so it is no surprise that you might not feel like getting on with your work at such times. It's probably right to take a nap or do something else to regain your energy. However, if the lack of motivation to get on with your work persists, then it's very important to take some time out to evaluate your balance, tiredness and perspective.

Establishing a sensible balance between work and relaxation is vital. You need life to feel as fun, interesting and positive as possible, and for this you need the right proportion of project work, other work, and activities and rest that are completely different.

Insist on taking regular breaks. Our concentration tends to wane after 15-20 minutes, so make sure you vary your activities, and get up and move around when you can. Don't work for long periods at your computer and expect your output to be equally productive. Although various people think they can multitask, it's really not advisable. If you're keen to communicate and catch up with social media - why not take a complete break to do it, rather than having your thought processes constantly interrupted by incoming messages?

However, if you're still tired after taking plenty of breaks and reasonably normal nights, you may wish to speak to someone about this (supervisor, doctor, university support network) to get some advice. It is not a sign of weakness to seek help, but instead is a very sensible managerial decision.

We've covered some ways to change your perspective - questions you can ask yourself to find a higher-level way of thinking about the task. Sometimes this can give you the motivation to make a start, or you may find that there is still a bit of work to be done before you can start on this task. If you have thought in detail about your weekly plans, then overall goals, then your whole project's success, then your degree's outcome - and you still cannot find the motivation to work, then you really do need to see your supervisor as soon as possible.

30.6 Further Reading and External Links

A web-page about when students should seek help:

http://studentsagainstdepression.org/get-support/building-support-networks/whats-stopping-you-getting-help/

An article about students with depression:

http://www.huffingtonpost.co.uk/2013/06/27/increase-student-depression-university-mental-health_n_3510291.html

This is a list of some of the common problems that students have (with links to useful advice) from the University of York (UK) Open Door team:

https://www.york.ac.uk/students/support/health/problems/

31. DISCOVERING SIMILAR WORK

A surprisingly common problem encountered by research students (who are trying to do something original) is the discovery (late into the project) of a paper or a product which appears to show that your work has already been done by someone else.

31.1 Someone else has done it already

If this happens to you, you will immediately worry about the validity of your project. You may feel guilty or annoyed that you did not discover this before, for example during the Literature survey. You may even worry about the outcome of your project and your whole course. Stop. Relax. Make an appointment to talk to your supervisor.

Remember that if this happens, then you are not alone. For whatever reason, you embarked upon your project in good faith that it was original, or had original components based on other work. Your supervisor knows this too and should be able to help you deal with this.

Sometimes you make the discovery yourself, and at other times someone else hands the paper to you, often with relish: "Hey look what I found – it seems to be *exactly* what you're doing!" But, before you despair, let's just look at the positives in this situation.

- The fact that someone else is working on this topic helps to show that it is a worthy and worthwhile topic to study.

- You now have more literature (and a highly related piece of work at that) which you can include in your literature survey.

- No two people (or research groups) do the same thing. Imagine a person in the process of inventing the violin. Now imagine someone coming up to them and saying *"Hey - I've found this great paper that does what you're doing. It's all about an instrument with strings stretched over a wooden body. You really should see this"*. Imagine if the violin maker gave up because their friend had found this description of a guitar[28]. Everyone's work is different, and the value of your work can come from the subtle differences.

Embrace the fact that other people are working on similar topics, and discuss with your supervisor how this might affect the focus of your work.

31.2 Updating your Literature Survey

In Chapter 19 we looked in some detail at the production of a Literature Survey. It is very likely that this took place in the early stages of the project. Towards the end of the process two important things may have changed:

1) Time has passed since you wrote your Literature Survey. In that time people all over the world will have been working in similar areas to your project. Some of this information will now have made its way into papers and onto websites. This new information is not yet reflected in your survey, so maybe this is a good time to bring it up to date.

2) Your perspective will have developed as you have carried out the work on your project. This means that you have new insights into what material is relevant literature for your project. While reading back over your original survey you may even find that some of it no longer seems connected with your project.

In both cases, don't be concerned, but instead use it as a driving force to update your survey.

31.3 Idea Particles

A very sensible and highly scientific colleague of mine once confessed that he had the notion that ideas appear to come into the world all at once, in showers of particles that float down from the sky and fall onto certain

---

[28] Actually it's really hard to say which came first, because there are so many precursors and variations that it almost does not make sense to say that one person invented it. And this goes for much of human endeavour. Really good inventions often evolve and are the products of a process of refinement and sharing / stealing / influence of other ideas. So (forgive the musical pun) if you're inventing the violin and someone shows you a guitar - don't fret !

Managing Your Project

random people who then have that idea.

Strangely enough, history is full of examples of people who did not know each other (often in different countries and with no chance of reading competing publications or communicating with each other) who seem to invent the same sort of thing at roughly the same time. This seems to happen not just in the area of science and invention, but in the arts and philosophy too.

An interesting article on Wikipedia talks about Multiple Discovery[29]. It seems that even the whole idea of mankind settling down from their nomadic existence and beginning farming and town-building seemed to spontaneously happen in many places around the world independently, starting from around 10000 BC. Many scientific inventions and papers are made and published, only to discover that someone else (or several others) has been working on similar or identical topics. One of the most famous examples was the invention of the telephone by Alexander Graham Bell who historically beat Elisha Gray (with his similar invention) to the patent office by a matter of hours[30].

It has been suggested that humans work on the combination of previous concepts and ideas and that this leads inevitably to new, similar works appearing in different locations at similar times. Clearly the gradual increase in worldwide communication - from travelling, to the printing press, to radio and television, to computers and the internet - has sped up this process. It is therefore *quite likely* that during the course of your project, you will discover something which is similar to what you are doing. I would estimate that between 50 and 75 percent of my PhD and Masters students have had this experience.

31.4 Using the new ideas

There are several things that you can do with the new discovery that can enhance your work. Have a read through this list, see if you think any of them might work for you.

---

[29] http://en.wikipedia.org/wiki/Multiple_discovery includes a summary, and an interesting set of references.

[30] If you're interested in this sort of thing, you might want to follow up the controversy that has raged for nearly 140 years about this. See, for example, http://www.loc.gov/rr/scitech/mysteries/telephone.html

31.4.1 Embrace the differences

Read the new ideas in detail. Take some time to note carefully how your work is different to theirs. During this process you may even realise that the new work only *superficially* resembles your own. When this first happened to me in my PhD I discovered that only the title was really similar. The concepts and even the meaning of the words in the title were very different to what I was doing.

Even if the concepts are similar, then look for the differences in the methods, the details, the analysis and the applications of the work. If it really does look very similar then your examiners are likely to ask you whether and how your work differs from this. So study it. Look for and expect differences, and learn from this process.

31.4.2 Improve your own work

On reading the new paper you may gain some new insights into the topic that you are studying. Note these down, think about them, and discuss with your supervisor whether it is appropriate to modify your own work in the light of what you have discovered.

31.4.3 Contact the authors

In these days of easy communication, you might even want to contact the person or people who have published what you have just read. Carefully discuss this with your supervisor, as there may be very good reasons not to do this. Equally, from my own students' experience, there have been several instances where the project was improved enormously by including some of the subsequent discussions in the final thesis, and then sending the other people a copy of the thesis after submission.

If, after discussion with your supervisor, you decide to do this, please re-read Chapter 22 - *Structuring your Communication*, and especially section 22.6, before you send off your message.

31.4.4 Reflect on how this happened

You can learn a lot about your topic by considering how this other person or group has made a similar discovery to you. Look at their references. Are they similar to yours? If so, this might go some way to explaining the similarities in their work. Alternatively are they very different? This is equally - if not more - fascinating, since they have reached

Managing Your Project

similar conclusions to you but starting from a very different background. Take a look at their research group and previous projects to see how the concepts overlap with yours. Look at their previous publications (or those of their supervisor) and see if you can notice any patterns in the development of the ideas. All of these things can help you to see your own work in a much wider context.

Whatever you do, try to quickly recover from the negative feelings of making such a discovery, and move on to positive action.

31.5 Summary

A very common experience is to find out, sometime during your project, that your idea you thought was original is being worked on by other people around the world. At first this can seem devastating to students who were thinking that they had the monopoly on a particular idea or invention. However, it is surprisingly likely that this will happen to you, just by the way that human beings tend to knit together existing ideas into new concepts.

As soon as you discover such a similar work, make an appointment to see your supervisor, rather than (what often happens) getting depressed and worried. Almost without fail this turns out to be a good thing!

If others are working on this idea, that shows that it's more likely to be a good one. In practice everyone does things differently and so it is most probable that your work will turn out to be subtly or even majorly different from the newcomer. You also have a new piece of literature which might prompt you into updating your Literature Review. You might learn something new about the subject by studying how this topic has been handled differently by someone else. In some cases you may even wish to make contact with the other researchers, but it is best to seek advice about this from your supervisor.

Whether 'idea particles' exist, or whether humans are just really clever at picking up on current inventions and situations and coming up with the next big thing - it seems as if it is completely normal to discover something and then find out that someone else has already done it. Your supervisor knows this, and your examiners know this. So, your job is simply to document what you discovered and to analyse your work in the context of that knowledge. It is very likely that you will learn something new and that this will (in the long run) be a help to your work rather than the massive hindrance that it appears to be when you first discover it.

SECTION 7
TOWARDS THE END OF THE PROJECT

This final section contains a set of chapters which come into play in the latter stages of the project, and after its completion.

- **Ch. 32 The Closing Stages** - *keeping cool towards the end.* Much of the earlier parts of the book rightfully concentrate on setting up a management system and 'getting going'. However, this chapter helps you to accept that running out of time is inevitable, and suggests ways of handling this positively and gracefully, thus bring the project to a successful and well-managed conclusion.

- **Ch. 33 Finding out how your Project will be Marked** - *allowing you to focus effectively in the latter stages.* Knowledge of your marking scheme and markers - if handled well - can give you an advantage by helping you to concentrate on the most important elements of your project in the last months and weeks. This chapter describes several strategies to discover your marking scheme and to use it to manage the closing stages.

- **Ch. 34 The Viva** - *talking about your project effectively.* Many projects conclude with a face-to-face spoken examination called a 'viva-voce' or commonly 'viva'. This chapter helps you prepare for it by giving you an idea of what to expect in that exam, what sort of questioning you may face, and how to handle this effectively.

- **Ch. 35 Publishing Your Work** - *sharing your project results with a wider audience.* This final chapter considers how to summarise your work in the form of papers, and how to present it at conferences. If your project is successful, then other people are going to want to hear about it, and this chapter gives some advice about how to make that happen.

32. THE CLOSING STAGES

This chapter discusses various ideas about how the management of a project needs to be handled and adjusted as you approach the end. There are various common behaviours that are best avoided, and certain elements of good practice that are advisable.

32.1 Running out of time

"What if I run out of time?"

"It's getting really serious now: I'm nearly at the end"

These are the sort of feelings, thoughts and questions that everyone seems to ask towards the end of the project.

Let me just say it so that we can get it out of the way . . .

You WILL run out of time.

The project is finite; it is going to end. It is not some sort of failure to run out of time - it's a temporal inevitability.

It happens to everybody, yet everyone seems to be surprised by it and to feel guilty about it. A good manager accepts that time ticks on and *will* run out. If your project is worthwhile there will always be more you can do with it, but time is finite, so you *are* going to run out of it. The trick is to ensure that you run out of time *gracefully*.

So the key behaviour is how you MANAGE that inevitability.

32.2 Don't forget to Manage

When you are in the final stages of the project, it is very important not to lose focus of the project as a whole. There can be a strong temptation to "just carry on a bit longer to get this section of work finished". Think about this for a moment – this is your inner Worker actually saying to your Manager *"Don't bother me now. I know we might be short of time, but I know what's best; I have to complete this"*. And there is the problem - you cannot get a high-level perspective when you're working on the ground.

So, here is a warning that is taken from many years' experience of watching students in the final stages of their projects. Don't be driven to blindly finish whatever you are working on; you may be making an unwise decision. Many a computing student has worked all hours to finish their computer program, apparently blind to the fact that it would be better to finalise their report. Of course the program is important, but the report is the statement to the examiners of what you have done and why you have done it. If the report is not complete you could fail – even with a working program! Now your Manager *knows* this, and has known it all along – it's written in your plan. But your Worker can sometimes take over near the end with disastrous consequences.

Here's a challenge for you to prevent the above from happening. Maybe when time is short you should have *more* Management meetings, not fewer. This will help to ensure that, especially when the deadline is approaching, you focus on the essential things.

As an analogy, imagine you had to tidy a room and you had half an hour before someone important came in. You should keep taking time out to go to the door and pretend to be that person entering the room – and noting what is the most obvious thing that still needs tidying up. When you run out of time, you know you will have done your best, and that the room is better than when you started. Beware the trap of getting really interested in sorting out a bookshelf in the far corner, and running out of time, not noticing that the important visitor will fall over a pile of smelly old clothes by the entrance.

The advice is clear. Do not abandon your Manager towards the end of a project when time is tight. Instead involve them *more* fully, having shorter meetings *more often* to ensure that the higher-level perspective guides the work being done, until the alarm clock strikes, and you can finally relax, knowing that you have done the best you could with the time available.

Here are four things you can do which will maximise your managerial control of the project.

Managing Your Project

32.2.1 Daily Management Meetings

When you're running short of time, it makes very good sense to start each day with a management meeting. It doesn't need to take very long, but it allows you to make a clear plan for the day. Start by looking at the date and your Critical Path and Countdown Plan (see sections 32.4 and 32.5) to remind yourself of the most important things that you have already identified to do. Check that this still makes sense, as some other issues may have emerged since you made the plans. Then decide what are your Aims for Today. By all means make a To-Do list just for today. The motivation you get from ticking things off becomes very helpful when you are tired and stressed.

32.2.2 Revisit your longer-scale plans

Every few days it is worth taking another look at your longer-term plans for the project. Remind yourself of the Aims and Objectives; Look again at the GANTT chart or Storyboard that you created. This can act as an antidote to the feelings of urgency that you get towards the end of a project, and can help you to focus on the most important things.

32.2.3 Optimise your work for your best time

In Chapter 11 - *Establishing your best times for working* we saw how to get the best use out of your time, taking account of your personal best and worst times for doing certain types of work. Now that your time is limited, it becomes even more important to allocate the correct tasks to each of your available time-slots. Some people find it very helpful to have a 'Day Planner' next to their ToDo list, so that at the start of each day you can allocate times to each task, taking into account how you're likely to feel in those slots.

So, for example if you've got two chapters of your report to do over a 3 week period you might wish to establish a 2-hour writing period every morning (maybe taking Sundays off). Using a Master Plan (or Contents page as described in Chapter 24 - *Organising the final report*) allocate each of the subsections to a particular day. In this way you split up the report into manageable chunks.

You can then allocate other tasks around this, for example relegating an hour of email and social media to your afternoon 'lull' time.

32.2.4 Use free time and holidays wisely

Occasionally the latter stages of a project fall across a holiday break (e.g. Christmas or Easter). Sometimes these university vacations can span several weeks. It is seriously worth planning out your use of these holidays into the following categories:

- Complete Rest (no project work; let your brain wind down for at least a few days and allow you to catch up with other people and things).

- Writing (finalising the report; proofreading; producing diagrams etc.)

- Final Project Work (any last experimental analysis or computer coding etc.)

- Other Assignments (some people have some other assessment work which needs to be handed in at a similar time to the final project, or maybe you have some part-time work to do).

Again, the more you plan when these blocks of time are to occur, the more you are likely to get something creative and productive done with the time.

32.3 Don't overwork

Just as it's important to not forget the managerial role, it's really important to be kind to your worker. Sometimes people are tempted to work flat out for several weeks towards the end of the project in an attempt to get everything finished, or to catch up for periods of low effectiveness earlier in the project.

Imagine you were employing someone else. I doubt that you would insist on them working 18 hour days for a few weeks, keeping their brain going with artificial stimulants. Yet this is what so many students do to themselves near a deadline.

As you can imagine, it's not good for your health (mental or physical) or your general quality of life.

Workers have rights - and you are a worker. Make sure that you get plenty of rest and exercise. Take regular breaks from your work-station. Stop completely when you get tired. Schedule in times to stop. Some students have not done this and have 'burnt out' just before the end of the project - a totally galling experience because they've worn themselves out over several weeks, AND have failed to meet the final deadline.

32.4 Identify the Critical Path

The Critical Path of a project is the set of activities that absolutely MUST happen in order for the project to be completed. The idea is - at any stage of a project - you can think about what this is, and then focus your main activities on completing it. The counter-side to this is that there are usually plenty of activities which are NOT on the Critical Path. Make sure you are not spending time on these distractions at the end of the project when there are critical things still to be done. This is a Management decision.

For some reason many students avoid the Management process towards the end of their project and often end up spending lots of time on non-critical activities at the expense of critical ones.

Some common examples that I have come across:

- (Computing) Working too hard on making the user-interface *look* nice, but neglecting the key processing (and thus purpose) of the program.

- (Computing) Working too intensively on part of the program that nobody will ever really see, at the expense of getting a usable user-interface.

- (Research) Trying to get more people to take part in an experiment at the expense of analysing the data that is already there.

- (Management) Suddenly getting a new idea about the project, and spending time investigating it, at the expense of finishing the final report.

Note that there is nothing actually wrong in principle with: making a nice interface; programming a difficult task; getting more test subjects; or having new ideas. It's the fact that these activities - when carried out at the time-critical end of the project - have caused something else serious NOT to be done.

Once you've identified all your critical activities, try to put them in priority order, write them down, and then (very importantly) track the progress of these every day in your Management meeting.

32.5 Form a Countdown plan

Much of the planning that you have done throughout the project has been *forward-looking*. This means that you try to think of all the things that will need to be done, and then you allocate time and resources to getting them done. You may make a Gantt chart to help visualise these tasks and their relationships to each other along a time-line.

At the end of the project, it is sometimes more useful to project your imagination to the END of the project and to think about the things that you will need to have done to complete the project.

Of course this still is forward-thinking because you're not actually there yet, but the change of perspective can be very helpful at the end of a project in making sure that you have made appropriate plans for everything to be done.

As an example, imagine that you are 3 weeks away from handing in your final report, and you take a few minutes to think about each of your upcoming deadlines. Let's imagine you have a report hand-in deadline; a viva voce exam; and an opportunity to show your work (in this example, to demonstrate some software you have been working on). This is how your Managerial thoughts might sound if we could look inside your head.

- **Report**: (Due in 3 weeks' time) I'm doing well writing the report. I have turned my Contents page into a plan, and I know how and when I'm going to write each chapter. Let's try to visualise handing this thing in. *(Imagines a beautiful report being handed in)*. OH MY GOODNESS the finished product is BOUND and I haven't done *anything* about the binding! Ok, write that down as a task to sort out today. Phew. Ok, imagining opening up my beautifully bound report, and turning the pages. Everything's ok. UH-OH it's got an *Abstract*, and a *List of Figures*, and I haven't scheduled in when to do this. Write that down. AAAGH - I've just remembered that some of the illustrations are only *draft*, and I need to go through re-doing them. Ok, write that down. Good. I think it's going to be ok. Mmm - I haven't contacted my proof-reader for about 6 months. I hope they're still ok to get my last two chapters done next week. Better email just to make sure.

- **Viva**: (Due in 5 weeks' time) My fellow students have told me that there's nothing you can do to prepare for a viva, but I'm not sure about that. Somewhere I have got a list of typical questions. I'll write down to schedule some time for preparation, otherwise I might get a bit too carried away with celebrations on handing in my report. Mmm - I wonder if there are things that my examiners might ask in the viva, that I can even prepare for by mentioning them in my report. Can't leave that til after the report hand in. Let's think this through tomorrow.

- **Demonstration**: (Due Next Week) I have to demonstrate my software next week to one of the examiners. Ok, what does that involve? Surely I can just show him what's working, as I know how to operate it? Oh - but what if he want to have a go himself? My interface isn't really friendly enough to let that happen? Can I do anything between now and then to improve this? Er, ok - if I change the wording on the screen to make it more obvious to a newcomer, and add one picture, I think this would improve how it looks and will prevent me from having to explain my cryptic terminology. Oh yes, and maybe I should remove that little pop-up box that says "Draft rubbish version". That might improve the overall impression and all those changes shouldn't take more than an hour.

In the above hypothetical example, the student has spent about 15 minutes thinking about (and - importantly - *visualising*) the 3 deadlines, and as a result has prevented a last-minute panic about a series of important tasks (which had been forgotten, or just not thought about).

So, the idea of having a Countdown plan is that you think things through backwards from your deadlines, and thus spot any loose ends that you hadn't thought of in your previous forward-planning.

32.6 Use Storyboards to gracefully manage Further Work

Sections 20.2 and 21.4 introduced Storyboarding as an excellent project planning tool precisely because it is about order and flow, and *not* about absolute time-scales. Towards the end of a project your Storyboard becomes a valuable way to help you to gracefully manage how you think about what *has been* done, and what has *not yet* been achieved. Given that you spent some time putting the Storyboard together into a coherent plan - arranged by logical time progressions rather than actual timings- you can now simply draw a line at the point you have reached towards the end of the project. Anything to the right of this line becomes Further Work.

This allows you to have a positive approach to the 'Further Work' section and to describe (in as much detail as you have time for) a coherent set of plans for what could (or will) follow this project.

This is in contrast to many Further Work sections, which seem to be a hastily put together list of things to complete what is currently in your head, e.g.,

- Finish software user-interface

- Debug program
- Find more test subjects.

This sort of list is not very helpful for the examiners as it really amounts to a brain-dump of currently unfinished tasks.

Instead, here are some ideas of how you might use the Storyboard as a springboard to a superb and insightful Further Work section.

- **Work to complete:** This is a version of the list mentioned above. Finishing off what is still incomplete is still something that can be written about; it's just not the *only* aspect to Further Work.

- **Future Projects**: For every major section on your Storyboard which is unstarted (or incomplete), write at least a paragraph (if not a page) on how this could be made into a future project. Maybe even phrase it in the way that your own project was originally suggested / advertised. This can help future students, could be of use to your supervisor and department, and shows the examiners that each of these undone sections really could be a whole project in its own right (so no wonder you haven't been able to complete it in the time available).

- **Project Insights:** While the abovementioned 'project' paragraphs outline the follow-up project specifications, you could also take the opportunity to summarise the valuable insights and ideas that you have had along the way. Think of this as helping future students who may well take up your suggested project ideas next year or later. These insights could include avenues of reading and research that you recommend; ideas for new experiments; people or companies to contact; recommended strategies to embrace and avoid. Don't underestimate your own experience, as you will probably have become rather a specialist during your time working on your project.

- **Grant Applications:** If you think that one or more of your undone sections has real promise (and you can always check this out in your next supervision) then you could write it up as a Grant Application for funding. You can learn a bit about the grant process in this way. Don't try to emulate all the necessary details and formatting, but present the idea in a one-page summary, particularly focussing on the area/s of innovation, the grant awarding body, and the supporting evidence from your project that led you to this idea.

32.7 Build in Review and Proofreading time

You have probably thought of this anyway, but it's worth mentioning because a few people forget to do it. If your deadline for handing in the report is in 2 weeks' time, remember that you will want to build in time for:

- any proofreading by other people
- you to make changes / corrections following that process
- adding references and diagrams
- a final read-through from you to make last-minute corrections
- time to print the report. Please remember if you're doing it yourself that printers are notorious for not respecting deadlines when they choose to run out of ink and paper, and when they break down. If you're relying on a central printing facility remember that many other people may be using to the full at exactly the same time as you. Always have a back-up plan.

32.8 Summary

All projects come to an end. You WILL run out of time, so rather than worrying (as so many do) "What IF I run out of time" you should manage the process so that the project finishes gracefully.

It is especially important to manage the project in its closing stages, as this will help you to avoid working away blindly on one thing while omitting to do other (and maybe more important) things. Schedule regular management meetings (possibly more than usual though the temptation will be to miss them altogether 'as time is short).

Best practice involves:

- having a daily management meeting to review progress and set tasks;
- revisiting your Objectives every few days;
- optimising your work to fit your best working times;
- using holiday time wisely, allocating certain periods for complete rest, project work, report writing, and any other assignments.

Make sure that you don't overwork. It's a common student failing to work madly for the last few weeks, skipping sleep and using chemical stimulants to keep going. This is not good for your mental or physical wellbeing, and rarely produces good work.

Identify the Critical Path - the set of activities that must be carried out for your project to be successful. Keep reviewing this and (in your daily management meetings) plan to do activities that are critical, rather than distractions.

Think backwards from your final deadlines by visualising each deliverable. This can often prompt you to be aware of tasks that you must carry out very soon, yet you had not identified up to this point. This is a Countdown Plan.

You can use your Storyboard to help you write an insightful Further Work section. It already contains a logical flow for the entire project, so you can take time to describe all those sections which have not been covered by the end of the project. You could write about future projects which could spring from your work, list recommendations for researchers in this field, and even try writing a grant application for particularly original work.

Finally, make sure that you build in enough time for proofreading, checking, printing, binding, and any other processes that you need to complete before the deadline.

33. FINDING OUT HOW YOUR PROJECT WILL BE MARKED

If you are being assessed on something it is generally very good practice to find out in as much detail as possible *what* the assessors are looking for. If you've ever watched a TV programme such as the X-Factor[31], you will know that the decisions are based around the opinions of the judges and the wider audience. The reason it's called the 'X-factor' is to express the concept of "we will know what it is when we see it". In education, while there are indeed certain parts of the process that look for an 'X-factor' (such as to which student to award a prize), much of the process is written down. In this chapter, you are encouraged to find out what you can, and to use this knowledge as an extra check for what you finally hand in.

33.1 Marking Guidelines & Markers

Anyone who marks your work will receive instruction on how to do this. In the 'old' days this was often passed down from academic to academic and refined by experience. More recently there is a move to making these marking procedures transparent - open and visible to all.

33.1.1 Official Marking Guidelines

Most educational institutions produce a set of guidelines to ensure that standards are kept and that different markers are guided to produce similar marks for work of similar quality. One of the first things you should do is to locate these guidelines and read them.

---

[31] http://www.itv.com/xfactor

Andy Hunt

Sometimes these are quite general, whilst others can be very specific. For example, compare the following three scenarios:

1. In a first-year undergraduate laboratory exercise there might be a marking sheet, with 20 specific criteria that can be ticked off (by different markers for each student) to decide whether each of the learning outcomes has been demonstrated in the student's work.

2. For a final year undergraduate project, there may be a series of categories (report, experiment, viva etc.) which have generalised 'performance standards'. Two markers may need to agree which standard category each aspect of a student's work falls into.

3. At PhD level it is usual that one or two external examiners (along with a variable number of guests, moderators or local examiners) read the thesis, cross-examine the student in a 'viva', and the outcome of that viva determines whether the student passes, fails, or is deferred, based on very broad criteria such as 'contribution to knowledge', or 'international significance'.

To the student it might, at first, seem ironic that the higher up the educational system you travel, the more generalised the marking becomes. The reason for this approach is that where *many* students are being tested on their fundamental knowledge or performance then it is reasonable to have something approaching a tick-list of those specific criteria. However, wherever the work is much more specialised, it becomes impossible and undesirable to have such simple criteria defined in advance in a check-list. Instead the work must be examined more deeply and thoroughly whilst looking for fewer - but more complex - quality standards.

What matters is that you make some effort to find, read and discuss these guidelines with your supervisor.

33.1.2 Can you talk to the markers?

It is important - at the very least - to find out something about your markers; who they are; what academic level they work at; what they would typically expect to see in a piece of work, etc.

This is something you should ask your supervisor about because supervisors typically know the local etiquette. The first thing to do is to find out *who* is marking you. Sometimes this is anonymised, but there will still be a 'pool' of markers so you can get an idea of what sort of person is looking at your work. If your supervisor is a marker then, yes, as early in the project as possible you should have a conversation about the marking process.

Managing Your Project

If you are allocated a second marker, find out whether it's ok to meet up for a chat in order to explain your work. If ever I am a second marker I always try to meet up with the student in advance because I can often find out a lot more by talking and discussing, than by solely reading the report. At such a meeting I would not mind at all being asked about the marking scheme or what I look for in a good project.

My etiquette suggestions for this process are as follows:

Ok to say

- what would you expect to see in a good project?
- for you, what would make the difference between a first-quality report and a 2:1?
- are there any sections of my work so far that you would suggest I improve?

Not **ok to say:**

- I desperately need a first; so I need both markers to give me a first. That's why I've come to see you today.
- What mark are you actually going to give me?
- How can you possibly assess someone else's work?
- I'm going to put so much effort into this that you're going to find it hard NOT to give me a starred first.

All of those comments above are loosely based on real comments I have heard from students.

In the 'OK' category there is a sense of humility, and this will usually work in your favour and draw out a good and detailed response from the marker.

In the 'Not ok' category there is a sense of arrogance and self-righteousness, mixed with a bit of threat and emotional blackmail that will not go down well at all. It's been my sad experience that many people who demand top marks or expect them as their right often actually submit substandard work.

If you follow the 'ok' category and take on the mantle of a life-long learner you will constantly improve your work and (in the process) won't end up alienating the very people around you who can help.

33.1.3 Talk to other students

If you can find a few ex-students who have been through (and survived) the marking experience, you could ask them what it was like. They might be able to tell you from a student's perspective the things they found difficult as well as the aspects of the assessment that they really enjoyed. Don't use this as a substitute for talking to your supervisor and markers, but as a complementary view.

You might also want to consider using your Special Interest Group to do some peer assessment of each other's projects. This takes time and trust, but can be extremely useful because it really is hard to spot weaknesses in your own work.

33.2 Using the Marking Guidelines

Study the marking scheme carefully. Make sure you understand what each section means. Discuss it with your supervisor if possible, to clarify what is being looked for in every category.

The next step is key. Work at converting the scheme into a checklist of things which will enable you to monitor your own work. The best way of using this is to become an examiner. If you take the time to 'stand back' from your work, almost pretending that it has been produced by someone else, then you could work through the marking guidelines (or your checklist) and honestly assess how you are doing against each criterion. This does not mean that you will get this mark because in practice it is very difficult to assess your own work. However this process will get you *thinking* like an examiner and you might begin to see deficiencies in your work that were not obvious while you were working on them.

When you've identified any problems or deficiencies, don't stop there and just feel bad about it (like so many people do), but turn them into a positive set of actions which feed into your Management process.

Be aware that it's very hard to 'reverse engineer' marking guidelines. For example if one criterion stated *"For a First mark the report will be produced to a professional standard of layout, grammar, structure and argument"*, then simply having that knowledge does not suddenly make this an easy process for you to produce that professional report. It will take a huge amount of sustained effort and regular review.

33.3 Looking at previous work

Try to look at examples of previous work where students did really well. Your supervisor may have examples of projects from recent years, and might be able to tell you what level of mark the project received.

Be slightly careful when looking at previous reports. Don't necessarily think "This got a first, and they used this font and spacing to make it look nice; so if I use this font and spacing I'll get a first!". Project marking is a lot deeper than that. It typically considers:

- the scope and ambition of the project
- the attention to detail in background research and context
- the diligence of the student throughout the project
- the logical flow and argument shown
- the amount of work done
- the quality and originality of the work
- the presentation of the final report
- the quality of argument under cross-examination at the viva

and much more.

You'll note that 'presentation' is one small element. Yet it is important, and you can pick up some really good tips for what works and what doesn't when looking at previous reports.

33.4 Summary

It is very sensible, with any assessment that you have to do, to find out as much as possible about how the assignment will be marked. This skill will travel with you into your career as you discover the importance of establishing how your customers assess your product or service. Modern institutions make visible a clear set of guidelines about how each assignment will be graded.

It's important that you located the guidelines for your assignment and read them, and very useful if you can discuss these with your supervisor. For a major project find out who will be marking you, and - if possible - examine the guidelines that they are given to assist in the marking process. Find out from your supervisor if it's ok to meet up with the markers in advance (as in some places this is actively encouraged, and in others it's more of an anonymised process). If you get such a meeting, ask detailed questions about what sort of things they are looking for, but refrain from being too personal or coming across as trying to manipulate the marker.

One of the best things you can do is to learn how to examine your own work, based on the guidelines for marking, or the stated assessment criteria. This will give you some experience in being an examiner, and will help you to spot deficiencies in your work before you hand it in. Schedule time in your planner to correct each of these. Try to look at examples of previous work that received a good mark, but be careful you do not conclude too much about the presentation of a report, as the marking criteria will typically delve much deeper into the originality, depth and achievement of the project.

34. THE VIVA

Many research projects are assessed not only by a final written report, but in a time of active discussion with the examiners. This chapter guides you through the preparation for such an encounter, and helps you to understand what the examiners are looking for. Such examinations are traditionally called *viva voce*[32] (or 'viva' for short), and take place by word of mouth, rather than in written form. However, a viva is by no means a simple spoken replacement for a conventional written exam, but rather a meeting of minds, and an opportunity for you to discuss the significance of your work in detail.

34.1 Purpose of the viva

Let us consider the reasons for holding a viva, both from the examiners' point of view, and your own.

From the point of view of the *examiners*, the purpose of a viva is to:

- Establish that the written report they have read actually *belongs* to the person sitting in front of them!

- Clarify anything in the report which is unclear;

- Determine the extent to which the student understands the contents of the report;

---

[32] from the Medieval Latin meaning "with the living voice" (The Oxford Compact Dictionary, 1996, OUP)

- Challenge the student's ideas, to find out how strongly or deeply the student believes them;
- Engage in general discussions around the topic area, to discover how flexible the student's thought processes are.

From *your* point of view the purpose of the viva is to:

- Ensure that the examiners comprehend the main purpose of your project and its most significant results;
- Show that you understand not only what you have written, but also issues surrounding the general topic area;
- Engage in conversation with someone who has read your work in detail;
- Clarify any misunderstandings about what you have written.

A few observations flow directly from the above points:

- The work you submit must be all yours, or properly annotated as someone else's.
- Anything you write is open to questioning and further discussion.
- You should *expect* to be challenged, and you have the right to answer.

34.2 Challenging Questions

The degree of *challenge* will be different according to your level in the education system. Viva exams at Doctoral level are often called 'thesis defences', where it is understood that someone (or indeed a group of people) will somehow attack or challenge the central tenet of your work to determine just how rigorous your thoughts and research procedures have been. You should spend time preparing for such a process, with your supervisor, your focus group, and with other people who have already been through such a process themselves. It really isn't as bad as it might first sound. Most people emerge from their doctoral vivas quite tired, but *glad* they went through the process, and pleased to have engaged with people who really understood what they were talking about.

At Masters level, there is usually less emphasis on 'defending your corner', and more focus on demonstrating that you understand the *significance* of what you have done, and how this fits in to the other work that has been done in this area.

At undergraduate level, you will still be challenged, but the main emphasis is on asking you to describe the *details* of your work, and on clarifying any misunderstandings.

However, at whatever level you are working, you should be prepared for challenging questions, and also those that appear to go off the subject. Also be ready for 'shifts of gear' in the questioning. For example you might be asked the following five questions, one after the other:

- On page 14, you say " . . . .", but this appears to contradict what Roxburgh says about it in his well-respected journal paper. How do you respond to that?

- Please explain how this <*pointing to the page*> bit of code works.

- What for you is the most significant finding of your research?

- Which paper in your literature survey is the most relevant to your work, and why?

- How do you see the future of this field of study progressing in the next 10 years?

Note how the 'level' of the questions changes; from a direct challenge, to low-level specifics, to a high-level overview, to engagement with the literature, through to speculation about the future of the whole research field. Now a real viva would probably operate with more of a conversational flow, but nevertheless the style and scope of the questions may change as rapidly as portrayed above.

34.3 Preparation for the viva

As you will gather from the depth of the questioning to be expected at a viva, you must take time to prepare for it. Some people go in without preparation, thinking "If I don't know it now I never will". Still others try to somehow 'learn' their report, as if they were revising for a written exam. Neither of these is an appropriate way of preparing for the viva.

What you actually need to do is to practise *talking* about your work with people who are reasonably knowledgeable about the subject area. This is the only real way to become confident at answering *questions* on your work. One of the best ways of doing this is to plan several sessions with your focus group (ideally with your supervisor in attendance).

Take turns in your supervision group to play the role of 'the examiners' and 'the person in the viva'. It is quite important for you to get some practice at formulating questions and comments *as if* you were an examiner. After all an examiner is not some special individual with magical powers of insight, but rather a person who is attempting to interact with you and assess your work. So try asking each other questions about your work.

At first your mind might be a blank, but try the following sorts of questions to begin with, then later invent your own:

- What have you achieved overall on your project?
- Which part of the work are you most proud of?
- How can you reassure me that your tests are reliable?
- Explain *that* section in more detail.
- Which parts of your work could be published, and where?

When I have run mock vivas with a focus group, it has always been amusing to see the range of responses from students who are pretending to be examiners. Some people do not seem to be able to ask a question. *"Er – I just can't think of anything to ask"*. Others seem to relish the new sense of power; *"Ha Ha"*, rubbing hands together, and smiling with an evil grin, *"your statistical analysis bears no relationship to the well-known guidelines. Why not ?"* However, most people find that they benefit from being made to think of questions, and indeed to answering questions, albeit delivered in a manner that a real examiner would never dream of.

When you have answered all these questions, and more, and you are feeling comfortable with the process, then you are probably ready for your viva.

Figure 34.1 shows a self-assessment form (similar to the one used in Chapter 29) which will help you to focus on the latter stages of your project, including the viva.

Managing Your Project

Project: Self-Assessment Form 2

Purpose: This form helps you think about the report submission and the viva.

1. What is your understanding of the purpose of the viva?
2. Explain how you plan to run the viva.
3. What equipment will you require, if any?
4. What sorts of questions do you think you'll be asked?
5. Which questions do you fear the most?
6. How do you plan to deal with them?
7. How much of the report have you completed?
8. What plans do you have to ensure that the report is completed on time?
9. Are you submitting any media (e.g. CD-ROM), and if so, what will it include?
10. How do you plan to use the time between report submission and the viva?

Figure 34.1: Self-assessment form to guide you through the project's final weeks

34.4 Presentation time within the viva

In Figure 34.1 the second question implies that you have some say over the structure of the viva. Sometimes the viva's structure is published and known and therefore fixed. At other times it is entirely up to the examiners. Whichever is true, you will probably be given an opportunity to explain your work, and it is important that you plan for this.

Some viva exams formally include a presentation time (say 20 minutes) before the questioning. At others the examiners may begin by saying "Give us a 5 or 10 minute overview of what your work is all about and what it has achieved". This is your chance to set the agenda for the discussion, so it is important that you prepare for it.

If it is a formal presentation, then you may wish to prepare a proper slideshow as described at the end of Chapter 23 - *Giving Presentations*. If it is an explanation around the table, then it is probably better that you prepare some cards containing the main points that you wish to communicate.

Even in the event that the examiners do *not* give you this opportunity, you will not regret the preparation. Imagine if you have two postcards containing every main point you want to get across, then the examiners say "Well, we're nearly finished; is there anything you feel we have not covered?" Rather than the (usual) response "er, no, I don't think so", you could scan down your main points and say something like "I think we've covered most things, but maybe I've not stressed this well enough..."

So, the sorts of things your notes (or talk) should cover are:

- The main focus of your study
- Why this is important
- What you have done / studied / proven / challenged
- How your work relates to that of others
- The significance of what you have achieved
- The weaknesses or limitations of your work[33]
- The novelty of your work
- The potential future implications of your work.

34.5 Summary

Many major projects conclude with a spoken exam - a time of detailed discussion where the examiners establish that you did indeed write the report, and where they challenge your ideas to determine how deeply you understand the topic. For you, it's an opportunity to ensure the examiners understand what you have done and to explain anything they felt was unclear.

For higher level qualifications, such as a PhD, the level of challenge will be harder and more overt. But even at undergraduate level you should expect to be questioned and probed about what you have done and about the wider context and implications of the work. Be ready for 'gear shifts' when the questions move from low-level details in your report to long-term speculation about the future of the research topic.

---

[33] It is *not* seen as a negative or damaging thing to talk about potential weaknesses in your work. It shows careful and objective analysis and is seen as being honest. This is much better than claiming that your work is better than it really is.

Managing Your Project

You should prepare for your viva, but not like revising your report for a conventional written exam. Instead, get some experience in talking about your work with people who know something about it. This is a perfect opportunity for the focus group members to take turns being the examiners and thinking up difficult and challenging questions to ask the student. This also helps you to think like an examiner and to hear what you think about other people's replies. We've shown some of the questions that examiners typically ask, and you can use these in your focus group sessions. Also included is a self-assessment form to guide you through the final weeks of the project and prepare for the viva.

Be ready to give a concise verbal summary of your work - its purpose, the main goals, the practical activity, the conclusions and the implications for further work.

The viva examination should be seen as an *opportunity* for you to talk in detail about the project you have been working on for a long period of time. After all by now, whether you *feel* like it or not, you are something of an expert! To maximise your chances of getting your message across to the examiners, you will need to practise talking about your project with others. In these practice sessions, the more you can cultivate an atmosphere where you ask and respond to probing and challenging questions about your work, the more confident you will be when it comes to the viva itself.

Andy Hunt

35. PUBLISHING YOUR WORK

In this final chapter we consider the options available for publishing your work. We discuss the different types of publication, and share some general advice about how to get your work published.

35.1 Why publish?

The writing and publication of academic papers is a central part of higher education practice. As a student you may be only aware of the *teaching* commitments of the staff (the lectures, seminars, exams and marking). However, it is *research* which is often the driving force behind much of the work done by universities and colleges.

One of the natural outcomes of finding out something new is telling others about it - sharing new ideas and discoveries with the international community; hence the need for publication. What is perhaps less obvious (from the point of view of students) is how important the activity of publication has become, because it is being increasingly used as a *measure* of creativity, productivity, and esteem in the academic community. Various exercises are in existence which link publication performance (amongst other things) to personal pay, promotion opportunities, departmental grants and overall university funding. The resulting figures contribute to 'league tables' which rank higher education institutions, and influence funding bodies and potential parents and students, thus determining future funding and admissions.

So, like it or not, publication is vital to the academic community. If you wish to continue to be involved in academic life after your current studies, then consideration of publication will play an important part in what you do.

Managing Your Project

For now, you need to consider whether or not you should publish the work you have just completed.

35.2 Should you publish?

Once you have completed your report, and have successfully come through the viva examination, you may wonder who else will read your report. Firstly, if your report has been bound it is likely to be available in your department for future students to borrow and look at. Higher level reports (most doctoral and some masters) are often kept in the university library, which means that they are available to all at the university and can also be requested by other universities via inter-library loans[34].

If, however, you (and your supervisor) are convinced that your work deserves to be seen by a wider audience, then you will need to consider publication. The first thing you should be aware of is that getting work into print is not an easy process. It is a time-consuming and mentally challenging procedure which usually involves the following stages:

- Selecting a publication to target (e.g. a specific journal)
- Finding out about the specific writing requirements of that publication
- Deciding which sections of your work are going to be put forward for that publication
- Editing a draft paper and creating an abstract
- Sending the abstract to the editor, and awaiting a reply
- Sending in the draft, and waiting for the referees' comments
- Re-working the paper according to the referees' recommendations
- Working with the commissioning editors to finalise the wording and layout.

The whole process can take a long time, even assuming your paper is accepted at each of the above stages. The writing and editing tasks are also quite significant – as you cannot just cut out chunks of your report and bolt

---

[34] Increasingly, students are being encouraged to submit their work (or a copy of it) electronically, but this is not usually considered as 'publication', because the work is normally uploaded to a private database, so is not accessible to a wider audience.

them together into a new document. Therefore you need to make sure that:

- you have got the *time* available to commit to this. Many students hand in their report, have their viva, then leave and go onto something else.

- your work contains enough *novelty* for publication. Discussions with your supervisors and with other experts in the area will help you to determine this.

- you really *want* to do this.

This last point is very important. You should have a strong reason for wanting to get your work published. For example, you may want to work for an organisation where your publication record is important. Or, it may be that you have discovered something in which you believe so strongly that you simply *must* get it 'out there'. The whole task of publication takes time and effort, so you should be sure that the benefits gained from getting your work into print will be worth that effort.

35.3 Which publication?

Every journal or publisher is different – with its own focus, readership, style of writing and presentation. Some students are so proud of their masters or doctoral thesis that they naturally think they have 'already written a book'. Editors are very wary of taking student work directly, and methods such as converting your thesis into a book, or taking a chapter out of it to make a paper, will rarely work. The report you have written so far (as described in Chapter 24 - *Organising the Final Report*) has been written for a particular readership, for a particular purpose, within a specific style and page-limits. Everything is different for an external publication. In fact you may have to radically re-write everything you have already written. Having recently spent so much time writing a huge document, the last thing you may feel like doing is *more writing*, especially re-working what you have just completed.

Assuming that you decide that publication really *is* for you, you will then need to consider the *type* of publication.

Chapter 19 - *The Literature Survey* describes the various types of publication, and how each addresses the reviewing process, highlighting the trade-off between refereeing quality and publication turnaround time. For an academic publication you are probably choosing between a conference paper, a journal paper, or a book.

35.3.1 Conference publication

You may decide that a conference is the best way to present your work to the world. Most conferences advertise their key topics and important dates on their own website (found easily by typing the conference name into an internet search engine). The first deadline is usually for a paper to be submitted. Therefore you need to organise your writing so that this deadline can be met. You often have to write the full paper *before* you have any idea of whether or not your paper will be accepted for the conference.

Remember to write for the *specific* conference, by reading carefully what the website says about the sort of delegates it attracts, and by talking to those people you know who have some experience of it, or ideally who have presented a paper there in previous years. You can learn a lot about the 'feel' of a conference from finding out about the atmosphere there, or the social events, or the type of people who attend. Remember that by going to a conference you will gain opportunities to meet other people working in your subject area. These personal links can become very important for your future work. You will also gain experience in how to present a paper in front of an international audience, and of course hearing about what other people are doing in your topic around the world.

At a future date you will be given an acceptance or rejection for your paper. Even if it's an acceptance there may be a list of corrections or suggestions for improvement from referees. A second date will be listed on the website for the 'camera-ready' paper to be submitted. This is a finalised and properly formatted version with all illustrations in place. Conferences generally haven't got the time to go through a full editing process and so your layout is usually what gets printed in the *'proceedings'* the paper and/or electronic record of the conference talks and topics.

You will need to register for the conference (fees vary widely), find out about travel arrangements, and liaise with the conference organisers about presentation facilities (such as the availability of computers and loudspeakers). A first conference can be a daunting experience, but most junior researchers find it very rewarding, and they have returned feeling somewhat 'grown up', proud that they have presented their work in public and had detailed discussion with the international representatives of their topic area.

35.3.2 Journal and book publication

For many journals you send in a full paper, so first of all you have to write the material you wish to get published! Some, however, initially just ask for an abstract, on which they will make a decision about whether to ask you for a full paper.

With your supervisor, you should explore a list of relevant journals, and then get hold of a few copies of each. Read the papers, the editorial, and most importantly the instructions for authors. These will often cover the journal's aims and objectives, describe the target audience, and give details about how to write for the journal and how to format your paper.

For a book, try contacting various publishing houses and discuss with them the need for a new book in your area. Prepare for many rounds of discussion, and refusals as publishers are looking for things that they *know* will sell. If the topic area is of interest to a publisher they may ask you to fill in a detailed Book Proposal. In this you will probably be asked to give some or all of the following information:

- a detailed overview of the intended readership
- some 'blurb' which could appear on the cover
- an outline of your book's contents
- a sample chapter
- an idea of the length of the book, number of illustrations, and any special publication requirements (e.g. special size, or CD attached)
- a date when the final manuscript could be complete
- an analysis of the book's competitors
- names of referees who would be able to review your proposal.

Nowadays there are many opportunities for self-publishing, but the pros and cons of this are hard to generalise and you should discuss this with your supervisor.

If you have decided to publish your work in a journal or a book, there is nothing quite like the thrill of seeing your work finally in print, in the official binding. However, as we discussed earlier, it takes a lot of effort to get to this point, so you really want to be sure that the process will benefit you.

35.4 Summary

Publishing new discoveries is an important part of letting other people know about the latest findings, but it is also built into the business and measurement of higher education. It is therefore particularly worth getting

Managing Your Project

published if you plan to be part of an academic research community.

Your project report will be available within your institution, but can also be borrowed by inter-library loan (and increasingly available on-line). However, if you and your supervisor agree that there is enough originality in your work to warrant wider dissemination then you should consider publication. This is not a decision to be taken lightly as it will involve a lot of time and effort in selecting an appropriate publication, approaching the editor, writing new material according to the guidelines, receiving reviewer's comments etc. You must *want* to do this and make sure that you have the time and support available.

It is very unlikely that you can just use some or all of your existing report, so this will require some significant re-writing. For academic publication you are most likely to be considering a conference paper, a journal paper or a book (or chapter). In all these cases, you will need to establish the readership and their expectations and experience. For a conference there is all the work of arranging travel and planning a live presentation, whereas for books and journals there is usually a more rigorous and lengthy editing and reviewing process.

35.5 External References

A nicely-presented quick guide to publishing research:

> http://www.wikihow.com/Publish-a-Research-Paper

A series of YouTube tutorials on Publishing Your Research. It's by the American Chemical Society but contains loads of generalised publication advice for researchers in any field:

> https://www.youtube.com/watch?v=q3mrRH2aS98

Publishing Your Research in Scholarly Journals - A Street Fighter's Guide by Richard Croucher, CreateSpace Independent Publishing Platform (2015), ISBN-10: 1514317613, ISBN-13: 978-1514317617

Andy Hunt

Final words

This chapter assumes that you have made it to the end of a successful project, and are now considering whether to publish your work. We have looked at some of the questions you should ask yourself before committing to a publication and have stressed the importance of writing the material especially for the chosen publication, not just taking it from your report.

In this book, we have seen that the management of a research project is a complex process that demands *much* self-management. If you have invested the time to put some of these ideas into practice you will find, like me, that they flow over into everyday life, and can improve how you operate in other areas of your life. If you wish to tune your skills still further, please look at the references at the end of each chapter for some ideas for further reading.

I'd like to wish you all the very best with your project, your career, and whatever you decide to do next. Give it your best shot, but don't forget to try and enjoy the journey.

ABOUT THE AUTHOR

Andy Hunt is a Professor in the Department of Electronics at the University of York, UK. He initially trained with Marconi Research Centre, then took a degree in Electronics at York. His final-year project involved creating a novel musical instrument for people with disabilities, and he stayed on to teach some of this topic on the new Music Technology Masters course in 1988, and which he subsequently led. Over the years he has been a Technician, Experimental Officer, Lecturer, Senior Lecturer, and Professor (Teaching & Scholarship). He has supervised hundreds of successful final year, Masters and PhD projects, and led curriculum development teams. His research interests include human-computer interaction, especially with music technology and sonification (the art and science of converting data into sound for analysis).

www.ingramcontent.com/pod-product-compliance
Lightning Source LLC
Chambersburg PA
CBHW070221190526
45169CB00001B/34